TWENTY FEET

From the Land of Ford to the Land of Cana

by
JOHN R.
GOODWIN

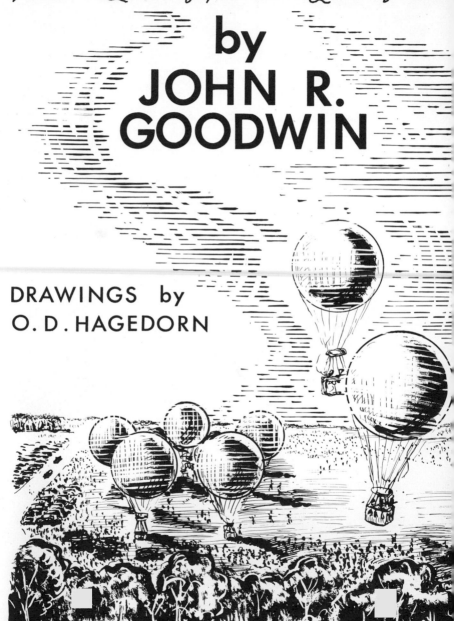

DRAWINGS by
O. D. HAGEDORN

ROM GLORY

Standard Book Number 87012-087-5
Library of Congress Card Number 78-122268
Printed in the United States of America
Copyright © 1970 by John R. Goodwin
Morgantown, West Virginia 26505

Available from
Betty Lou Goodwin, D/B/A
Betty Lou's Country Store
1300 University Avenue
Morgantown, W. Va. 26505

and

McClain Printing Company
Parsons, W. Va. 26287

TO
JOHNNY
AND
PORKY

TABLE OF CONTENTS

FOREWORD

Twenty Feet From Glory had its beginning at John Me-
halic's Restaurant in Granville, West Virginia, in 1967. J. S.
Cooper, Frank Fisher, Jr., and John R. Goodwin stopped
there for lunch. Antique gun collecting has been Goodwin's
hobby for many years and mention was made of an antique
"Kentucky Rifle" acquired the previous day. Cooper remarked, "I have two guns; one that my father gave me, and
the other, the German flyer gave me after he crashed in the
Canaan Valley."

The story was uncovered! Fourteen months of travel,
study and research followed. During this time many persons
gave freely of their time, records, photos and information,
and mention must be made of their names. If a name is
omitted, it is an error for which apologies are given.

First, thanks to J. S. Cooper for telling about the pistol.
Had it not been for this lead the story would (in all proba-
bility) have been lost. Next, to Andrew G. Fusco, for diligent
newspaper research and careful proofreading; Walter L. (Bill)
Hart who took time from a busy schedule to provide a lead
on a flyer who died in a crash at Everettville, West Virginia;
John R. Sanders, Jr., whose combat experiences in the South
Pacific as a Navy man, brought recollections of Amelia Earhart which led to discovery of important material (he remembered "scuttlebutt" about the "white lady" captured by the
Japanese); to Lieutenant General William E. Kepner for patience and kindness in writing at length about the '28 race;
Charles G. Worman (a gun collecting friend and historian at
the U. S. Air Force Museum) for taking time to find valuable
material in the files; to the U. S. Air Force Museum, Wright-

Patterson Air Force Base, Ohio (a wonderful place to visit),
for permission to use the materials in the files found there;
The New York Times for permission to use the July 8, 1928,
Rotogravure as a cover for the book; Mike Magro, Jr., Es-
quire, fellow member of our local Bar, who provided encour-
agement when it was badly needed; John H. Brickner of
Edison Institute who was kind enough to sacrifice a lunch
hour to provide research assistance; Robert Blake, *The Salem
News*, Salem, Ohio, for research on background material of
Captain Bertram; James C. Cooper, Jr., and Louise, his wife,
for spending a day in March, braving four-foot drifts in the
Canaan Valley in search of material; to J. S. Cooper's wife,
Katherine, for enthusiasm, which came at a time when it was
appreciated; to Richard A. Raese, executive of Greer Steel
Corporation (and coach of the 1942 "Cinderella" Basketball,
and all-time great, team at W.V.U.) who was most patient in
the beginning and suggested a pattern to follow during research; to Robert C. Raese, of Davis, West Virginia, for remarkable photos and information given by him; to William
Sembella, a student at W.V.U., for difficult German transla-
tions; to Walter M. Raese (a well-known Morgantown
businessman) and his wife, Pauline, for photos and other information; to James R. Browning (a prominent businessman
in Morgantown and long-time member of its City Council)
and his gracious wife, Reba, for the use of letters, photos, and
the German flag; to Donna Agah for a brilliant job of typing
(which she did seven times); to Stan Kloc of the Bureau of
Better Business Research at West Virginia University, for
proofreading, valuable suggestions and material arrangement;
to O. D. Hagedorn for patience in working out line drawings
brilliantly executed; and to Myrtle Edwards and Fay Graham
for kindness and patience on a very cold winter day in March.

Without suggesting their contributions were of lesser importance, thanks to Professors Edward A. Johnson and Fred
E. Wright of the College of Commerce, West Virginia Univer-

sity, for suggestions and encouragement; C. Glenn Zinn, The Farmer's and Merchants' Bank, Morgantown, who gave a hand when it was needed the most; to Betty Lou Goodwin for valuable typing performed at a time when it was the hardest to do; William Sayger, the barber at Davis who supplied old photos and new ideas; Ken McClain of the McClain Printing Company, for patience in working out details of the book; Mr. and Mrs. John J. Deutsch, Severna Park, Maryland, who were at Lakehurst, New Jersey, the day the *Hindenburg* burned; Frank Fisher, Jr., and his wife Elaine, for the suggestion that O. D. Hagedorn do the drawings; and last to Matthew, Mark, Luke, John, Jr., and Elizabeth, who waited almost two years to see what it was that their father spent so much time working on.

PREFACE

Early in the year 1928, three German balloon racing teams traveled to America with their flying equipment to participate in the James Gordon Bennett International Balloon Race. This race was scheduled to begin at 4 P. M., June 30, 1928. The location was set at Ford Airport, Dearborn, Michigan. At stake was a world's distance record for a free-flight balloon as well as an international trophy. The story told here is—at first glance—an eyewitness report of the flight of one of these German teams. But as the events of this flight unfold, a larger, more significant and—in some ways—beautiful story is found underneath.

As research into the basic balloon flight began, convincing evidence of the nature, attitudes and beliefs of Americans during their most energetic decade—the Twenties—was uncovered. Discovered with this evidence were serious overtones of the First World War—information about events from that war that had become almost obscured by the passage of time.

Another War—the American Civil War—was suddenly seen as having a direct link with the year in which the flight occurred. And a realization that the first Moon Landing had its beginning within this almost forgotten race emerges with startling clarity.

The picture painted in this story contains many dark spots because research has not provided all of the answers. Many witnesses interviewed in the course of investigation hesitated to answer questions. It is assumed that they had good reason—possibly international ones—for their reluctance. In a striking example of this a foreign nation refused to disclose the service record of one of its prominent military men.

Twenty Feet From Glory is a story that takes a close look at the social, political and economic trends affecting the 48 hours in question. In this respect the story is unique since it is a rather complete history of a very short period of time. And the flight of one balloon provides the cohesion with which these events are brought together.

A turbulent and sometimes violent American era was involved. It was a true age of spectaculars since nothing ordinary happened in the Twenties. The story told provides an accurate description of the beliefs, attitudes and feelings of Americans living in the days written of. Sporting events were "King" and flying events were taking their place with the other sensations of the time.

Daredevil flyers—sometimes called "Barnstormers"—flew their biplanes under town bridges, and often upside down. Some crashed them into flaming barns sacrificed for the occasion—thus the origin of the term. Daring women rode the wings of looping planes or performed acrobatics upon a trapeze swinging below. Many arrests followed these antics in the sky, evidence that public approval was not unanimous. For example, law enforcement agencies could not ignore an airplane that flew the length of the main street of town scant inches over the heads of those below, sending autos and pedestrians scampering in all directions. It was during this era that free-flight ballooning, that unique form of flying, was making its contribution to the growing list of sensations. But with "sensations" often travel "dissents"—thus creating differences.

Sharp contrasts characterize the events told of here and these weave in and out of each other as the story is told. For example, what once was "heroic" would probably be labeled "trivial" in a later age. Witness the Mah-Jongg craze and the crossword puzzle mania. The headlong plunge of Americans in the Twenties seems exciting, colorful and one finds that he envies them in some ways. But pity must follow because their blind rush for pleasure took them to the breakwater of the depression in 1929, where the strength of their past ten years was suddenly tested against cold, hard and unexpected facts—facts which emphasized their recklessness.

A new era followed the crash of 1929, and unbelievable mass production geared to the effort of the second "war to end wars" provided the momentum to push the flying machines of men into earth and moon orbit and to the surface of the moon itself. The realization of man's ancient dream of flying found reality within a remarkably short period of time. Only sixty-six years separated Kitty Hawk from the Moon Landing—a span of one lifetime.

In an age of expanding space travel, free-flight ballooning and general flying of the Twenties tends to fade into the vast realm of insignificance. And yet when one realizes that the lack of safety devices and modern equipment made these flights constantly perilous, the thought arises that perhaps the almost fearless spirit of our astronauts might have had its origin in times when aeronauts[1] found the courage to "bump the clouds" in lighter-than-air craft—both in peace and war.

In the ten years following the Armistice of November 11, 1918, a new set of values unfolded in America. The age of "ballyhoo," "bathtub gin" and the "speakeasy" had arrived. It was a time when rich and poor turned to sports, exciting current events and neighborhood scandals to fill their hours. The sex magazine, the radio, the closed auto and slipping concepts of morals brought violent change to the American scene. One hundred fifty thousand persons would gather at an airport to watch the start of a balloon race; the nation would go into hysteria when one man flew the Atlantic alone and mothers would do their best "to save their daughter." But these facts faded with the passage of time.

The story told here was almost forgotten. Fortunately it

was uncovered at a time when there was still an opportunity to gain enough information to tell it accurately. In another ten years it would have been lost in the deep shadows of a fabulous valley in West Virginia, to be told only by the ghosts there who guard the forgotten events of yesterday.

The story reaches from the timberland of West Virginia to France and the grave of a son of a former president of the United States. It goes back in time to the lumbering days on the slopes of West Virginia's mountains, when hard-drinking "wood hicks" fought their way through Saturday night in early lumbering camps. An early crossing of the Atlantic is involved, causing a military man to lose his temper with a priest. The fifth largest city in America finds itself linked by a straight line with one of the smallest. Tales from an ancient land find their way into the story and the Bible provides an answer to what really happened.

This is the story then of one racing balloon, why it was brought to America, what it did, where it went and who flew within it. It is told in detail against the backdrop of the two days during which the flight occurred. The excursion told of here started at Ford Airport and ended in the "Switzerland of America"—West Virginia. It is the story of "a German airship painted gold, just twenty feet from glory."

THE TWENTIES[2]

*The warmth of it was a false warmth because
the values upon which it was founded were un-
real and destined to be self-destroying, and because it deepened the gulf between the fortu-
nate and the majority.*[3]

The third decade of the Twentieth Century began at one
second past midnight January 1, 1920. Only 415 days had
passed since the end of World War I. The new decade was
soon labeled the "Roaring Twenties" for good reason. As a
reasonable man looks back at the events of those ten years, a
startling spectacle unfolds. Millions of American youths who
had just finished fighting the "war to end wars" came home
united in a promise to live life as fully and as rapidly as possible. The war had convinced them that the opportunity to do
so might last only a short time. And live it quickly they did.
The social, political and economic events of the ten-year span
in question read like a fairy tale of fun, replete with thrills of
every nature but contrasted sharply against the terror, scandals, immorality and lawlessness bred by the times.

Of note is the fact that the first Miss America was selected
in 1919. This provided an excellent preview of the social
events of the new decade opening. Her name was Edith Hyde
and the prize awarded was a golden apple. An ordinary apple
painted gold seems an appropriate symbol to award to the
first winner of an important social event of the future. The
idea of something ordinary being covered by a false front was
an example of the nature of the events that followed
shortly. If something might in fact be ordinary, why not call
it something else and thereby make it extraordinary? The

decade became one of innocence in values; lowness in standards and apparently almost everyone wanted to be fooled.
Why concern oneself with an important problem if it could
be shoved away by simply ignoring it?

On the financial scene, the stock exchange on Wall Street
had closed on May 31, 1919, out of fear of what had apparently been speculation. The day before the exchange had
experienced an unprecedented "one million and a half share
days" and many were concerned. Within eight short years the
"Big Bull Market" of 1928 would provide better reason for
concern about speculation.

On January 1, 1920, the driver of the latest model automobile found that the roads available for his use were either
non-existent or in such bad shape that it would be better to
leave his car in the garage for four or five months of the year.
In addition, the only paved roads available might be a small
strip or two in the center of town. If this driver looked
carefully around he noticed a lack of other autos on the
roads that he traveled. But in just ten years the number of
autos would triple; better roads would be in the offing and
the open car of the 1920's would become a closed car. This
combination of places to go, roads to go on and a closed car
to go in would carry a large share of the blame for some of
the things that were to happen. And coupled with Prohibition, the result was going to be even more precise.

The first Great War had generated a true "Spartan fever"
among both the young and the old of America. A nation that
had caused Lincoln concern about "enduring" had just conquered the mightiest military power of all time. With strength
goes virtue and the people of America unanimously joined in
a fantasy dream (coupled with a promise they had no intention of keeping): the dream and promise of a "dry" America.
Here was a real spectacular with which to start the new decade. What difference did it make if no one really believed in
what they were clamoring for? After all, it was a time to be

fooled. President Herbert Hoover, speaking of Prohibition in a letter to Senator Borah in 1928, stated: "Our country has deliberately undertaken a great social and economic experiment noble in motive and far-reaching in purpose." Could it be that Hoover was fooled too?

The 18th Amendment was reduced to Constitutional mandate and ratified rapidly by 36 states. It took effect July 1, 1919. In prior years drinking by women had been non-existent—at least publicly. After the Amendment men and women alike suddenly turned their attention to the creation of bathtub gin, the maintenance of roadhouses and the successful operation of speakeasies. It was a classic example of "saying it one way and doing it another." This Amendment would carry a heavy share of the blame for many problems of the approaching decade. In the meantime President Woodrow Wilson had something to say to all Americans.

On November 11, 1918, President Wilson delivered a message to the people of the United States. He told them that the Armistice had been signed that morning and spoke in his message of "sober, friendly counsel" and of "the establishment of just democracy throughout the world." The news media exercised caution however, because a false report four days earlier had triggered a gigantic nationwide celebration. But this was straight news and there followed once more a wild, hilarious, thankful nationwide celebration that surpassed even the first one. Sirens, whistles, bells, firearms and every conceivable means of making noise were turned loose across the land. A heated celebration started that was destined to continue for a decade—until the tragedy of 1929 would put out the fire. Girls kissed every soldier they came upon; Barnard College girls snakedanced through the streets of Morningside Heights in New York; and the Kaiser had been burned, drowned and hanged in effigy. America had had enough of the Hun. A new era of "lasting peace" had finally arrived. At least the President felt it had.

Woodrow Wilson dreamed of a League of Nations and carried this great hope with him on his postwar trip to Europe. Unfortunately, his idealism was not shared by others. "The tide of events, had Wilson but known it, was turning against him. Human nature, the world over, was beginning to show a new side, as it has shown at the end of every war in history. The compulsion for unity was gone, and division was taking its place. The compulsion for idealism was gone, and realism was in the ascendant."[4]

Wilson's idealism, soon to be rejected by those he felt would support him, dragged him into a distortion of facts. He no longer saw the world as it was—rather only as he thought it should be. On March 19, 1920, the Treaty of Versailles was offered to the United States Senate and ultimately rejected. Americans were sick of the entire European matter—tired of the Germans—fed up with the idea of further responsibility to other nations. They were more interested in such matters as the Willard-Dempsey fight and the arrival of the British dirigible *R-34* at Mineola, Long Island—the first transatlantic dirigible flight. A serious change in values was under way. A decade of fun, scandals, celebrations and tragedy opened and more than ten years would pass before the nation's collective sense would be regained.

As an example, the Ku Klux Klan had been founded in 1915 by Colonel William Joseph Simmons, a Georgian, and the following five years had been lean ones. When the Twenties opened, Edward Y. Clarke of the Southern Publicity Association had been given the job of getting the organization on its feet. It was an ideal time to enlist more members to serve as defenders of white against black; the Gentile against the Jew; and Protestant against Catholic. The organization became a paying one for the first time and the terror that it caused is still in the minds of those who know of the tragedies that followed in its wake. But the time was ripe because the concepts of the K.K.K. dovetailed with the newfound attitudes of Americans who were beginning a new social revolution. And other changes were taking place.

By the end of the summer of 1920, the "Big Red Scare" was over; women's suffrage had become a reality and dinner table conversation included the subject of making gin in the basement. In addition—being practical—most Americans were interested in learning how good Canadian whiskey could be brought across the dry border.

On September 16, at lunchtime, near the junction of Broad and Wall streets in New York City, a gigantic explosion rocked the nation's financial center. A huge bomb had exploded in the street in front of the Assay Office and thirty persons died outright, hundreds were injured. The tragedy was attributed to an anarchist gang, bitter against private finance and bitter against capitalists. "They showed them" with this deed it was rumored. The next day the stock market opened and prices were higher than the day before as though nothing had happened. The resilient Twenties were under way, as radio stock began a fabulous climb.

On November 2, 1920, at East Pittsburgh, Pennsylvania, KDKA was born—the first radio station in the world. Its transmitters beamed the Harding-Cox election returns and radio stock started an uphill climb that would reach a pinnacle in 1929. Other nations were not experiencing such activity, however.

In Europe other young men had returned home—but to families that had either been lost or hopelessly scattered during the terrible war that had recently raged like a terrible flame across that continent. Americans would try to forget the war—immunized by a wide ocean. But many persons in Europe would live very close to the terrible scars of the war for the balance of their lives. A young German officer, limping from leg wounds caused by Allied machine gun fire, had returned to his home in Chemnitz, Germany. The young man had flown on Zeppelin raids over London and knew how to

fly lighter-than-air craft—both motor driven and free-flight.
He turned his talents to the building of a business in steel and
iron and his success and luck would be great—at least at first.
In less than eight years he would travel to America to take
part in an International Balloon Race. In America, collective
attentions were "tuned in" on sports.

Man O' War broke all records in 1920, and the "Sport of
Kings" was off and running as never before. Babe Ruth raised
his home-run total to 59 and the 1921 World Series shattered
all records for both attendance and receipts. Sports was
king—and so were court trials.

In April, 1920, at South Braintree, Massachusetts, two
guards were killed during the course of a robbery. The tragic,
but relatively insignificant, crime almost went unnoticed. It
eventually gained international proportions and caused up-
heavals around the world. In 1927, Judge Webster Thayer denied final motions for retrial and on the evening of August 22,
1927, Sacco and Vanzetti died in the electric chair. The world
prayed for their salvation—but these prayers would not be
answered. Man responds to man's accomplishments—as well
as to man's mistakes. It was only one of many sensational
trials of the decade. In the meantime other events were making headlines.

The American woman demanded independence and had
been successful in obtaining it. Coupled with a "devil-may-
care" attitude encouraged by the closed automobile, the demand fed fuel to a new revolution and the young women of
America went on the rampage. Sex movies and sordid maga-
zines fanned the flames; promiscuous drinking by both sexes
lowered inhibitions; the closed auto provided the vehicle and
the new order rolled on. The skirt raised from the shoe sole
level to the knee and there it remained for the balance of the
decade. The "Flapper" had arrived. The amount of material
required to clothe a woman had suddenly decreased from
about 20 yards to seven or less. The beauty parlor made its

first appearance and the sales of cigarettes doubled. The divorce rate started to climb and would reach 16.5 divorces for every 100 marriages by 1928. "The old bars were down, no new ones had been built, and meanwhile the pigs were in the pasture. Some day, perhaps, the ten years which followed the war may aptly be known as the Decade of Bad Manners."[5] The saxophone crooned its lusty tune; the autos were rolling; parents were alarmed, shocked and dismayed—and justifiably so—at what was taking place. The Church and state—and parents—could *not* provide the answers. And the youth of America were not interested in answers. They were not even interested in questions!

For example, at Davis, West Virginia, a group of young men overturned a new car to simulate a crash. After the car was on its side, they posed beside it for photos. While the identity of these residents of Tucker County has not been disclosed, one of them recalled that his neighbor who had seen this incident had stated, "I certainly hope that no one was hurt in that wreck." Modern youth would lack the strength! (See Figure 1.)

Since it was a time of fun and pleasure for both young and old, why not elect a fun-loving president? On March 4, 1921, Woodrow Wilson, worn and crippled, rode down Pennsylvania Avenue in an open auto to attend the swearing-in of his successor, Warren G. Harding. Thus Harding became the first president to ride to his inauguration in an automobile—and Wilson, the first to bow out in one. It was a time to do things differently. On this particular day a state of war technically existed between the United States and Germany. America had suddenly dropped into a depression and the population was aroused over the high cost of living. But Harding took office and was soon being called "the friendliest man who ever entered the White House." By resolution signed on July 2, 1921, peace with Germany became a reality.

In the meantime Harding had surrounded himself with

many capable men, such as Herbert Hoover, Secretary of
Commerce. Yet he had made some unfortunate choices. On
August 2, 1923, Harding died suddenly of an alleged stroke
of apoplexy. The nation mourned while the martyred President was given the burial of a hero. Shortly thereafter, the
Tea Pot Dome and Elk Hills oil scandals broke. One of the
constant sensations of the decade was uncovered. Involved
were Harry F. Sinclair's Oil Company, Edward F. Dohney's
Pan-American Company and the mysterious Continental
Trading Company Ltd. of Canada. Fortunes in bonds were
involved and Albert B. Fall, Secretary of the Interior, was
destined to occupy a poor rung on the ladder of political
history. Perhaps Harding had died out of fear of exposure of
the acts of some of those who made up his very liberal ad-
ministration. In any event, Calvin Coolidge took the oath of
office.

In America, "Coolidge prosperity" began while in Europe
the German beer garden became the rallying ground for German politics. Here were nourished Communists, Nazis and
Freikoros—and all at the same time. The coup of Hitler was
attempted out of the Burgerbrau-Keller in Munich in 1923. A
political revolution was under way there.

In America the new social revolution continued as families
learned for the first time what foods had vitamins and what
foods did not. The habit of serving fresh vegetables, such as
carrots and spinach all year round was here to stay. Auto
manufacturers turned from utility to beauty—and even Henry
Ford gave in. The Model "A" was introduced in 1927, and
the first model was shown publicly on December 2, 1927.
Niagara Blue and Arabian Sand were offered as color options
to offset the traditional black. Even the disciplinarian Ford
was caught up in the spirit of the Twenties.

The "spirit" rolled on as the Mah-Jongg craze of 1922 was
gradually replaced by the crossword mania of 1924. The tragedy of Floyd Collins trapped underground made headlines

during each of the 18 days of his ordeal and the nation mourned when news of his death became known. And Clarence Darrow threw his reputation on the line in the defense of Leopold and Leob, charged with the death of little Bobby Franks of Chicago.

Darrow was back in the headlines in the summer of 1925 in the Scopes trial at Dayton, Tennessee. Tennessee law prohibited teaching in schools that man had originated from a lower species and the law was upheld—but many were skeptical. Could there be another answer? The sensational trial cost the now famous defendant a penalty of $100. A small price for a place in history! This trial concluded, the people of America looked elsewhere.

As 1925 drew to a close, the public gasped as news of the wreck of the U. S. Navy Dirigible, *Shenandoah*, became known. Although 20 had survived, 14 had died. Two days after the crash the farmer whose land was then occupied by the 450-foot stern of the ship, charged one dollar per car and two bits per pedestrian for admission to his field. Commander Lansdowne had been opposed to the September flight because he knew what weather conditions could be like in his native Ohio. He died with the other thirteen near Ava, Ohio. In other news, the Florida real estate boom was reported to be at its height; Red Grange galloped into football history and Byrd flew over the North Pole in a German airplane. But the big flying news was yet to come.

On the morning of May 20, 1927, Charles A. Lindbergh climbed into the *Spirit of St. Louis* and flew solo from Curtiss Field to Paris. For this accomplishment he was awarded the Congressional Medal of Honor—the highest award that America can give to its heroes. This award was denied to the first American to land on the moon—but 1969 wasn't 1927 and there will be no more Lindberghs; no more grandsons of Swedish immigrants who will fall heir to a nation's worship and devotion. Alcock and Brown had flown the Atlantic nonstop in 1919, and others had done it in lighter-than-air dirigibles. But the feat of the "Lone Eagle" was the brightest moment of the Twenties. Apparently he symbolized all of those things that the people of the era wanted to believe. Nothing could have been more sensational.

One who clearly recalls the event would later say: "Facing any man who would try this feat was 3,000 miles of stormy sea. Only 24 years had passed since the first successful flight by the Wright brothers. Would any motor hold steady for the hours required for such a flight? Or would it freeze—as could be expected—thus dropping its commander into the sea?" Charles A. Lindbergh provided the answer.

"Lindy" had been a mechanic—a self-styled pilot—a "barnstormer." He had not lived too well because the fees that he earned were small. When Raymond Ortieg offered to pay $25,000 to the first man to fly the Atlantic alone, it was logical for Lindbergh to respond. But, fly alone? Six men would die trying.

A group of St. Louis businessmen had decided to back Lindbergh in his attempt. He kicked in $2,000, they added $13,000 and the group then turned to the Ryan people in San Diego after hearing that Ryan made good airplanes.

"Can you build a plane capable of flying the Atlantic?" Lindbergh had asked. The answer was a simple, "Yes." Don Hall who designed the plane said at the time, "If he will risk his life, I will build it." After preliminary design and subsequent construction, the question changed from "Will it fly the Atlantic?" to "Will it fly at all?"

As one stands today under the wings of the *Spirit of St. Louis* as it hangs unceremoniously from the rafters of the Smithsonian Institution gathering dust along with relics of other years, this question takes on a precise meaning. The *Spirit of St. Louis* carried an unbelievable load of 451 gallons of gasoline and twenty gallons of oil; a payload of 3,157 pounds of gas and 160 pounds of oil—in addition to other cargo. It was a miracle that it left the ground.

"He socked it right up into the blue but no one in America expected him to make it." Lindbergh was unknown at the time—yet he represented the American pioneer reborn. "People were put to prayer across the nation. It was a sleepless night. There he was—one man alone trying to do what no man had done."

The news broke the next day. Lindbergh had crossed the Atlantic and had landed in Paris. There was a rolling and swelling sense of pride and relief throughout the nation as the news spread. Modern aviation was born and a grateful world paid homage to its hero. As a reporter stated at the time, "Man answers to man's accomplishments." The honors extended to the "Lone Eagle" matched his singular accomplishment. After all, this truly significant event happened in a special decade—and the American public needed this.

The year 1928 opened unceremoniously—since nothing could top Lindbergh's flight. But it soon became apparent that this year would occupy a unique position in the Twenties. Serving as a mirror for what had happened in the previous years, 1928 was a sounding board for what was coming. The symptoms were there but they apparently went unnoticed. Further, as viewed from today, 1928 occupied a position that might be thought of as a buffer between the sensational—often hysterical—events of the first seven years of the decade and the disaster that followed in 1929. It was a year in which to "cool off" and take it easy; a time to play a little and to appreciate the good things of life. For these reasons, 1928 seems clouded out of the Twenties. It is almost as if 1927 plunged headlong into 1929 with only lip service being paid to 1928 and even by the greatest social historians. In spite of this, the year 1928 had its sensations; its court trials; its trivial but interesting moments and its small and often personal tragedies. Some miscellaneous statistics of the events of this "sounding-board" year prove interesting when viewed objectively. In fact, the social, political and economic events mirror what had gone before so clearly that 1928 might be called the "Crystal Ball of the Twenties."

January, 1928, was ushered in by a demand for personnel. Shields Agency, 11 John Street, Room 11, New York City, offered $37.50 a week for a secretary for "an executive." A regular stenographer in the typical bank earned $30 per week; library clerks, $25 to $30, and typists, $15 to $20. Beginners in most lines started at $13 per week. The average wage for six days was $26. The *New York Times* was selling for two cents in Greater New York, three cents within 300 miles and four cents elsewhere in the United States. Bread was selling at eight cents a loaf; steak forty-six cents per pound and margarine twenty-seven cents a pound. Coloring for the margarine was supplied in a small extra package. The kids at home were given the job of whipping the white margarine until the yellow coloring sprinkled into it produced a butter-colored product. Due care was taken to be sure that real butter was not confused with something that wasn't! Meanwhile, the question of what a "work week" should be was discussed constantly.

At Dearborn, Michigan, Henry Ford was asked if the increased pressure in the production of his Model "A" cars would force his Ford Motor Company to depart from a five-day week and go back to a six-day work week. He replied: "Absolutely not. Our shop week is still a five-day week. Five days a week and no Sunday work—that is our program." A letdown in sales of the "T" eighteen months previously had prompted Ford to go to a five-day week—but at six days' pay. He was criticized for this shortened work week but stood fast. Rumors that he was about to go to a seven-day week were dispelled by this February 5 statement. And Ford appeared in other news.

Associated Press reported on April 13 that the "cobblers

stall," mentioned in *The Countess* by John Greenleaf Whittier, had been acquired by Henry Ford. This one-room shack had guarded the way at Rocks Bridge and the tollkeeper had collected a fare for the privilege of crossing this New England bridge. Operating from 1828 to 1889, it often served as a meeting place for neighboring farmers. The stall was dismantled and shipped to Dearborn, Michigan, to join other New England antiques in Ford's growing collection. More important news items followed quickly.

On May 30, in a special to the *New York Times*, it was announced that the inquest into the murder of William McSwiggin, an assistant state attorney at Chicago, had been reopened. The killing attracted nationwide attention, had never been solved and the first inquest had never been completed. Those who understood organized crime in Cook County hinted that solving the murder would provide a lead to a positive connection between politics and crime there. Significance was also being attached to the fact that the Chicago Bar Association asked Chief Justice William V. Brothers to call a special grand jury at the same time. At Belgrade, Yugoslavia, one person was killed and 30 others were injured the same day when police attempted to break up demonstrations against the Treaty of Nettuno. A large group of students had gathered demanding that the government abandon its plans to ratify the treaty with Rome. The police ordered the crowd to disperse and a confrontation had been inevitable. Youth was fighting for principles that it lacked in maturity—and experience—to understand. In March, 1928, Colonel William Avery Bishop, U.C.—the Canadian Ace who officially destroyed 72 German planes—was a guest of a number of German Aces in Berlin. As proposed by Ernest Voet, Bishop was made a member of the German Ace Association. Three months later Bishop was in turn dinner host to eight leading German flyers. It was a true age of chivalry[6]—as well as business.

Radio sales had risen from $60,000 in the first part of the Twenties to more than $650,550 in 1928. Colonel Robert W. Stewart waited until 1928 to disclose to his directors that he had received $759,000 out of the oil scandals of the Harding administration. Apparently business ethics were mirrored in the morals of the decade. Harry M. Blackmer, who received a similar sum, had lodged it in the Equitable Trust Company in New York, but still had not disclosed this to his directors. Radio Corporation of America stock held at 85¼. It would reach a high of 549 in 1929.

In the meantime Americans were searching for pleasures elsewhere. Some went to Ontario "where vacation dreams come true" (and where good Canadian whiskey was available). Others chose Japan with its oriental atmosphere or Mexico with a 25-day all-expense-paid trip for $275. Many traveled to South America, Europe, Hawaii, New Zealand, Spain, Italy—it was traveler's choice. More than 437,000 Americans left the United States this year with some 14,000 visiting Mexico and Canada on more than a one-day basis. No count is available of the cars that traveled in and out of Canada and Mexico on one-day trips. In the meantime there was plenty of action at home.

The Kiwanis Club had almost 1,800 clubs by the end of 1928. Stocks offered on the market were high priced and this caused concern. Was the nation in trouble? By March 4, the stock market had entered a sensational phase and by spring a fever of speculation had set in. Buy or not? Could this continue forever? Some felt it could. While Coolidge prosperity had truly been prosperous, hadn't Coolidge declined to seek office again? By the latter part of May, the pace slowed, prices fell, leveled and then fell once more. On the first of June, a serious collapse was predicted.

On June 14, Herbert Hoover was nominated for president and the market made a partial recovery. The presidential campaign of 1928 was under way and in seventeen days an international balloon race also started. Meanwhile, at White Sulphur Springs, West Virginia, a most successful summer unfolded. The golf course was occupied constantly and various tournaments were held there with many persons from across the land in attendance. At Lake Placid, New York, the first boat races of the season started by July 8. Expanding construction on the main highways in Connecticut drew an increasing number of summer motorists to the Berkshire resorts. This made it much easier to get there and the same was true in other states.

The Bedford Springs Hotel, Bedford Springs, Pennsylvania, offered "Championship Tennis Courts, enclosed tile swimming pool, picturesque mountain trails and medical baths in the world-famous Bedford Mineral Waters." Virginia Beach was advertised as the "Ideal Summer Resort." The Pinewood Hotel and Traymore Apartments fronting on the Boardwalk at Atlantic City were "places to visit." The Hotel Jefferson was billed as "Atlantic City's newest fireproof hotel."

About 400 miles west of Atlantic City at Tucker County, West Virginia, subscribers of the *Parsons Advocate*, a weekly newspaper, received the June 21 issue. The headlines told them that the first crossing of the Atlantic by a woman had been accomplished. Miss Amelia Earhart co-piloted the *Friendship*, a German Fokker, and had been accompanied by Wilmer Stultz and Louis Gordon. "Doesn't she look like Lindbergh?" But there will be no more Lindberghs (And there will be no more Earharts.[7]) She had left Prepassey, Newfoundland, and landed at the Burry Estuary, off Burry Port, Wales, at 12:40 A. M. Wales time or 6:40 A. M. Eastern Standard Time. The crossing had taken 20 hours and 49 minutes.

Three hours before this landing judgment was entered on the law side of the docket in the Circuit Court of Tucker County in favor of the Tucker County Bank. At Republican Convention Hall, Kansas City, the June 14 nomination of

Hoover was reported as a landslide. Hoover served as wartime food administrator and had spent seven years as secretary of commerce under Harding and Coolidge. He emerged free of scandal.

Back at Parsons, River City Chevrolet on First Street advertised the 1928 Imperial Landau at $715 and the Coach at $585. John W. Smith, West Virginia's Commissioner of Agriculture, announced an outbreak of rabies in Tucker County and warned everyone to guide themselves accordingly. Harold Shaffer, a student in agriculture at West Virginia University in Morgantown, returned home to spend the summer and Attorney A. G. Bolten of Thomas, Republican candidate for prosecuting attorney, attended court at Parsons and visited friends there. In the meantime the Democratic Party selected a candidate.

On June 28 the Democrats named Al Smith on the first ballot. Mrs. J. Walter Barnes, State President of the Women's Christian Temperance Union in West Virginia, said she would not support Smith for president. On the Tucker County scene notice was given to all candidates in the primary election that campaign expenses had to be filed with the Clerk of the County Court no later than June 29. Henry the Magician, with a new program, was scheduled to appear at the Parsons Chautauqua on Tuesday evening, July 10. Admission was seventy-five cents for adults and forty cents for children. "How does he do it?" A small quote in this issue warned: "You may not need a prescription to get liquor from a bootlegger but you are pretty sure to need one after you drink it."

Fourteen days later the *Parsons Advocate* for July 12 related how Amelia Earhart had been welcomed home on her July 9 arrival at Boston.[8] A listing of county officials of Tucker County in this issue showed A. Jay Valentine serving as judge at Parsons; Clara Rightmire as clerk of the circuit court; Riley Harper as sheriff; Sylvanus Harper as his deputy and R. D. Heironimus as prosecuting attorney. The prosecutor's platform had been "anti-moonshining." Many persons in the laurel-covered hideaways of the Alleghenies had reason to fear his name, and some in town for that matter. He promised that he would prosecute "moonshiners" . . . and he was going to keep his promise.

And so the warm, peaceful summer of 1928 had arrived. Ted Lewis and his musicians played in New York that summer after sessions at Los Angeles and in Europe. In other major cities the playhouses were quiet during the first days of June. Patrons were spending leisure hours away from the congestion of the cities with the heat being the major reason. The days and evenings were sweltering—and the nights were just plain hot. Air-conditioned comfort would arrive in another age.

Carroll McComas continued in the cast of *The Ladder*, although her fellow actor, Reginald Owen, temporarily deserted the drama to play Cardinal Richelieu in the cast of *The Three Musketeers*. In London, Van Druten's dramatization of Rebecca West's novel *The Return of the Soldier* received favorable reviews.

Sportswear became fancier this summer of '28 and "modernism is the new vogue." Helena Rubinstein, world famous beauty scientist, granted personal consultations at her New York studio during the first week in July. Banks advertised 4½ percent interest on savings and urged everyone to "invest your money in the safest way." The painting *Woodland Stream* by Wilson Irvine, ANA, was displayed at Grand Central Galleries. The *Blackbirds of 1928*, featuring Bill Robinson, was advertised as playing at the Liberty Theater in New York. The same day this ad appeared the Boy Scouts marked the entire Lincoln Highway with signposts promoting highway safety. Covering 3,100 miles, the task was accomplished in one day.

Meanwhile in Detroit, the gaiety of the decade was

mirrored by the activities of its residents. Thomas Meighan appeared in *The Racket* and *Wings* was a best-selling Paramount movie in its forty-eighth consecutive showing. Cecil B. De Mille's *King of Kings* was billed as a "new sensation."

On Saturday, June 30, large crowds converged by car and foot on Ford Airport at Dearborn. There was an exciting day awaiting them. By noon 100,000 persons were crowded inside the airport and another 50,000 lined the highways for miles in all directions. The trip to the airport had taken the spectators past great subdivisions that had been laid out in the mid 1920's—some of which were abandoned. The Florida land boom of the early Twenties had affected other sections of America. The main event at Ford Airport that day was the National Air Tour scheduled to start in the morning. But the James Gordon Bennett International Balloon Race, scheduled to start at 4 P. M., attracted many, many spectators. Airplanes always attracted attention because they were a recent and novel experiment of man. But when word circulated that balloons were going up, the crowds would swell to tremendous proportions.

MICHIGAN, DETROIT AND FORD AIRPORT

L'etat c'est moi! (I am the state!)
Louis XIV 1655

The combined land and water acreage of Michigan makes it the largest state east of the Mississippi. It has two peninsulas, a 3,200-mile Great Lakes shoreline, 17 million acres of forest land, 11,000 plus inland lakes and more than 80 skiing centers. It is a vast recreational wonderland. The "Wolverine State" contains a total of 58,216 square miles ranking 23rd in size. Michigan was admitted to the Union on January 26, 1837, thus becoming the 26th state.

In ancient times the Indians dreamed of bridging the Straits of Mackinac, a five-mile span in the upper peninsula that was a major obstacle for them. Their age-old dream was realized for use of modern man in 1957 at a cost of $100 million. A majestic bridge now connects the Mackinac with the Sault-Green Bay across from the upper peninsula.

The majority of the population of Michigan is in the southeastern part of the state. Detroit, the "Motor City," is the hub of an eight-county section that contains 50,000 acres of public land and hundreds of inland lakes. (See Figure 2.) Founded in 1701 by Antoine Cadillac, Detroit was captured by the British in 1760 and other French settlements were taken in 1761. On July 17, 1787, Michigan, and its growing city of Detroit, became part of the Northwest Territory. Detroit and Mackinac were surrendered to the United States by the British in 1796. At the site where Cadillac and his hearty Frenchmen landed in 1701 is found a 75-acre civic center. The Veterans Memorial Building located there marks the site of the landing.

Thus the flags of France, Britain, and the United States have flown over Detroit. Further, Windsor, Ontario, is just across the Detroit River making Detroit an international city while deep in the heartland of America. With this colorful and varied history, Michigan is a favorite with tourists. Old forts, covered bridges, mining towns and historic monuments capture the imagination of thousands of visitors each year. With 110,000 miles of well-kept highways and 1,000 miles of free expressways available, those who visit can travel to historic points quickly and easily—and Detroit is also a tourist favorite.

With the title of the "Automobile Capital of the World," Detroit is the nation's fifth largest city. Here Henry Ford began the motor revolution that changed the course of mankind. In June, 1928, Henry Ford stated: "I'm not a success. I am not yet a success, except as an assembler of tools. My real work remains to be done."[9] His prophecy was accurate and in many ways his work is still not completed. But his contribution was to be greater than he could have realized at that time. The executive offices of three American giants of industry are located in the "Motor City": Chrysler, General Motors, and American Motors. Their assembly plants are well-visited tourist attractions. The giant Ford River Rouge plant at Dearborn is a particular favorite with tourists.

The history of Detroit can almost be relived first-hand by visitors. For example, at the Historical Museum in Detroit, on a cobblestone street of the 1840's, is found the gunsmith shop of William Wingert with its original fittings. Old-time barber shops are there with mustache cups lining the windows. At Dearborn, the Henry Ford Museum, Edison Institute and Greenfield Village have become leading tourist attractions. One enters the fabulous Ford Museum and Edison Institute through a replica of Independence Hall. After the city fathers of Philadelphia refused to sell Henry Ford the original, Ford ordered his engineers to reconstruct Independence Hall in the middle of a beautiful field at Dearborn. The final cost of this project is unknown even to those who supervise the Ford Archives. It is a strikingly beautiful and fitting memorial to not one great man—but three: Thomas A. Edison, Luther Burbank and Ford.

Under the main steeple of the structure, on the first level just inside the main entrance, is a large, glass-covered block of concrete. On September 27, 1928, Edison placed his footprints in the soft concrete and signed his name in a large, scrawling fashion. After this, the silver shovel used by Burbank to turn the first ground for the museum was thrust deep into the concrete. Today the shovel, the signature and the prints remain: a fitting memorial for future generations. Glass encloses the cornerstone, but the shovel, with its silver "D" type handle, protrudes through an opening.

The workshop of Thomas Edison has been reconstructed at nearby Greenfield Village. The country courthouse in which Lincoln once practiced law, the Wright brothers' cycle shop (See Figure 3) and many other historical buildings have been rebuilt for posterity. In the basement of Ford Museum is found the power plant that once supplied electricity to the residents of Davis, Tucker County, West Virginia. On one of his fishing trips to the beautiful hills of West Virginia, Ford had seen this plant. Some older residents of Parsons, West Virginia, still recall that Ford, accompanied by Edison and Harvey Samuel Firestone, had stopped at the drug store opposite their aging county courthouse. The three giants of American industry were interested in only one thing at that time—a cool drink. In later years J. S. Cooper, Oakland, Md., explained how the power plant found its way to Edison Institute:

> The power plant was located in the West Virginia Pulp and Paper plant at Davis. It was powered by steam from the paper plant and as I remember the generator was 3 or 4 feet high and a wide belt from a 10 or 12 foot high fly wheel ran the generator and for years only

operated at night, no day service. A man by the name of
Harry Hunter, who worked for the Paper Company and
later moved to Detroit and was a top engineer for Edison Electric in Detroit, was the one who made the arrangement with the Town of Davis and the Ford
Museum. When I visited the museum many years ago
this plant was in the basement in the same building with
the old cars and railroad equipment. At that time I visited with Harry Hunter who is now deceased but he told
me the story about how he had arranged for the moving
of the plant to Detroit.[10]

The Davis Electric Light Company had been incorporated
with a starting capital of $50,000. With F. S. Landstreet as
President, H. A. Meyer as Secretary and C. E. Smith as Treas-
urer, the plant was operated under careful and judicious management. Electric light was furnished by the plant as early as
1895 and the cost to the users at Davis was very modest.

In June, 1928, Ford Airport at Dearborn was being called
"A Model of Efficient Organization." Aircraft flying both to
and from the airfield often passed over Detroit. Because of
this, the average person residing in Detroit had seen more
airplanes than any three or four persons in New York City.
Detroiters were said to be "air conscious" and the modern air
age had truly arrived at Detroit. The great percentage of
Americans elsewhere had yet to see their first aircraft. While
it is true that air events of this decade made constant headlines yet the unforgettable sound of the grinding and thresh-
ing of a wood propeller against turbulent air would not be
heard by many for years to come. It was estimated that by
1925 less than one percent of the population of America had
even been near a real airplane. The few aircraft that were in
use usually belonged to a "barnstormer" or a circus flyer, and
these were few in number. But this wasn't so at Detroit.

Located eleven miles out of downtown Detroit, Ford Airport had been constructed by Henry Ford and was by far the
most efficient airdrome east of the Mississippi. The field had

been constructed upon part of three hundred and fifty acres owned by Ford and was surrounded by high brick walls. Within were four main buildings. At the aircraft factory, four tri-motor "Tin Geese" and fourteen monoplanes were produced per month. Adolph Hitler later flew in a Ford Tri-Motor on one of his trips across Europe although his regular flights were made in a Fokker Tri-Motor. On May 9, 1926, Commander Richard E. Byrd, accompanied by pilot Floyd Bennett, made the first flight over the North Pole in a Fokker Tri-Motor. The ship had been named *Josephine Ford* in honor of the wife of Edsel Ford.

Today, the German Tri-Motor sits in Edison Institute beside a Liberty V-12, 400 H.P. engine designed and constructed by Henry Ford in 1917. This was a powerful engine and it would be used successfully in other planes which made historic flights at different times. The Byrd-Fokker Tri-Motor had been powered by three Wright Whirlwind Engines. To the right of this Fokker sits the Ford Tri-Motor that had been used by Byrd on his next successful flight: the flight over the South Pole. A 12-inch, oval aluminum plate is riveted to the left side of this ship. On the plate these words are found: "Stout Metal Airplane Company, Division of Ford Motor Company, Dearborn, Michigan." This plane was constructed of corrugated dura-aluminum riveted at close intervals. Five windows run along the lower side of the plane. The two side engines have two-bladed propellers while the center motor has three. Attached to the landing gear struts are two giant, laminated wood skis used in the South Pole landings. The name "Floyd Bennett" is painted on the side. Under the right wing of this plane sits the "Second Spirit of St. Louis" flown by Jimmy Stewart in the movie of the first solo flight across the Atlantic. (See Figure 4.) The left wing of the "Spirit" extends over the left wing of the German *Bremen* (see Figure 6), the first plane to cross the Atlantic East-West. These

planes are all part of one story—a story that finds Henry and
Edsel Ford—and Ford Airport—deeply involved.

A second large building at Ford Airport in 1928 was a
huge metal and concrete hangar. Large enough for fifty or
more planes, it contained several efficient offices. Near the
giant hangar were testing laboratories, a power plant and
other equipment needed to meet the requirements of the
operation of a major airport in 1928.

About one mile south of the center of the main runway
stood a dirigible mast or mooring tower. While it had cost
$100,000 to build, it had only been used twice in two years.
At the top of the tower was a beacon that could be seen as
far as 50 miles on some evenings.

Three runways had been constructed at Ford Airport. Two
were laid out in a southeast direction and the third southwest. The prevailing winds from Lake Erie had been a factor
in the final location of the landing strips. The main strip was
3,500 feet long, the other two less than 1,000 feet. The
shorter runways had not been completed in 1928. Hardy
North Dakota grass had been planted in the earth between
the strips but the wheels of the huge planes kept the turf
ground into dust. On dry summer days the arriving and de-
parting planes caused dust clouds that could be seen for miles
and the airplanes of the Stout Company were kicking up
their share of the dust.

The name Stout was familiar to those who visited or used
Ford Airport. The Stout All-Metal Airplane Company was
not only the builder of the Ford Tri-Motor but constructed
freight, passenger carriers and monoplanes as well. In August,
1925, Ford purchased all of the stock of the Stout Metal
Airplane Company and Edsel Ford played an important part
in his decision. Edsel had been impressed with the fact that
the company had been using dura-aluminum to build the
large, sturdy monoplanes. Such an innovation proved worth-
while and the company, under Ford management, looked

forward to the production of one plane a week and later, one per day. In 1926, the Ford Tri-Motor had gone into service and remained a major plane in commercial aviation for more than a decade. And tri-motor Fords still fly in parts of the world today. The "Tin Geese" are about as sturdy as any airplane ever constructed.

At that time a German professor named Junkers stated that air freight would never pay unless it was done on a regular basis for the public, accompanied by passengers on the same flight. Ford's temporary reply to the prediction was to permit only air freight at his airport which concerned Ford business. Maybe he didn't know American history too well, but he knew how to run his own airline! But Ford knew the German was right and his long-range plans included plans for regular passenger service.

In the meantime Stout Air Service operated a 30-mile sight-seeing tour from Ford Airport over Detroit and back. Also two daily round trip flights were made to Cleveland, some 60 miles across Lake Erie. Flights to other major cities were soon added.

The Stout factory worked eight-hour shifts, twice each day except on Sunday. The same schedule was followed by the Ford and Lincoln car plants because Ford would not permit Sunday work. But the policy caused problems for Stout. Many would-be Sunday passengers were turned away because of this policy. It was no secret that the personnel who flew for Stout were looking for another field to fly from on Sunday and maybe permanently. The reason was an economic one—the Stout flyers were losing considerable revenue because they were not permitted to fly on the one day that would-be passengers were free to come to them—Sunday.

As it turned out sight-seeing flights and not freight and air-mail provided the bulk of the Ford Airport revenue. From May 27 to December 1, 1927, Stout personnel flew 19,000 persons. The company expected to carry over 50,000 in 1928 with an expected gross revenue of over one-half million dollars. These figures would have been much higher had Sunday flying been permitted. But Ford firmly believed in the day off. Enough profit—and wages—were made the other six days of each week.

Passenger buses left Detroit regularly 50 minutes before scheduled flight time and pickup points were plainly marked at the main hotels and restaurants. Upon arrival at the airport, travelers saw as many as 20 planes leaving in one day—a record for those times. Sight-seeing tours were available daily until dark—except on Sundays. The 35-minute bus round trip from Detroit to Ford Airport soon prompted others to plan another airfield closer to downtown Detroit. The general feeling was that the drive to Ford Airport was a waste of time. In the meantime, Ford Airport with adequate waiting rooms, bus service, excellent hangars and other modern facilities—including Dearborn Inn—served the flying public well.

The National Air Tour had been scheduled to start from Ford Airport on Saturday, June 30, 1928. There were simply *no* exceptions to the Ford Sunday rule. All sight-seeing flights were cancelled this day in order to avoid hazards to both participants and observers. Many spectators arrived in the early hours of the morning and by noon every open field inside and adjoining the airfield was crowded with men, women, children, cars and dogs. Indian blankets and picnic lunches dotted dozens of acres inside the airport. Several high school bands were present in their colorful, military style uniforms. Vendors circulated through the crowds selling soft drinks, popcorn, gaily colored balloons and small American flags. The day had taken on a gay, colorful carnival atmosphere.

Those present were about to witness the start of the Fourth Annual National Air Tour. At stake was the Edsel B. Ford "Reliability Trophy"—an outgrowth of the Ford interest in aviation and "engine engineering." After leaving Ford

Airport on June 30, the participants followed an air route that took them to Indianapolis, Wichita, Tucson, Los Angeles, Tacoma, Fargo, North Dakota, Chicago, Battle Creek and back to Detroit by July 28. "America First in the Air" announced the program sold by circulating vendors.

The size of the constantly swelling crowd was attributed both to the publicity of the National Tour and the second double feature—the James Gordon Bennett International Balloon Race that was scheduled to begin at four o'clock. Both events were sponsored by Ford Motor Company as had been the case in 1927. The 25 planes in the National Air Tour had all taken off without incident and faded into the distance headed for Indiana. The crowd shifted its collective attention to the second feature of the day—the International Balloon Race. It was a lovely June day for the start of any type of race.

Overhead, light fluffy June clouds drifted lazily across the brilliant blue summer sky as a gentle breeze from the direction of Dearborn Heights helped them along. These patches of white in the sky provided cooling shade to the inquisitive crowds below who systematically explored the airfield. In the dusty areas of earth between the hangars several aircraft were being given close scrutiny by those who crowded around them. Here and there a dog yapped as lively children darted back and forth around and under the planes and through tie-down ropes securely fastened to iron anchors driven into the hard, summer-dried ground.

As the morning passed the activity increased. At the far end of the main runway several military style tents had drawn the attention of many spectators. Flags of several nations flapped near the tents as the gentle breeze lifted their colorful folds first one way, then another. Here a flag of Germany, there a flag of France, a flag of Argentina, and flags of other countries as well. Many persons guessed wrong in their efforts to tie a flag to a nation. The tents were the field headquarters of the balloonists while some held equipment and personal gear of the participants in the race. Tents, contestants, flags and gear were all under the watchful eyes of inspired spectators. It was a true spectacular.

Near the center of the airport large canvas ground cloths were unfolded. Small boys were hired from the crowd to sweep the dust from these cloths, some of which were as large as 100 feet square. Occasionally large air bubbles had raised up within the folds of the canvas covers as they were unfolded. The problem was solved by attendants who directed the small fry "sweepers" to run these bubbles right out of the canvas. It proved great sport as spectators cheered their progress.

The balloons had been stored at the main hangar and several Model "T" trucks delivered large, canvas-covered bundles to the proper ground cloths. The milling crowds made driving difficult and the drivers were forced to repeatedly use their "OOGAH" horns to clear a path to the proper location. Service help unstrapped web belts from brass buckles, allowing the contents of the bundles to spill onto the ground cloths. Great care was taken to make certain that sharp objects or other foreign matter did not get under or within the unfolded bundles. The balloon within each bundle was carefully tugged across the proper ground cloth until the unfilled gasbag was spread out in near-perfect circles. None of the teams present wanted to be eliminated by some careless mistake at this point. For this reason, all contestants were carefully overseeing the preparations and each flying team closely observed their balloon as it was tugged into position for filling.

The flyers of the three American teams present carried the hope of capturing permanent possession of the James Gordon Bennett trophy. Since America had won in 1926 and 1927, a win in 1928 would provide the three straight victories required under international rules to give permanent possession of the coveted balloon trophy to America.

One of the American balloons and its two flyers captured the attention of the milling crowds. *The United States Army Entry No. 1* was piloted by a strikingly handsome 35-year-old Army captain, William E. Kepner. Born in Peru, Indiana, on January 6, 1893, the captain had a brilliant service record behind him. From Mexican border service as an infantry private with the National Guard, he had gone to France in World War I to earn the Distinguished Service Cross for heroism. His promotion to captain, Regular Army, followed on July 1, 1920, exactly eight years lacking one day before the starting date of the 1928 balloon race.

This handsome aeronaut took the "first large step toward the moon" in *Explorer I* on July 28, 1934. A section of material from his high-flying balloon of that year was carried by the United States astronauts during the first moon orbit in 1969. His distinguished career elevated him to the rank of Lieutenant General of the United States Air Force and command of the Eighth Strategic Air Force Command. The talent of true leaders is often uncovered during the course of dangerous sporting events. And it is said that the 1934 flight became a reality only because of Kepner's success in the 1928 race. So the first step to the moon was made on June 30, 1928.

Captain Kepner's aide in the 1928 race was a dashing second lieutenant, aged 28, by the name of William O. Eareckson. A spirited man, "Eric" had the deepest admiration for his captain. Born in Maryland, May 30, 1900, "Eric" was the subject of later gentle memories of General Kepner.

Henry Ford visited Kepner's inflation point that morning. Having met Captain Kepner on a previous occasion, Ford asked the captain to accompany him as he visited other flight locations. Ford expressed particular interest in the German teams and since Kepner spoke German, a friendly acquaintance between Ford and the flyers developed as Ford warmly greeted each of the German contestants. Kepner recalled 41 years later that Ford had been particularly impressed by the thorough preparation made by the German flyers. Ford toured the other inflation points and personally greeted a representative of each nation that had an entry in the race.

At a study room in the main Ford hangar, several flyers were busy scanning weather maps. The maps covered the eastern United States reaching from Michigan to Florida. With luck one of the contestants might set a new record within two days. As it stood, the world's distance record for free flight in a balloon had been set by a Frenchman in 1912, in a spectacular flight across Europe. The distance covered?—an unbelievable 1,358 miles! The record stood at the close of the 1928 race. The weather was and is the primary and constant concern of balloonists. For this reason, C. G. Andrus, weather forecaster for the Air Mail Service, was present at Ford Airport.

It was his job to fully advise the contestants as to weather conditions. Being a former international balloonist, Andrus was well qualified to act as a consultant for the flyers. Flying a free-flight balloon was hazardous, and knowing this, Andrus made it a point to be accurate and completely fair and impartial to each contestant. It would have been wrong (criminally so) to give advantage to one contestant at the expense of another. Death might well result from such partiality. While it was true that each contestant was there to win the race, they nevertheless did all they could to assist each other. Ballooning is a sport that lends itself to cooperation between competitors and the dangerous nature of the sport makes it so. Therefore, the pre-race activity at Ford Airport was careful, deliberate, and even friendly. It was as though all of the contestants were on the same team.

Across from the main hangar, Andrus had set up a radio broadcasting station. Since some of the flyers carried radios in their gondolas, or baskets, he could keep them informed on weather conditions after the race began. He was prepared to broadcast reports that evening (June 30) of weather conditions over the Lake Region consisting of Lake Erie, Lake Michigan, Ohio, New York State and Pennsylvania. On the next day (July 1) he would forecast the weather that would likely prevail further to the South and East. If all went well, one or more of the assembled flyers would benefit directly from the information.

Seven nations (and Aero clubs within those nations) had sponsored entries in the race and Germany was represented by three teams. It was only the second race since 1913 in which Germany had participated. The intervention of the First World War and the German defeat was an obvious reason for this. The German entries were the *Munster*, piloted by Ferdinand Eimenacher, and his aide, Carl Zeck; the *Bremen* (named in honor of the plane now at the Edison Institute, see Figure 6), flown by Hugo Kaulen and assisted by his son, Hugo Kaulen, Jr., (the only father and son team in the race); and the *Brandenburg*, piloted by Captain Otto Bertram, assisted by Lieutenant Georg Frobel—a German military team consisting of a former military dirigible pilot and an artillery officer.

The other entries, the nations they represented and their crews were:

> *American Business Club*, Akron, Ohio. A. C. Chalmers, pilot; Lieutenant F. M. McKee, aide.
> *The Detroit*, Detroit, Michigan. W. C. Naylor, pilot; Rund Wherritt, aide.
> *The Lafayette*, France. Georges Blanchet, pilot; Alphonse Coquois, aide.
> *The Denmark*, Denmark. S. A. U. Rasmussen, pilot; Tracy W. Southworth, aide.
> *The Helvetia*, Switzerland. E. S. Magg, pilot, who flew alone (the only solo flight in the race).
> *The United States Army*, the United States. Captain W. E. Kepner, pilot; W. O. Eareckson, aide.
> *The Argentina*, Argentina. Don Eduardo Bradley, pilot; Huberto E. Elliff, aide.

The Wallonie, Belgium. Joseph Thonnard, pilot; Profes-
sor Maurice Boel (a flying doctor), aide; and
The Blanchard, France. Charles Dolifus, pilot; Georges
Carmier, aide.

What had caused such diversified persons from so many
nations to gather at Ford Airport? The Atlantic had been
conquered by both man and woman and heavier-than-air flying made constant news. What type of sport was it that drew
flyers, former artillery officers, fathers and sons—and even a
doctor of philosophy? The answer to the question would
vary as each contestant might formulate his own ideas of the
reason. But one thing seems certain; the background of the
race and a brief look at the history of free-flight ballooning
provides insight into the reason why that variety of persons
gathered there to compete in the race.

SOME HISTORY

In ancient centuries, down the deep corridors of time, man lived in a wilderness surrounded by beasts of all kinds. Long ago he must have noticed two things: the winged creatures that successfully used the air to avoid the pitfalls that constantly confronted him, and the rising smoke and flames from fires created either by an "Act of God" or his own efforts. Here, in wings and air lighter-than-air, was ultimately found the answer to an age-old question: Will man ever fly? It is theorized that primitive awareness of flight, in some form, contributed to the ancient and recurring subconscious nighttime dream of man—the dream of flying. Each man—and woman—has experienced this.

Before man could conquer the air some type of propelling or "lifting" force had to be found. The force would have to be either vertical, or horizontal, or a combination of both. Successful forward propulsion came first in the form of the internal combustion engine, sprocket chained to a wooden propeller, and later in the form of jet and rocket power. The first effective vertical power came from lighter than normal air—hot air—captured within a container. In the meantime, before successful and later practiced flight, man flew in legend.

Khenso, the "navigator of the skies," was carefully shoved into immortality by artistic Egyptians who recorded his flying feats in paintings created many years before the birth of Christ. At least these unknown artists left the impression that Khenso could fly since they recorded the fact that he had wings.

In 885 B.C., Ashur, the leading Assyrian deity, was carved

into a bas-relief wall scene showing him with the head of a warrior—but with the wings of an eagle.

In Greek legend, Icarus, with wings of feathers attached to his body by wax, flew so high that the sun melted the wax, causing the feathers to fall thus sending him to his death in the sea below. Daedalus had told his son Icarus not to fly too close to the sun! Dissenting youth quite early learned the art of ignoring competent advice from experienced elders!

And there was Elijah[11] who ". . . went up by a whirlwind into heaven," and this probably happened. He may not have reached heaven but the event is based upon enough fact to conclude that he went somewhere.

Centuries passed and legend gave way to primitive scientific research. Flight by man might yet become a possibility and man continued to try. Early theories of flight had been developed by the Chinese in their use of kites since 200 B.C. Fashioned in the form of dragons and demons grotesquely painted with brilliant dyes and pigments, their kites presented a striking spectacle once placed into the air. Here was a form of flight—but it lacked practical use. In later centuries many travelers to the Orient purchased kites and carried them to other nations. At first they were used for amusement only but scientific use followed in more modern times as man learned basic principles of heavier-than-air flying from them.

Many centuries ago Father Galien of Avigon discussed one possible formula for flight.[12] He theorized that rarefied air would be found on the mountaintops. If this air could be captured in a container and brought back to lower ground, upon release, the air and the container would return to the mountains from which it came. Carrying this to a conclusion, Father Galien suggested that if enough rarefied air could be captured, it could lift a chariot, a man or two and a team of horses, thus providing the whole assemblage with a free ride to the mountaintop. Apparently the horses would be needed for the ride home. The trip up would be on air—the trip back on saddles.

Albertus Mangus, writing on the subject of "Wonders of Nature" in the 13th century, suggested a plan that had possibilities. He wrote: "Take one pound of sulphur, two pounds of willow carbon, six ounces of rock salt, grind very fine in a marble mortar. Place when you please in a cover made of flying papyrus to produce thunder. The covering, in order to ascend and float away, should be long, graceful and well filled with this fine powder." He recognized that the shape of the container would have an effect upon its performance in flight. The ingredients listed would probably have caused a rocket-like explosion with some form of propulsion resulting. He did not mention that the plan had met with any success. However the fact that he wrote of it is evidence that experimentation along those lines was carried out in the years before Columbus discovered America.

Man's dream of flying persisted. Even though man had not been successful there was no reason why he should stop trying. And try he did. Gliders or wings were constructed from willow limbs and other materials. Covered with fine linen fabric, these wings were sometimes attached to foot-powered devices. Other times the wings were simply held by straps placed around the arms of the would-be flyer—and the "flying pioneer" went out to the field to try his luck. Men threw themselves down the sides of steep mountains, into rivers and even over the edge of cliffs with the flying device clutched in some manner. These early attempts to fly are sometimes comical as recalled today but usually tragic then for those who tried. Success waited for a relatively recent time and it first came in the form of lighter-than-air flying.

Joseph Michael Montgolfier (1740-1810) and Jacques Etienne Montgolfier (1745-1799) were brothers living and working in Paris, France. They had been successful in the manufacture and sale of all types of paper products. As young men they had spent many hours of winter evenings in front of the massive fireplace in their father's villa-type home watching the ashes of burned parchment rising up the chimney. They suggested to each other that an open mouth paper bag placed over hot air would rise up the chimney just as the ashes did. Experiments quickly demonstrated that this was so. They further observed that in almost all cases the bag would be destroyed or damaged by the fire that lifted it. The fire source had to be controlled in order to prevent the paper bag from igniting. They began to reason that a small fire, mounted underneath an open mouth container of light fabric, would place man into the air. Experiments continued.

Turning to silk material, the Montgolfier brothers constructed a large teardrop-shaped balloon with a relatively small open mouth. Suspended below the open mouth was a platform upon which a small fire could be started and maintained. The platform was attached to the silk material above by ropes.

On June 5, 1783, the Montgolfier brothers made the first public ascension of a lighter-than-air balloon over Annonay, France. The flight was made without passengers—and as it turned out, luckily so. The large balloon rose to about 3,000 feet, literally pushed upward by the hot air rising from the fire crackling and smoking below the open mouth of the balloon. The lumbering airship stayed up for 45 minutes and traveled some 15 miles. There had been no news of the first attempt to fly and when the balloon descended near a neighboring hamlet the populace was terrified. The people concluded—and justifiably so—that they were being attacked by some kind of monster from the skies.

Concerned first about women, children and incompetents, the braver members of the "home guard" eventually attacked the gasping hulk of the downed balloon with pitchforks, knives, stones and other convenient weapons. As the "victim" was torn to shreds, black, smoky gas belched from its wounds. Assured now that this creature from above had been overwhelmed, the heroes continued their destruction. The "coup de grace" was administered to the "monster" by tying the ragged remains to the tail of a plow horse. Now followed a sharp "crack" across the hindquarters and the startled creature scampered for its life across the green French countryside. The first balloon ascension was history.

Legend, scientific experiments and facts began to fall into place as history continued to be made. On September 18, some 105 days from the first ascension, the Montgolfier brothers were ready for a second try. The "battling neighbors" had left the brothers nothing to salvage and they had been forced to start all over again. Learning from experience they circulated word throughout the countryside about their next flight. The name "Montgolfier" became synonymous with free-flight ballooning and those who learned of the bold new experiment watched the sky. Man was causing something to happen there for the first time.

This second flight is known as "the first passenger flight." Carefully selected, the passengers consisted of a sheep, a rooster and a duck. The second balloon and its startled crew, rose 1,500 feet above Paris and traveled two miles before the hot air cooled within the container dropping the ship and contents safely to earth. One observer at the event was an American by the name of Benjamin Franklin. He was both interested in and impressed by what he saw.

The first true manned flight followed on November 21, 1783. A French scientist, M. Pilâte de Rozier, and the Marques d' Arlandes acquired a Montgolfier hot air balloon. The balloon was gaily decorated with colorful designs that reached around the large exterior establishing a custom that would be followed two centuries later. With apprehensive passengers hanging on for dear life the fragile ship rose to an altitude of only 300 feet but drifted five miles in 20 minutes.

The King of France originally refused to allow de Rozier, a

brilliant scientist, to risk his life in the flight. The King commanded instead that two criminals sentenced to death be sent. Arlandes interceded and agreed to accompany de Rozier and his gallantry won the King. Ben Franklin was there again and became the first American to see an air voyage of human beings. (This same year the British granted the American Colonies their independence. Thus American freedom and the freedom of flight were realized in the same year.)

The balloon in which man first ascended measured 85 feet high and 48 feet in diameter—a large one by today's standards. The lift, or buoyancy power, was supplied by a fire located below the open mouth of the balloon. With a capacity of 100,000 cubic feet, the balloon had a neck of 16 feet in diameter. Around this neck was a three-foot wide wooden balcony with railings upon which the first aeronauts walked. Stockpiled on the circular walkway were bundles of straw used for fuel in the fire along with pails of water and sponges to extinguish any flames that might spread from the central heating unit into the balloon itself.

On November 22, 1783, Franklin wrote to Sir Joseph Bank about the first flight of man:

> There was a vast concourse in the garden who had great pleasure in seeing the adventurers go off so cheerfully, (sir) and applauded them by clapping Sc., but there was at the same time a good deal of anxiety for their safety. Multitudes in Paris saw the balloon passing; but did not know there were men in it, it being then so high that they could not see them.
> One of these courageous philosophers, the Marquis d' Arlandes, did me the honor to call upon me in the evening after the experiment with Mr. Montgolfier, the very ingenious inventor. I was happy to see him safe. He inform'd me they lit gently without the least shock, and the balloon was very little damag'd. [13]

After the flight, d' Arlandes reported:

> After crossing the House of the Invalides, we passed

along the island of Cygnes, reentering the principal bend
of the river. I stirred the fire and took with the fork a
truss of straw, which from being too tight, did not fire
easily. I lifted it and shook it in the middle of the flame.
The next moment I felt as if I were lifted up from under
the arms, and said to my companion, "Now we mount."
I felt a shock, which was the only one I experienced. I
said then: "What are you doing? Are you dancing?" "I
don't stir," said he. "So much the better," I replied, "it
is then a new current, which, I hope will push us over
the river." In passing over Paris, we approached the tops
of the houses, very sensibly we increased the fire and
rose with the greatest ease. A rising current of air carried
us toward the south.[14]

The first manned flight was history and a few persons in
other nations became interested.

On January 9, 1784, just 49 days after the first manned
flight, Jean Pierre Blanchard of France made the first manned
flight in America, traveling from Philadelphia to Woodbury,
New Jersey—a flight of 45 miles. A large, gay group of persons had assembled that day. In attendance and dressed in
appropriate finery for the occasion was President George
Washington. The ascent of the balloon was exciting to those
who witnessed it—but apparently it wasn't much more than
that. The big craft was too delicate, unstable and could not
be controlled. The balloon appeared to Washington to be
little more than an instrument for Sunday amusement.
Blanchard carried a personal note from the President asking
the people "to aide this gallant flyer." A crossing of the
English Channel by air came next.

Approximately one year later, January 7, 1785, Blanchard
teamed up with Dr. John Jefferies of the United States in an
effort to fly the English Channel. The ascension from England was made without mishap and prevailing winds carried
them toward their destination. However, not knowing that
free ballooning is always more successful in warm weather,
the flyers suddenly found themselves losing altitude in the

cold of January despite emergency efforts to stoke the fire
under the balloon. All loose gear and ballast were frantically
thrown overboard in an effort to keep the ship out of the
freezing, chopping waters nipping at the bottom of their gondola. Arriving in France by a narrow margin, the flyers had
nothing of any substance left in their basket. Even their
clothes had been thrown overboard. There was quite a stir at
the landing site as two embarrassed and shivering flyers scampered for cover. One eyewitness newsman reported, "Ballooning is not a sport for women."

The channel crossing began a series of "firsts" which continued until the first man stepped onto the moon. Credit for
the first air flight by a woman was given to Madame Thible of
France. On June 4, 1784, she co-piloted a hot air balloon on
a successful flight accompanied by W. M. Fleurant. The first
parachute jump (something that had to follow successful ballooning) was made in 1797 when Andre Jacques Garnerin,
jumped from a balloon over Paris at an altitude of 2,230 feet.
Born in 1769, Garnerin would live a fairly long life to die in
1823. (The first jump from a heavier-than-air craft waited
until March 1, 1912, when Captain A. Berry, UC, dropped
from an airplane over St. Louis, Missouri.) One who is "first"
can never be anything else—not "second"—and cannot be
placed in any other position. The nature of the "human"
(being what it is) leaves no place for one who finishes
second—or even third. "One who finishes second is a loser."

The years passed, the United States of America flourished
with newly won independence and the new century opened.
Another war with England (the War of 1812) was resolved
and the new nation settled down to enjoy a relatively long
period of nervous peace. By 1859 the nervousness was replaced by unbridled anger. The young and great new nation
of America separated at midpoint: The North turned and
faced the South. Anger and separation led to a holocaust and
hundreds of thousands of American lives were consumed in

resolving the issues: issues of states' rights, cotton—and slavery. It was the greatest of American tragedies—American vs. American had met on the field of battle.

Overshadowed by events of national importance a small incident occurred August 17, 1859. That day John Wise flew a lighter-than-air balloon carrying mail from Lafayette, Indiana, to Crawfordsville, Indiana. Thus the United States Air Mail Service was born prior to the American Civil War. One hundred years later the event was commemorated by the issuance of an appropriate stamp at Lafayette. The stamp marked the almost forgotten event—a first in air mail history. John Wise tried for a better place in history a few years later when he challenged Professor Thaddeus Lowe in the attempt to establish the "United States Air Force."

Balloons found use at other stages of history. For example, the Franco-Prussian war raged during the years 1870 and 1871. As will be mentioned later an associate of Thaddeus Lowe had been a German by the name of Zeppelin. After flying in battle with Lowe during the Civil War, Zeppelin quickly realized the military potential of balloons. In the new war in France, Zeppelin used balloons to establish communications between besieged Paris and the outside world.

Peacetime ballooning flights set records and in 1910 an American crew flew more than 1,100 miles in a flight from St. Louis to the Quebec wilds of Canada. The haggard flyers struggled their way to civilization after five harrowing days on foot. The flight stands as a distance record for free-flight ballooning upon the continent of the Americas.

Balloons were widely used by both sides in World War I for observation and aircraft defense purposes. They saw limited use as a weapon of offense as long, ghostly gray, Zeppelins bombed London on several occasions. But the price paid by the Germans was too high. Flyers such as Frank Luke of Arizona (See Figure 7) made ballooning one of the most hazardous occupations of the war for those who flew them.

The Germans made pre-war threats in reference to destruction of London by means of Zeppelins. In the end the threats proved more fearful in words than in action and many Germans perished in the flaming folds of hydrogen-filled monsters. A few survived, and one of them, Otto Bertram, flew in a balloon race in America ten years following the close of the First World War.

During the Second World War, English balloons pulled steel wires aloft in an effort to clip the wings from German Dorniers, Stukas, and Messerschmitts as they winged across the Channel to deliver destruction to the English cities—and especially so on "Eagle Day."[15] Occasionally an errant Spitfire pilot found himself desperately flying between silver wires that looked like tracer bullets fired vertically into the air. This "second" war saw the last extensive use of balloons as an implement of warfare. There would be no use for them in Korea or Vietnam.

Between the two great wars, balloons, in the form of dirigibles, were used successfully for many Atlantic crossings. Luxurious saloons inside the gondolas complete with finest silver and glassware were available to the passengers who made those trips. The safety record of the crossings in terms of passenger miles was excellent even by modern standards. World War II would have stopped the crossings—but instead, a tragedy in 1937 slowed the flights to a standstill. The explosion and flaming destruction of the *Hindenburg* at Lakehurst, New Jersey, and the loss of life that accompanied it, for all practical purposes ended trans-Atlantic travel by balloon. The tragedy had occurred as the dirigible was mooring in preparation to discharge passengers. Reporters present reported the tragic event firsthand. The flaming, exploding hulk of the *Hindenburg* had been filled with volatile—but inexpensive—hydrogen. Only a spark from an overheated piece of equipment—or a carelessly tossed cigarette was needed to cause the holocaust. The death of the *Hindenburg* was tied by a direct link to a balloon flight of the Twenties.

The *Hindenburg* disaster almost spelled finish to trans-Atlantic balloon travel but balloons were destined to play another role in coming years. Altitude exploration and scientific experimentation while circling the earth in orbit were jobs that would be accomplished by use of balloons. Other than this the major use of lighter-than-air balloons shifted to peacetime balloon racing—a sport that has few followers today.

1928 PITTSBURGH ELIMINATION RACE

When the Gods destroy, they first make mad. [16]

In all major racing events some plan is developed whereby the sponsoring association may eliminate all of the hopefuls except those who make the best showings in semi-final races. So it was in international balloon racing. The 1928 National Balloon Race was held May 30, 1928, at Bettis Field, Pittsburgh, Pennsylvania. The event was presented and directed by the Pittsburgh 1928 National Balloon Race Committee, the National Aeronautic Association and the Federation Aeronautic Nationale.

The program issued for the race reported that it was "Pittsburgh's First Annual Air Classic." As it turned out it was going to be the last. The colorful blue-backed program carried photos and brief histories of "The World's Greatest Pilots." But death was lurking over the airfield that 30th day of May as the "Grim Reaper" carefully scanned the program for victims.

Laying out of the balloons started at 10 A. M., with the first flight scheduled to begin at 5 P. M. The usual pattern of starting the balloon race late in the day in order to obtain maximum lift from the gas the following morning was followed. At stake was the Litchfield Trophy—and the privilege of representing the United States in the International Races at Detroit on June 30.

The fourteen airships at Pittsburgh took to the air as scheduled but were immediately hit by a severe lightning and wind storm. All of the craft were out of touch for several hours and racing officials, and others, feared the worst. Lieutenant Paul Evert of Langley Field, Virginia, flying in *Army Entry Number 3*, was killed when struck by lightning but his aide, U. G. Ent, Northumberland, Pennsylvania, was unhurt. Walter T. Morton, aide in the *Goodyear V*, flying with Ward T. Van Orman was also killed by lightning. Van Orman received a fractured leg as the ruptured balloon plunged to the earth. James F. Cooper, Akron, Ohio, flying as an aide with Carl K. Wollam of Cleveland in *The City of Cleveland*, was severely burned by lightning which forced their entry down. *Army Entry Number 1*, piloted by Captain William E. Kepner, landed at Weems, Virginia, at 6:10 A. M. the next day, and was a sure bet for first place.

Immediately following the Pittsburgh victory, Kepner wrote an account of his adventure, calling it "Riding the Storm in a National Balloon Race." He reported, in part:[17]

The day broke cloudy to overcast with an occasional spit of rain to dampen the ardor of the fourteen pilots and their equal number of aides.

As each contestant earnestly searched the sky, each no doubt wondered what the day would hold for him. Fourteen giant gas bags were being spread out on the respective starting places with all the care that could be given in an effort at perfect preparation for the race. Even the ground crews contested in an effort to give their respective pilots the best possible break through getting the bags perfectly centered in the net. Then the valves must be leak proof, because once inflated it would be too late to correct mistakes that could easily be the cause of a failure, even in starting, let alone finishing creditably in the race. A bag not properly started in the net or carelessly handled might even roll out of the net and sail off skyward, leaving its passengers-to-be to gaze forlornly off into space at its retreating shape. Or a valve that is to be a means of control once in flight, if not properly seated and secured to the fabric, might leak and, by a continuous loss of precious lifting gas, rapidly bring the flight to an end.

The entire weather is governed by atmospheric pressure areas and temperature changes. These are con-

stantly changing and must be studied not only up to the
moment of the take off but even during the flight. The
winds in a high pressure area usually accompany fine
weather and circle the area's center with a clockwise
motion. At the same time the entire area will move
generally eastward, following the low pressure areas that
dominate all weather and produce storms. The winds in
these low pressure areas circle anti-clockwise toward the.
center of the "low" area. These low pressure areas always produce clouds and often rain. When colder winds
come into contact with them, they produce line squalls
and frequently during the summer months violent thunder and lightning. Woe to the balloonist who is caught in
such an area. Happy is the one who can accurately forecast it ahead of time and mayhap dodge it by going to
an altitude that is not affected by it. The center of a
thunderstorm produces strong upward currents of air,
naturally the winds near the ground flow directly into
such centers. The higher one goes when some distance
away, the less this tendency to be flown into the center
of the storm. Good judgment and an accurate forecast
when in the air at some distance from it will often enable a pilot to avoid storms that are local in their nature.

About noon conditions were less encouraging. The
sky was thickening up some and the wind was becoming
more and more west. We were all anxious to get off
before it came out of the northwest. Such a wind would
carry us south of New York City and the coast would
certainly cause the race to be a short one. The sky did
not look particularly threatening at the take off. Certainly there was scant warning of the terrible experience
we were to undergo. The sun was even shining through
occasionally.

Our balloon, *The Army No. 1*, was starting at position number nine. We were ready early, thanks to Lieutenant McCormick and his squad of Army lads who had
been sent there to help. Two civilian balloons and then
Lieutenant Paul Evert with Lieutenant U. G. Ent as his
aide took off in five minute intervals. As we watched
Evert sail away in a perfect take off little did we dream
that he was to land a couple of hours later dead from
lightning, the balloon on fire, the terrible hydrogen in a
grim race to explode before the courageous Ent could
safely land himself and Evert.

Van Orman took off number five. I went over for a last word and incidentally to check my watch with his. We both navigate by use of the sextant and accurate time is most necessary. I also checked my map variations with his to be doubly sure. Little did we realize that within two hours "Van's" beautiful balloon would go up in the smoke at an altitude of two thousand feet, leaving the basket with its two occupants—Van unconscious and Morton dead—to hustle downward to the ground.

We were maneuvered out to the starting point. Each balloon started separately and at five minute intervals. This race counted distance and rules alone. A middle-aged and serious-faced lady walked quickly up to the basket and, addressing "Eric," said "Will you take this little token for luck, with my prayers?" Having little time for anything, "Eric" thanked her and put it in his pocket. It turned out later to be a little disc with miniature figures of Christian saints imposed in relief upon it.

Five forty-five! At last the starter's signal and we were off. A perfect get away. As we gazed around, taking stock of our position, one hour after take off, we observed Captain Hill's balloon to be following us. He had gone higher and we, staying low, had passed him on our way north-eastward. We had not long to reason for the cause, a vicious-looking cloud appeared in the north-west.

At a little over a thousand feet altitude we were enveloped in the cloud. Up we went, the hydrogen expanding and pouring out of the appendix due to the decreasing atmospheric pressure as we went higher. This meant that we were also getting heavier and the balloon must sooner or later start a more rapid fall.

I looked up at the bag, scarcely fifteen feet above my head. Its huge, silvery shape had practically disappeared in the inky blueness that completely enveloped us. Only the barest portion directly above was the least distinguishable. The impression was ghastly. The air had become icy cold. In fact had we been suddenly transplanted to the inside of some refrigerating plant it would have been as cold and perhaps as dark.

It dawned on me that this was no ordinary storm such as we had, upon numerous occasions, ridden out. I felt like a child with the goblins about. I heard "Eric" laconically remark, "Well, guess I might as well get into my parachute as that's what it is meant for." He put on his parachute, tied the release ring to the rigging and sat on the edge of the basket. I hastily did the same. If the balloon was struck, we might not be sufficiently conscious to get out of the basket. We reasoned that by sitting on the edge of the basket we would fall into space and the rope attached to the release ring would automatically open the "chute."

The lightning was crashing all about us. The inky darkness had changed to a greenish-yellow color. The giant bag over our head was whirling and being thrown to right and left. Of course the basket, acting as a fifteen hundred pound pendulum attached to the bag, followed it all over the sky. A blast of air would strike us first on one side, then on another.

Death seemed near, in fact at our very door. Apparently the grim specter was in search of others and only paid us a passing glance. However that little glance was awesome, magnificent in its apparent terrible reality. But there is no way to adequately describe it in mere words. Suffice it to say that the impression is burned upon my soul and will always remain. Once in the World War I saw a stream of blood the size of my finger pouring from my own mouth; I was sure my jugular vein had been opened by the bullet I had received. I expected to die and had, to some extent, made my peace with God. It left a most distinct impression with me of what the portal was like. Yet the interior of this storm left a greater picture upon my soul than that.

I have said this turbulent condition existed for us but a few minutes. Then down we came faster and faster. Where normally we should only require a couple of bags of sand thrown out to stop our descent, we threw twelve bags as fast as we could open and pour the sand out. We did not know where we were, we might be over a town and pouring out sand. It could hurt no one, whereas if we threw a whole bag from such an altitude we stood a good chance of killing some innocent person below.

We came falling out of the cloud a few hundred feet above the ground. Thank goodness we were over a woods and not a town. The heavens still reverberated with the thunder's roll while the smoky tongues of fire continued to dart across the sky, alternately looking out at some particular spot on the hills below.

Finally, after what had seemed an age, our balloon appeared to be checking its precipitate fall. The sand that we were throwing overboard was making it light. We hesitated about one hundred feet off the ground and, being light, started to rise again. There was one chance that we might, by flying low in this valley, let the storm go by.

We started to maneuver by valving hydrogen and alternately throwing sand. We didn't have to valve very much because the basket was catching lots of water and was getting heavier all the time. About a hundred yards off to our left another balloon came dropping out of the clouds, and another followed almost immediately. The first was Lieutenant Evert's balloon, the second was a civilian balloon. They both apparently intended staying down and we laughingly agreed that they had had about the same experience as our own. The wind caught them and both balloons appeared to be chasing each other as they careened madly over the ground up a small ravine to disappear in the rainy distance to the north of us.

I heard, about this time, a remark from "Eric," "Here comes another and it looks like he might hit us." We were then about 500 feet above the ground and going rapidly east by north in this small valley. The balloon was Van Orman's. He went by on his drop, the loose edges of the bag flapping and cracking in the fall. He must have been pretty high for he seemed to have lost about a fourth of his gas. That meant probably nine thousand feet by a density ratio of atmosphere. What had he been through at such a height. Only Van can tell you, but I'll venture it was plenty.

Our temporary peace was short-lived. We were caught in a down gust and down we came. The lightning continued if possible with renewed vigor. It was terrific and appeared to cross the sky just over our head. Would it never end? But now our drag rope was draggling one end on the ground. "Eric" received a couple of light shocks of electricity from somewhere but it was not serious. The valley was a regular wind tunnel and we were traveling at very high speed, just clear of the ground and following the valley. Our drag rope caught, momentarily, then free, it would leap up so that the lower end was higher than our basket. The end dropped again, this time it wrapped securely around a tree top. The top of the tree broke with a report like a shotgun. The valley turned, we banged against the ground in front and burst both air pontoons on the basket, while both "Eric" and I scrambled to stay in the basket.

The balloon by now was positively heavy. I somehow managed to get a bag of sand and throw it over just as two high tension lines suddenly appeared in front of us. The basket cleared them, thank goodness, but the drag ropes didn't. As it crossed the wire a blueish flame about two feet long shot up the wet rope. Our speed saved us because the rope was off the wires in a second. Hardly had we caught our breaths when another electric line assembly appeared. This time there were six lines. We had no chance to lift over them, we smashed into them, our basket went just below the lines, the huge bag above and there we formed a perfect jack knife around the wires, as helpless as we could possibly be. There seemed to be absolutely no chance to get out alive. In fact we bid fair to be first electrocuted, then cremated. I hadn't been able to guess, when in the clouds, what was going to happen, but now I was certain that death was a matter of a second away at best. However Providence had ordained otherwise and for some mysterious reason there was no fire. Our next experience was to hit a railroad telegraph pole. We broke it off and it hung from our basket while we dragged a few feet. We swung outside the basket by our hands while we pushed with our feet and were barely able to dislodge the pole.

There was a gentle wind blowing us to the south. We had practically reversed our course. It was 7:50 p. m. All that I have written here had occurred in a little over a half hour.

The storm was still active to the southeast of us but we were going south and it was a comfort to know we were not going into it.

About midnight we accidentally spilled some water and rose to 3800 feet. The rigging froze so that a rope would crackle as it was bent. The wind was taking us farther south up there so we stood it for a while, but there is a limit to flesh and blood, and finally we had to come down. We valved and descended to just off the surface. It was much warmer there and a wind was blowing us to the southeast at the rate of 25 miles per hour. This would take us to the coast much quicker, but we could do no better.

A little later we again ascended to an altitude of 7000 feet. Above 6400 feet it was snowing. We did not linger long at this altitude as our misery increased with the cold and once again we valved down to the tree tops. Here we remained until daylight not knowing our exact location except that we were over forested mountains. At daybreak we crossed a large body of water. To the east of us was a large city so it could not be Chesapeake Bay. Besides, it wasn't large enough to be the bay. The height of the hill tops diminished rapidly until we were well below the altitude of Pittsburgh. This proved that we were nearing the Atlantic Coast in spite of the fact that we did not reckon our distance traveled as so far. We found a thin strata of air 400 feet thick that was flowing south and managed to stay in this strata until it disappeared near the mouth of the Rappahannock River. We had gone as far as we could in this craft and landed in the last field of dry land, near Weems, Virginia.

We headed for home. As I stepped up to the ticket window in Richmond, Virginia, a tired and weary traveler, I gave my name to the agent, he started, then asked, "Are you the fellow that won the balloon race?" I could scarcely believe it but there in his hand was a newspaper with my picture on the front page. We had won! The hectic night that had just passed didn't seem quite so terrible in the thrill of success and possession of the National Balloon Trophy.

The race was one to remember by those who survived the storm. But the terror of the storm did not discourage Ed Hill even though he lost at Pittsburgh.

Hill made the winning flight in the 1927 international race giving America the international trophy for the second straight year. One more win and possession would become permanent. Since Hill was from Detroit he had a double interest in winning at Pittsburgh. He would represent the United States and as a bonus, would start the race from his hometown. However, a combination of savage, death-dealing weather and just plain bad luck ruined his chances of bringing the international trophy to America. But Hill was a good sport—if not a good loser—and he promptly volunteered to fly the "pilot balloon" at Detroit. A pilot balloon serves the same purpose in free-flight ballooning as a "pacer" in auto or foot racing. Such a balloon provides a guide for those who follow to observe and make adjustments by. Ed Hill served well in this capacity at Ford Airport and made a good showing in the international race at Dearborn.

Two Germans at Ford Airport.—Drawing by O. Dale Hagedorn

NEAR STARTING TIME

I never saw a man who looked
With such a wistful eye
Upon that little tent of blue
Which prisoners call the sky,
And at every drifting cloud that went
With sails of silver by.
Oscar Wilde, *Ballad of Reading Gaol*

Brilliant, shimmering rays of the noonday sun plunged through openings in the masses of June clouds that gathered above, converged and parted once more. Polished metal on numerous autos, flat glass plates in the cockpits of airplanes or smooth objects carried by spectators reflected sun rays laterally across the "fields of Ford" causing temporary sun blindness to many.

Tall grass that stood away from the runways was reduced to a flat mat by the crowds that moved from one place to another as the pattern of spectator interest shifted first to one point on the field and then somewhere else.

A total of 23 experienced aeronauts were present and ready to fly. Each was busily engaged in performing some last minute task associated in some way with increased performance of his ship. Each crew—with one exception—knew and understood the flight characteristics of the ship that would carry them skyward. The exception was E. S. Maag, the Swiss pilot. His balloon had been seriously damaged in transit to the United States. The only balloon available was one of a mere 35,000 cubic-foot capacity, capable of carrying only one man.

Maag was presented with an alternative: fly the smaller balloon alone or drop from the race. He chose the former but since all of the other balloons exceeded 80,000 cubic-foot capacity, he had little chance in the race. His early elimination did not come as a surprise to the race officials. In the meantime, the other flyers were busy with their preparations.

Kepner's *U. S. Army Entry No. 1* was in position and ready for filling. It was flown this year (1928) by the same flyers who had participated unsuccessfully in the 1927 race which had also originated at Ford Airport.

The German ship *Brandenburg*—at least in name only—was familiar to those who had been present at Ford Airport the previous year. On September 10, 1927, the first *Brandenburg*, piloted by Dr. R. B. Halben, assisted by Hugo Kaulen, Jr., (who flew in 1928 with his father) had lifted off easily. But disaster struck quickly when a gas valve stuck in an open position. Since the valve could not be reached from the gondola, the result was an almost downhill flight from lift off, direct to Sugar Island in Lake Erie, just 21 miles from Sandusky. Fortunately, the ship had not landed in Lake Erie. The 1927 crew had not carried a life raft. The 1927 ship was the first entry by Germany in international racing since 1913 and the disappointment that resulted from the poor showing was very pronounced. After spending the night in a cottage on the island the flyers journeyed back to the point of liftoff the next day. Balloon pilots have a feeling for successful flight that results in disappointment in failure that is always bigger than the letdown of the craft itself. Such feeling is reserved for those who know what free-flight ballooning means. The three German teams present in 1928 were hopeful that they would make a better showing than their brothers had in 1927. And many others became interested in the outcome of the race.

High ranking military officers, consular and diplomatic representatives and other dignitaries (including officers from the Ford Motor Company) were present. They were about to witness the start of a race considered to be the greatest event

in the field of lighter-than-air flying—and they were interested in what they saw. The June 30, AP report stated: "On
hand as one of the officials was Brigadier General Frank P.
Lahm, winner of the first international race which started
from Paris in 1906." Therefore the first international race
was connected by a positive link with the 1928 race. Perhaps
the more important accomplishments of man are tied to
insignificant events of the past. And if this is so—the lesser
events should be considered part of the larger achievements.
But maybe this is never the case in practice since the events
of yesterday are always forgotten too easily by those who
should have remembered them.

The point at Ford Airport where the racing balloons were
unpacked was east of the main field. This position had been
chosen for two reasons: first, it would avoid the danger of
contact with the airport buildings and dirigible mast; and
second, the distance to the main road was relatively short. A
gas company crew from the City of Detroit had dug open a
four-inch gas main that lay near the curbline and about two
feet under the street. A series of extensions were installed
and these ran near the site occupied by the balloon teams.
Gas valves had been installed at the ends of these lines and
these were connected by appropriate fittings to 13 filling
lines. The filling lines were made of petroleum impregnated
canvas and had been supplied by the contestants. The lines
were securely attached to the "appendix," or small spout, at
the bottom of each balloon. As the gas valves at the main
were gently opened, the illuminating gas flowed into the
canvas lines. The lines expanded under the gentle pressure
from the main allowing the gas to flow into each balloon.

Attendants on duty issued warnings against smoking near
the filling lines and they admonished the spectators to keep
clear of the lines. A recent gas-main explosion in Detroit had
ripped apart an entire city block and the gas people knew the
hazards and took all possible precautions. However, the

milling crowd would not cooperate. A flaming, natural gas explosion within their ranks was the last thing they had on their minds that lovely June day.

The job of filling a balloon can be very difficult on a windy day. But the breeze that gently blew across the open fields of Dearborn was very mild and comfortable. The filling progressed with little difficulty, although great care was exercised to see that all valves were sealed on each entry.

At the site of the *Brandenburg*, Captain-Lieutenant Otto Bertram supervised the laying out and filling of his gold-colored balloon. To the far side of the ground cloth sat the wicker basket in which the Captain and his aide would hopefully spend many mile-covering hours. The basket was five feet square and almost four feet high. The wicker had been woven around a strong willow frame which contained a slatted board floor. The completed basket resembled the wicker porch swings, chairs and porch couches so popular at the time. The gold-colored cotton of the entry was positioned in a careful circle so that the appendix pointed toward the filling line. At the center of the deflated balloon was a three-foot valve cover that would cap the inflated balloon. Resembling the "flying saucers" of later years, the device was designed to keep the elements away from the top gas valve. [18] The valve could be opened manually by rope to allow gas to escape as the need arose. A second valve at the mouth of the appendix would also allow discharge of gas during flight. The "rip panel" of the balloon, used for quick deflation upon landing, and its accompanying rope, were carefully positioned on the ground cloth.

A large crossed netting of thin cotton strands was carefully unfolded by Frobel. Like a fisherman casting for his catch in the shimmering light of a summer evening, the lieutenant threw the net over the deflated balloon. It was carefully spread out by the Germans. Improper positioning of the net over a balloon might result in the filled balloon rolling out of

the net, spelling a sudden finish for the entry. White canvas
ballast bags filled with about 25 pounds of fine sand, were
positioned in a circle around the net. The bags of sand were
fastened to the net at about two-foot intervals by means of
small curved hooks which in turn were secured to brass eyelets in the edges of the ballast bags.

As gas rushed into the *Brandenburg* through the appendix,
the gold cotton began filling the net that covered it. The
netting, held firmly to the ground by the ring of ballast bags,
quickly stopped the inflation of the balloon. It was then
necessary to unhook the ballast bags one by one placing the
hook at a new location lower down on the net. The balloon
continued to fill—but the filling was controlled at all times
by moving the hooks attached to the ballast bags. A similar
procedure was followed by the other entries.

As more of the *Brandenburg* was released to the filling gas
the Germans carefully walked the circumference of the balloon. It was apparent to observers that they were looking for
any indication that the cotton of their balloon had been
damaged in transit from Germany. The close scrutiny enabled
them to check the netting for frays or other signs of weakness. Their caution was quite obvious.

The filling continued as the sun moved into a position that
indicated midday had passed. The *Brandenburg* had almost
assumed its full, round shape as the appendix dangled gently
below the balloon although still attached to the filling line.

Other entries had taken on full proportions and the giant
balloons swayed gently overhead providing large pockets of
shifting shade for spectators crowded below. (See Figure 5.)
The baskets—or "gondolas"—were carried into position inside
the weighted-down netting of each airship. While the Germans of the *Brandenburg* stayed close to their ship, other
flyers visited the flight station or carried on conversation
with enthusiastic spectators. Some of the flyers purchased
extra rations and personal items from vendors operating on

the field, and others worked on various equipment. Captain Kepner carefully checked his watch with the official time-keeper. While the race was constructed around distance and not time, Kepner navigated by a sextant and needed to know the precise time.

The gondola that had been positioned under the gasbag of the *Brandenburg* had ten heavy manila ropes braided to the top edge. At the loose end of these short ropes were found three-inch braided loops. A link—or connection—was required to secure the basket to the ship above. The link was provided by the load ring; a solid, hickory ring, about two and a half feet in diameter which had been steamed into a circle under pressure. The joint of the ring had been expertly spliced to form a solid wooden circle and around the outside and inside edges of the ring had been tacked a rope split in half lengthwise. The purpose of the rope was to reduce friction on the ring by the rigging that would be attached to it. Two heavy ropes had been securely fastened across the center of the ring in the shape of an "X". The reinforcement was designed to keep the ring from being pulled apart by lateral pressure that was exerted against it.

Spaced around the load ring were ten stout ropes of shorter lengths. To the ends of the ropes, five-inch pieces of turned walnut that closely resembled rubber dog bones had been securely braided. The walnut connectors were inserted end first into the loops of the longer basket ropes. The wood pieces were tugged into place creating a firm connection between the basket and the load ring. The loose ends of the netting were securely fastened to the load ring. The completed arrangement was not unlike the rigging on ancient sailing ships. But the ships at Ford Airport would navigate in the skies.

After the rigging was completed the ballast bags were removed one by one and either tied on the outside of the basket or stored on the floor inside the basket. This process continued until the balloon pulled the rigging taut while the ballast held the ship to the earth. The balance between the total lifting power of the entry and the weight of the ballast was adjusted until the removal of one ballast bag would allow the ship to be airborne. Captain Kepner carefully recorded in his log the delicate balance that was reached prior to the flight of his airship.[19]

According to Kepner the lift of gas per 1,000 cubic feet was 42 pounds in his balloon. Therefore, based upon the total cubic footage of his entry, the total ascensive (gross lift) force was 3,360 pounds. He reported that this total was broken down as follows: pilot and aide, 350 pounds; instruments and supplies, 225 pounds; balloon and equipment, 1,400 pounds; ballast, 1,375 pounds—a total of 3,350 pounds. The balance was such that a scant 10 pounds held the entry to the dusty surface of Ford Airport. Release of this small amount of ballast permitted the airship to reach for its natural place, the atmosphere above. In the meantime the spectators stood and sat open-mouthed as the airships assumed racing form. The complexity of preparations added increased importance to the event that unfolded before them.

The site of the race had been carefully chosen by the international race committee. The size of Ford Airport and the absence of obstacles that might snare a free-flight balloon made the location ideal for the start of an international race. The geographic location of Detroit was also important since it was inland far enough to permit flight over hundreds of miles of land in any direction. The proximity of the Great Lakes to Detroit provided an exception, but all of the flyers were confident that their ships would fly beyond the Lakes—even at worst. The experience of those who flew the *Brandenburg* the previous year was ignored by some of the contestants. In addition, the race officials of the 1927 race had experienced difficulties that they had prepared for in 1928.

A recurring problem at previous international races had been that of broken netting. Often a break would go unnoticed until filling had almost been completed. Such a break would cause an entry to be eliminated if the break could not be reached—and it might be near the top of the balloon. For this reason, Ford had arranged to have two fire trucks present, each equipped with extension ladders capable of handling such an emergency. The trucks were parked near a Ford Tri-Motor and the combination of trucks and planes drew a crowd of young and old alike as hundreds of spectators milled about the brilliant red trucks and the shiny aircraft.

The day was beautiful, there was much to see and the spectators took in as much as they could. From a distance the airships looked like children's balloons tied at the base by strings which were fastened to the ground. But these racing balloons were not for children. As preparations neared completion, tensions mounted both among the flyers and the spectators. As the race date had drawn nearer, interest grew. Now that the day had arrived, interest took on a new pitch of excitement as each minute passed. The crowds grew larger, the bands played prominent military tunes while small boys dressed in knee stockings and knickers scampered among the adult spectators causing considerable irritation. The temperature had been over 80 degrees since noon and menfolk present pushed sleeves to the elbows, some using black garters to hold them in place. Younger women were dressed in the scant garb of the "flapper." Older ladies present preferred ankle-length dresses decorated with silver pins and sparkling colored stones while large brimmed hats topped off the outfits. The carnival atmosphere prevailed as flags whipped and snapped in the soft breeze. The 13 entries in the race shifted as though reaching for new records and the spectators milled continuously like an excited June circus crowd moving from the merry-go-round to a free side show.

Captain Bertram and his aide made last minute checks of

their gear as loose items were secured. Their weather map was placed in a special pocket at the side of the basket. And the Germans looked skyward. Although the illuminating gas had ceased its noisy flow into the golden folds of their balloon, Bertram had decided to leave the filling hose attached as long as possible. He knew that gentle pressure from the main would continue to insert gas even though it would do so at a greatly reduced rate. Further, he theorized that as the afternoon wore on the temperature would drop, even if only slightly. As the gas cooled, it would contract, thus allowing more gas to enter the balloon. If his theories were correct, the extra cubic feet of gas gained would give his balloon maximum lift. After all, Bertram wanted to win this race— and so did his aide. A few extra feet of gas might make a huge difference in a free flight.

Both Germans at the *Brandenburg* were dressed in knee-length highly polished boots. Two straps at the top of Frobel's boots were characteristic of the German artillery uniform. Dark, almost black, canvas riding-style breeches were laced along the side at the top of their boots. Their officer-style military hats were decorated by an oval silver insignia. The emblem carried a slim German eagle topped by the letters "D.L." Around the bottom of the oval was a carved design. It was the flying insignia of the DEUTSCHES LUFTS-PORT VERBAND—the German Air Sport Club—and was similar to the World War I flying insignia of the German Imperial Air Force.

Captain-Lieutenant Otto Bertram, a German naval flying officer, served the German cause in the First War as a pilot of dirigibles. Taking part in several bombing raids over London, he later remarked in America, "Yes, I have been to London— but I was there when they did not want me."[20] He suffered machine gun wounds in the left ankle and walked with a slight limp. Commissioned in 1911, he was one of the first of the German navy flyers. In 1913 he served as the

Commandant of the combined land and sea operations at
Augersee in Riga. Following the war he had been associated
with the airline Deutschen Luftreederei. His main job was to
recruit wartime flyers into the airline service. Successful in
this venture, he further served his nation by establishing
way-stations between Germany and Brazil. These were used
by German seaplanes making overseas air service flights. His
small stature led close friends to call him "der kleine Bertram"—"the small Bertram."[21]

The captain's aide, Lieutenant Georg Frobel, had served in
World War I as an artillery officer. Those who remember him
on the visit to America recall that he did not speak English
and was quiet and reserved. His home was in the same town
as Bertram, Chemnitz in Saxony, Germany, and he shared a
common interest in free ballooning with the captain. He had
traveled to America with Captain and Mrs. Bertram and had
stayed with them at the Pennsylvania Hotel in New York
prior to the trip to Detroit. The three arrived in America on
June 18, 1928, having made the crossing on board the North
German Lloyd steamship, *Stuttgart*. Their team had been selected as one of three finalists in runoffs held in Germany in
the early months of 1928. Was "gangsterism" on the rise in
America as claimed by German newspapers? The question
had been discussed by them before their trip.

General lawlessness of the Twenties prompted many citizens in America to carry revolvers or automatics in their
automobiles—and often on their person. In addition to this
experienced balloonists knew that people often became hos-
tile to them at the end of undirected balloon flights. For
these reasons both Germans traveled to the race armed. One
pistol carried by the flyers of the *Brandenburg* was a 7.65-
caliber seven-shot Bayard automatic. Manufactured in Belgium, it had a patent date on the top of September 8, 1908.
On the right side, forward of the ejector and above the trigger,
was carved the number "24". (See Figure 8.) This indicated

that it might have been a military issue piece. The weapon carries serial number 137820 and is now owned by J. S. Cooper, Oakland, Md. It was lent by him for photographs. The top of the grip on the right side had been partially broken away from the top screw. The damaged grip ties the weapon to a significant historical event.

The three o'clock summer sun leaned seriously toward the west as great shimmering shadows of the race entries shifted cooling shade gently from one group of spectators to another. Crowding onto the ground cloths, the spectators caused considerable concern in reference to the gas lines as well as other equipment. Constant reminders of the danger of smoking were heard around the field as Lieutenant Frobel tried desperately to keep the gear of the *Brandenburg* out of reach of the curious. Souvenirs were in constant demand and since the balloon crews had not expected this close confrontation with the spectators, it all added up to serious inconvenience for the contestants.

By 3:30 P. M., most of the crews had disconnected the filling lines from their balloons. Their gas supply had then been cut off from the main at the branch line. After the white canvas filling lines collapsed they were carefully rolled and taken from the field for storage. One line, however, still snaked across the dry, grass-starved turf to the *Brandenburg*. As four o'clock neared the temperature began dropping. Bertram stuck to his theory that the cooling would cause some shrinkage of the gas already within the balloon thus allowing more to enter. (It is because of this fact that balloon races are generally started late in the day.) Even a little extra gas would help carry an airship through the cooler night. As the morning sun warmed the balloon the gas would expand giving the flyers additional lift for the following day. It was a sound theory.

Starting time was at hand!

BASICS OF BALLOONING

The atmosphere is very massive by ordinary standards: thus the portion directly above one square foot of the Earth's surface weighs almost one ton; and the whole weighs about five thousand million million tons, enough to provide each of the world's inhabitants with two million tons of air. [22]

The atmosphere that surrounds the earth has been classified into subspheres based upon variations of temperature. The first layer, or region of air, is called the troposphere. Above this lies the stratosphere followed by the mesosphere and then the thermosphere. Balloons have played a major part in the exploration of some of these layers of the atmosphere. In 1938, *Explorer II*, carried by helium, gained the remarkable altitude of 13 miles. But balloons suffer one weakness in altitude climbing: The fall of the buoyancy of air as altitude increases limits the performance of balloons. In addition, the requirement of protection for the persons manning the balloons at high altitudes places a serious limitation upon their use. The following chart indicates the loss of buoyancy lift as altitude increases: [23]

Displacement Of 1,000 Cubic Feet	Buoyancy Lift In Pounds
Ground Level	80
10 miles	11
20 miles	1
30 miles	1 ounce

In spite of this, unmanned neoprene-latex balloons have flown as high as 20 miles.

As a hypothetical ascent begins into the troposphere the temperature drops sharply. It then levels off at about 8 or 10 miles, remains constant for a time and then begins to rise at about 16 or 17 miles. At about 35 miles the decreasing temperatures resume and at about 45 miles the temperature is at its lowest. From this point on, the temperature begins to rise and becomes extremely warm. This is well beyond the height that any balloon can attain in free flight from the earth, presenting no problem to balloonists. Thus the Greek legend of Icarus referred to in the third chapter has scientific backing because there is a very warm region at about 60 to 100 miles altitude.

The highest altitude attained by the *Brandenburg*, based upon the later report of its captain, was 4,400 meters, equivalent to 14,440 feet, or just short of three miles. At this altitude temperature is on the downgrade and buoyancy of the air is very low.

Assuming the temperature is 75 degrees at the earth's surface, the drop in temperature as the altitude increases would be approximately as follows: [24]

Height In Feet	Temperature °F
0	75°
2,500	68°
5,000	54°
7,500	51°
10,000	43°
12,500	35°
15,000	25°

At 4,400 meters the *Brandenburg* was flying in almost freezing weather. If the temperature at ground level is low it doesn't take much altitude to cause the thermometer to slide to zero—and lower.

The pressure at every level of the atmosphere must be capable of supporting the weight of the air that lies above it. Thus the pressure decreases as the altitude increases. "The amount of matter contained may perhaps best be appreciated by noting that if the atmosphere were compressed until it became as dense as water, its thickness would be more than 30 feet. To pass through so much matter is not easy. Hence the atmosphere acts as a powerful shield."[25] The flaming reentry of the astronauts into the earth's atmosphere bears witness to this fact.

It is within this sliding temperature and lowering density that a free-flight balloon must operate. Coupled with this is the fact that hills and valleys produce different effects upon a balloon as it passes over them. The same is true with the cooler air that lies above a body of water. Coolness causes a lighter-than-air balloon to drop—and sudden descents can be fatal. In addition, constant attention is required to maintain equilibrium in order to keep the craft from running wild on the recurring up and down drafts. Factors such as these make free-flight ballooning a scientific sport.

A free-flight balloon in the basic sense is some type of cloth container, impervious to the passage of gas, that is inflated with some substance such as helium, hydrogen, or natural gas which is lighter than air. After being attached to a basket or gondola, this combination of equipment is capable of being forced into the atmosphere because of the density of the air closer to the earth. Since the gas within the container is lighter than the air that surrounds it, the denser air "squeezes" the balloon causing it to move to an altitude where its weight equals that of the air it displaces. This is called the point of "equilibrium." The balloon will then remain at this level until some change occurs in the temperature or pressure of the air. At one time it was believed that a cork popped to the top of water "to see the light of day." The physical force that causes a cork to come to the surface of water is very similar to the force that operates on a free-flight balloon. The cork, being lighter than the water that it displaces, rises as it reaches for the equilibrium point. This point cannot be attained within the water, thus the cork comes to rest upon the surface.

Therefore a balloon does not "lift" into the air. Rather it is "pushed" as a heavier substance replaces the space previously occupied by the lighter substance.

As indicated, the equilibrium point can be disturbed by many factors. For example, heat from the sun will cause the gas to expand thus making the balloon rise. Coolness found over water, or under clouds, will cause a balloon to fall. Ballast can be discarded making the craft lighter, thus allowing it to rise. Gas can be valved making the balloon fall. Therefore, a racing balloon can only be controlled vertically. Horizontal direction is determined by wind and chance. The only control that a balloonist can have over this element is to determine the wind in advance and fly when it is favorable. These factors, most of which cannot be controlled, must be thoroughly understood by one who would successfully fly a free-flight balloon.

The bag of the usual balloon of the Twenties was made of fabric such as silk or "goldbeater's skin"—plastic today. A network of fine woven lines was constructed to ride over the bag when it was inflated. The network was in turn connected by a series of lines that supported the basket below. The load ring was used as a connector.

One other piece of equipment found in the racing balloons of the Twenties was the drag rope. This was very heavy Manila rope and about 500 feet long. When a balloon was within 500 feet of the earth the drag rope was thrown over the side. Since the balloon thus had less weight to carry, it tended to move upward. As altitude increased the balloon again carried the weight of the rope dangling and whipping below. Thus the balloon would descend. This counterbalancing action at low altitudes resulted in fairly level flight without the necessity of gas release or the discharge of ballast. (See Figure 16B.)

A hypothetical flight on a make-believe day will illustrate the factors involved in a balloon flight. Liftoff begins when attendants remove enough ballast from the basket of the craft that the dense air at ground level begins to exert force on the conical-shaped balloon. The force pushes the balloon into the atmosphere so "liftoff" would more accurately be called "push off."

As altitude increases the air becomes more and more rarefied. Eventually the point of equilibrium is reached. This is the point where the weight of the craft and its men and equipment equals the weight of the air displaced. At this point the craft is no longer "lighter than air" but is in fact equal in weight to the air that it displaces. The ascent will stop and after settling motions, the balloon will hang suspended. As long as the temperature remains even and there is no movement of air, the balloon will remain motionless.

If a slight amount of gas is released the balance will be disturbed. Less air is displaced and the equilibrium point is below the craft. The balloon will drop to a point where the density of the air increases to a point sufficient to cause the craft to stop once more. A "bouncing" would occur, but after settling motions, the ship would be motionless once again.

A rise in temperature will cause a change. Increasing heat will expand the gas causing displacement of the air surrounding the ship. This will cause the balloon to rise since it displaces more air than before expansion.

A cloud passing between the balloon and the sun causes gas contraction and the balloon to drop. For this reason, clouds are of constant concern to balloonists. Balloons will literally bounce from the underside of clouds because of the cool, moist condition found there. Flying through clouds is almost impossible and flying between clouds requires great skill and judgment. Split-second decisions must often be made in order to avoid disaster.

Continuing with the hypothetical balloon flight, assume that it is motionless once again, the air is still and temperature steady. The balloonist decides that the ship should move to a different altitude Ballast can be dropped gently over the side and the craft will rise. Such movements are often made in search of a favorable wind current. Any sudden dropping of ballast is avoided except in emergency situations. The result might be a rapid rise that could rip the cloth of the balloon. With death waiting thousands of feet below, such a move is considered foolish. Old-timers warned balloon passengers at fairs "not to even spit or we will all go to Kingdom Come."

Assume that a gentle wind begins to blow in an easterly direction. The craft will be pushed in front of the wind causing it to move in that direction. Assume that as it moves eastward a low-pressure area builds in its path. This is usually caused by changes in temperature coupled with other meteorological factors. As the balloon reaches the low-pressure area, a downward sliding move usually follows. The movement is much like a child on a sled who shoves off at the top of his sled run. The sled will slide down the slope (responding to any irregularities in the earth) at an increasing rate of speed. As the balloon hits the edge of the cone-shaped low-pressure area the balloon will suddenly and often without warning, start a dangerous slide down the side of the cone. The equilibrium point is constantly replaced in a downward line as the craft reaches for this point. Stopping such a descent in a balloon requires split-second decisions. If the descent becomes too rapid the gasbag may burst. If the balloon is too close to the earth it may crash violently into the ground. Either of these events could prove fatal to the occupants. The usual solution is to discard ballast in order to check the descent. But wholesale discharge may cause the race to end early since in the coming morning, as the gas warms, this same ballast may be needed to keep from valving gas. If ballast is short, gas will be lost which might be needed to allow the ship to rise over mountains that may be in the flight path.

An experienced pilot may decide to "ride out" slides and conserve ballast for future use. This is usually the case where the slide is not violent and the altitude is high. In riding one of these slides the balloon will often be tossed up and down like a small boat in a rough sea.

In rapidly sliding balloons men have been known to throw everything overboard—even their clothes. Others have climbed into the netting and cut away the gondola. The decision to ride out a slide is always made in direct relation to the altitude of the ship. If an overcast situation exists the dangers multiply rapidly, especially for the balloonist who does not carry a statoscope.

The statoscope is an instrument used for measuring altitude. (See Figure 9F.) A small bubble rides in the center of a curved glass tube. If the balloon is flying level the bubble will ride in the center of the glass—much like the bubble in a carpenter's level. If the balloon should start upward the bubble will break to the right in the glass, thus warning the flyers of the need to release gas to check the ascent. If the balloon starts down the bubble will reverse, permitting the flyers to take appropriate action. An experienced flyer can predict rises and falls by watching the bubble and take action accordingly. Unfortunately not all balloonists of the Twenties had statoscopes.

The lift or—more accurately—the push of gas is directly related to the purity of the substance. Hydrogen is the lightest gas—and at the same time, the most volatile. Under bad weather conditions hydrogen will lift about 68 pounds per 1,000 cubic feet while helium will lift only 63 pounds.

During the cold winter months, 14 percent more lift is obtained from hydrogen because the air is denser and thus heavier. A balloon will never lift as much in warm air since the warm air is lighter and does not produce good buoyancy.

The "illuminating gas" used to fill the balloons in the 1928 race was natural gas piped from storage fields near Detroit. Just how pure the gas was is unknown today, but records kept from that time show the lifting qualities of normal gas as compared with hydrogen. The General Regulations, Article 26, issued prior to the Pittsburgh Races on May 30, found in General Kepner's files at the U. S. Air Force Museum, set out the following formula:

The category of free balloons inflated with other than illuminating gas, shall be determined by the volume of a balloon filled with illuminating gas having the same ascensional force. The ascensional force of illuminating gas shall be taken as 0.7 kilograms per cubic meter.

In figuring the fictitious volume (f.v.) which will determine the category of any balloon filled with other than illuminating gas (il.g.) multiply the true volume (t.v.) of the balloon by the ratio of the ascensional force of the gas actually used (g.u.) to fill the balloon and that of illuminating gas (il.g.), i.e.

$$\frac{(TV \times GU \times FV)}{IL.G.}$$

Example: A balloon of 1500 cu. meter, inflated with hydrogen, which has an ascensional force of 1.05 kg., using the formula:

$$1500 \times \frac{1.05}{0.70} = 2,250$$

corresponds to a balloon of 2,250 cu. meters filled with illuminating gas which has an ascensional force of 0.7 kg.; this balloon filled with hydrogen would then fall with the 6th category.

Converting this into simpler terms permits a more positive understanding of the formula. Allowing 20 percent less buoyancy for the gas on a given day, 1,000 feet of hydrogen will lift 63 pounds at 20° Fahrenheit. Therefore at this temperature, 85,000 cubic feet of hydrogen will lift 5,355 pounds; natural gas, 4,284 pounds. If the two flyers weighed 300 pounds, the basket 100 pounds, the bag and netting 500 pounds with 1,000 pounds of ballast, there would be 2,384 pounds of buoyancy power. This buoyancy would vary with the temperature and the density of the air. It is understood that this power would be curbed at the takeoff point by the addition of sufficient ballast to keep the balloon earthbound until liftoff. At higher altitudes the power would decrease; as the ship came down it would increase; as gas is valved the power decreases; as ballast is discarded power increases. The result? A flying device capable of traveling great distances guided vertically by the skill of its passengers: and guided horizontally by destiny.

FLYING TO KILL

While it is true that the airplane had been invented by the Wright brothers, America had lagged behind in preparing for World War I in the air. In the end, France did most of the building—although many Americans did the flying. By December, 1917, 325 Americans had fought in the French Lafayette Escadrille. Many had become aces (one who shot down five or more aircraft or balloons). The largest flying field of the war had been located at Issoudun, France. Offering primary training among other things, the complex was made up of 14 separate fields which contained 84 hangars, many warehouses, shops and barracks.

By July, 1918, the Germans had broken through at Chemin des Dames and had slugged their way to the Marne River. The Allies, constantly pressed by the new model German Fokkers, were in dangerous shape both on the land and in the air. The loss of Allied air superiority was costing a heavy price in the ground war—air victories were desperately needed. On April 14, Lieutenant Douglas Campbell and Lieutenant Alan F. Winslow each made a kill. One of the Germans shot down that day could not believe that his assailant had been an American. The Germans did not believe that Americans would fight.

Major Raoul Lufbery had 18 kills to his credit when he took to the air on May 19. He was killed six miles from Toul as the Germans shot his plane from the sky. On the following day the 94th Aero Squadron, including a young flyer by the name of Rickenbacker, dropped flowers upon Lufbery's grave from the air as they flew over in a final noisy tribute.

An argument had raged among the flyers, the statisticians and others, in reference to the duration of life of a flyer at the front. Some argued that the life span was 60 hours, others said 40 hours. Regardless of who was right, the time span was all too short. Lieutenant Charles Hastings Upton of the 50th Aero Squadron had written: "I do not fear my own death; there is too much beyond; but I fear to see my brothers go." He died shortly thereafter at the front. Lieutenant Louis Bennett, an American fighting for the Royal Air Force, removed two planes and nine balloons from the skies before his death.

These men flew and died. And they not only flew in the skies but they flew on the ground as well. Perpetual "barracks flying" led to an Army directive that flying was to be done in the sky only. The men should forget flying when off duty. Wasn't the real flying strain enough?

Hatred for the "Hun" was more pronounced at home than it was at the front. In combat it was more a matter of respect for the other side and pity for those who died. Who had time to hate when life was so short to begin with? The answer was clear and the mutual concern for the fallen of either side was forceful evidence of this.

Outnumbered Americans went into combat flying the inferior Nieuport 28's against the superior Fokker D-VII's—and they fared badly. The Nieuport fighters carried only 1.5 hours of gas. For this reason a flyer of one of these planes always kept one eye on the gas gauge—an eye that was needed to look for "the Hun in the Sun." To make matters worse a Nieuport would not glide well. This prompted flyers to conclude that "it was cheaper to land in a peach tree than a grape vine."

While the errant Nieuport carried a compass, it nevertheless vibrated with the motor. Therefore, north might in fact be south, or east might be anywhere. Because of this, the flyers relied upon visual observation of roads, railroad tracks and other landmarks. To make matters worse, the altimeter did not work well—and the tachometer did not work at all. Little wonder that German fighters had a field day! Americans were flying on the wings of the mistakes of France. The result was bitter pain to many American families who finally came to realize that their sons would not be returning home.

Colonel Billy Mitchell argued long and hard about this situation before the Nieuports were finally replaced with the famous Spads. After the war ended, it was discovered that 10,000 airplanes had not in fact seen combat. Thousands of these planes were put to the torch! Many were sold for pennies—and Mitchell objected again. His objections fell on deaf ears—and precedent was established for others to say later, "The man is crazy; war with Japan will never be possible." Mitchell was a prophet—but he suffered from the pains of other prophets: Those who should have listened, refused to do so. And America was to pay a terrible price in the end.

From May 6, 1918, until the end of the war, two American squadrons, the 94th and 95th, occupied the same aerodrome. Commanded by Captain John Mitchell of Boston, no other two squadrons in France would equal their total victories and total hours over enemy lines. The men in these squadrons flew and killed anywhere within their range. As pilots were killed or wounded, new replacements were sent into action. One of the newly arrived replacements had been assigned to Squadron 95. This smiling young man quickly became the most popular man in that group. From the beginning he flatly refused to rely upon the fame of his father, Theodore Roosevelt. Feeling he could do what he had to do, Quentin Roosevelt had no intention of asking for or relying on favors. What was good enough for other Americans was good enough for this son of a former president of the United States. Those in command gave Quentin the title of "Flight

Commander" before he had flown his first mission. Roosevelt resented this and disclaimed the title in flight and dropped back to fly behind his more experienced flyers and under their command. Another American flying with the 95th would later write in defense of both squadrons after the death of Quentin Roosevelt. Eddie V. Rickenbacker strongly resented any insinuation that the men of these two squadrons had caused the death of Quentin because of their cowardice.

During the four-week occupancy of their sector of the Chateau-Thierry line, the two squadrons lost 36 pilots killed or wounded. On Bastille Day, July 14, 1918, Roosevelt went down mortally wounded. The cost to the Germans during the same period had been 38 planes plus the men that these machines had carried.

Some believed that Roosevelt would not be fit for battle because of his famous father. They felt that Quentin might use his father—in some way or another—to avoid danger to himself. A few believed that the father would surely "pull strings" to protect his son. It quickly became apparent that the skeptics were wrong. Quentin was often brave to the point of recklessness, for which he was constantly reprimanded. He often flew headlong into fights that others avoided. It was clear to those who served with him that he was either going to become an ace—or die very quickly. (See Figure 10.)

Roosevelt made his first kill just a few days before he died. On a return trip to the lines, he suddenly left his companions to scout a group of planes circling in the distance. Twenty German machines made up this group and Quentin wisely decided not to get involved. Turning away, he spotted what he believed to be his own group and flew into the last position. He had decided to follow his comrades home and stay out of trouble for the balance of the day. After some 15 minutes of flying the lead plane suddenly turned, diving to the right. Roosevelt observed the black Maltese cross on its wings and tail for the first time. He had been flying with an enemy patrol! Later he related that he fired a long burst which flamed the nearest German plane. Diving away, he returned to Allied lines leaving four angry Germans circling in the distance. For this victory he was awarded the Croix de Guerre with palm.

On the day Quentin Roosevelt died, he had left the aerodrome with a formation of five planes and crossed the lines east of Chateau-Thierry. Both the Allies and the Germans were busy strafing trenches and supply lines and a major fire-fight was never far off. Seven Fokker machines were sighted in the air—and the group of five Americans took them on. The German flyers stopped their strafing mission and a tight circle of aircraft developed. Circling, sliding and "soul searching" combat continued for 10 minutes when Quentin suddenly spotted another group of German aircraft with bright red painted cowling, approaching from the east. Leaving the formation to meet this new threat, he was not missed immediately. Lieutenant Burford, the leader of Quentin's formation that day recalled later that he saw a Nieuport falling through the clouds from above him. At the time he did not know who it was but stated that the airplane passed out of control. Realizing there were Germans above the clouds, Burford signaled his men to break and they returned to their lines since the odds were bad enough as they were. After these planes landed it was discovered that Quentin was missing.

A wireless message was received that evening by the 95th stating that Lieutenant Quentin Roosevelt had been shot down by Sergeant K. Thom of the Richthofen Flying Circus. The message further stated that he had been buried with full military honors. The news startled and shocked the world. The son of a former president of the United States had been killed in action. Rumors circulated. Many persons felt that

Roosevelt had been abandoned by his four fellow flyers. Rickenbacker denied this forcefully when he later stated:[26]

A story came to my attention later which deserves a drastic reply. New York newspapers gave wide publicity to a statement made by a certain noncombatant named Hungerford who claimed to have been employed on the Chateau-Thierry sector of the front at this time. He not only attempted to describe the fight in which Quentin Roosevelt lost his life, but even intimated that had Quentin's comrades not fled, thereby leaving Quentin alone against desperate odds, the whole German formation might have been destroyed. He stated that he saw the fight and that Quentin before his sad death actually shot down two of the enemy planes.

This whole story is absolute piffle. Nobody saw Quentin's last fight except the Huns who shot him down. The fight itself occurred ten miles behind the German lines over Fere-en-Tarden. Quentin did not shoot down two enemy planes nor did his comrades desert him in time of trouble. It will be very unhealthful for Mr. Hungerford to meet the members of 95 Squadron upon their return to New York. A more gallant lot of boys never came to France, as this noncombatant gentleman will discover when he meets them.

A dispute was beginning to mount. Who in fact had scored the victory against Roosevelt? Thom was only the first German name to be linked to his death. The German newspaper, *Kölnische Zeitung*, reported the following story:

A formation of seven German aeroplanes, while crossing the Marne, saw in the neighborhood of Dormans a group of twelve American fighting aeroplanes and attacked them. A lively air battle began, in which one American in particular persisted in attacking. The principal feature of the battle consisted in an air duel between the American and a German fighting pilot, named Sergeant Greper. After a short struggle Greper succeeded in bringing the brave American before his gunsights. After a few shots the plane apparently got out of his control; the American began to fall and struck the ground near

the village of Chamery, about ten kilometres north of
the Marne. The American flyer was killed by two shots
through the head. Papers in his pocket showed him to
be Quentin Roosevelt, of the United States Army. His
effects are being taken care of in order to be sent to his
relatives. He was buried by German aviators with military honors.

In his book, *Fighting the Flying Circus*, Rickenbacker
states that Roosevelt was shot down by Sergeant Feldwebez
Karl Thom, a member of the Richthofen Circus.[27] This was
taken from the wireless message received on the evening of
his death. The German records after the war gave credit for
the kill to Feldwebel Christian Donhauser, a sergeant in the
Imperial Air Force. At the time of Roosevelt's death, Donhauser had eight planes to his credit and finished the war
with a total of fifteen. At the time of the Roosevelt kill,
Thom, despite his low rank, was the commander of Jasta 21
of the Flying Circus. He finished the war as a lieutenant with
a score of 27 official victories. Donhauser was the only member of Jasta 21 to be officially credited with a victory on
July 14, 1918, the date of Roosevelt's death. The mention of
Thom's name probably arose out of the confusion of the
event since he had been in command of the German group on
this day. But what about Greper? The facts may never be
known for certain.

The death of this young son of an American President has
been clouded in controversy since it occurred. Quentin had
fallen behind enemy lines, and what had taken place at his
death scene has not been accurately determined—at least in
published material. At the U. S. Air Force Museum in Dayton
is a small file that carries the name "Roosevelt, Quentin." In
this file is certain scant information, some of which has not
appeared in print before. There is a letter from Burdick
Heytz of 4493 E. White Street, Fresno, California, dated
May 19, 1966, and addressed to Maurer Maurer, Chief, His-

torical Studies Branch, U.S.A.F. Historical Division, ASI-HS,
Maxwell Air Force Base, Alabama, 36112, which reads as
follows, partly paraphrased:

> Thank you for your letter of May 16. I was one of
> the first American soldiers to reach his plane after it was
> shot down northeast of the Reddy farm and headed
> toward Belgium. I was attached to Co. M, 128th Infan-
> try, 32nd Division. There was a hole in the upper left
> wing, the left wheel was smashed, the propeller was in
> good condition, the radiator was full of water, there was
> plenty of gas—Roosevelt had been shot in the back.
> The Germans buried him before our arrival, placing
> his body in a grave with his head toward the west. They
> had fashioned a wooden cross on which was a card bear-
> ing writing in German and his name on the bottom.
> Three German soldiers, unarmed, had been left as cour-
> tesy guards.[28]

The cross at Quentin's grave had been hastily erected out
of two pine logs tied together. (See Figure 11.) The file at
Dayton indicates that the cross was later replaced with an
elaborate carved, fence-like affair erected by the French.
Painted below the cross at the top of the new fence were the
following words:

> L.Q.R. Escadrille 95
> Tombe glorieusement
> In combat aerien
> Le 14 Juillet 1918
> Pour le drout[29]

The paint apparently had been applied hastily since it had
dripped, or "run," at several places.

In the file mentioned is a photo of the crashed plane with
the flyer lying beside it, face up. The top wing in the photo is
collapsed downward and the elevator is missing. Lieutenant
W. W. Tanney of Pittsburgh, a prisoner of the Germans at the

time, later said the Germans had a postcard made of the death scene and used it in Germany for propaganda purposes.

July 14, Bastille Day, had been a holiday in France—but not for the American flyers. The orders for this patrol directed them to fly at high patrol—5,000 to 5,500 meters—between Dormans and Belleau Woods at 11:00 A. M. Captain Philip Roosevelt, a cousin of Quentin, saw his plane fall not realizing at the time who it was.

Conflicts in the evidence are apparent. For example, Lieutenant Hamilton Coolidge, who later fell in the Argonne Forest, claims that he saw Quentin's grave. "At the foot of the cross was a bent and twisted axle of the machine, with the wire wheels attached; all that was left after his fifteen thousand foot fall." This squares with the graveside photo—but what happened to the balance of the plane as shown in the German photo? Some theorize the latter photo may have been posed.

Lieutenant Alden Sherry of the 94th claimed that he met the man who killed Roosevelt. This meeting allegedly occurred at Coblenz and the lieutenant does not recall his name. He does relate that the German said, "I am sorry, but if I didn't, he would have gotten me."

The death of Roosevelt was mentioned by a German offi cer ten years later during a conversation in a small West Vir ginia town. The officer related that he had been present at the burial. He made a gift of a 7.65 automatic pistol stating he had carried the gun at the burial of the American in France. The German officer also displayed a photo that pictured himself at the burial site. The broken right handle of this small automatic showed clearly in the photo. While the clouded story of the death of Quentin Roosevelt fades deeper into the obscurity of time one fact remains: One of the two flyers on the *Brandenburg* of 1928 had been present at his burial. The pistol is forceful evidence of this.

By September 12, 1918, Colonel Mitchell had almost

1,400 airplanes under his command and the Americans had started the St. Mihiel offensive. On the western front, the flyers on both sides were "busting" observation balloons. (See Figures 12A, 12B, and 12C.) Tracer bullets fired into a hydrogen-filled balloon accompanied by the resulting flaming explosion presented a once-in-a-lifetime spectacle for those who observed. American artillery observers, flying hydrogen-filled balloons, were not ignored by the German flyers. By the end of the war a total of 116 parachute jumps had been made by Americans from burning balloons. (See Figures 12A and 12B.) But only one man had died as a result of these jumps—a remarkable record. The American Balloon Corps had served well. (See Figures 13A and 13B.)

The Great Crusade was drawing to an end. On November 11, a fearful silence descended across the battlefield as the "war to end wars" came to an end. The total cost in lives to Germany in balloons and planes had been 927—the United States, 316. The nervous peace that followed provided an opportunity for two million Americans to discover Europe. What they saw there molded their future—and the future of America. What had this savage war meant to those who fought it? Only time would provide an answer. In the meantime, the Americans moved into German towns and most were startled by the reception extended to them. There was no outward feeling of hostility or anger. While there were exceptions, the Americans and the Germans had met each other for the first time. The warm treatment of Americans there in the "land of castles" (see Figure 14) was repaid ten years later when two Germans visited the Switzerland of America—West Virginia.

NAMING A RACING BALLOON

Prior to World War I, ballooning in Germany had been a favorite sport and thousands participated. But nine years passed following the Armistice before they became active again. The aero club that sponsored Bertram's entry in 1928 had been faced with two practical problems: first, the construction of a suitable balloon was almost impossible since there was no ready supply of reasonably priced silk or gold-beater's fabric; second, they had to choose a suitable name for the entry. The first problem was overcome by the use of cotton fabric (very dangerous for the flyers) coated with gold lacquer. The second was resolved by turning to German history. The name chosen was the *Ernest Brandenburg*—the same name used by the German entry in 1927. The name had a particular meaning for this crew as well as their nation. The origin of it provides insight into the background and causes of the First World War, as well as the decision to use the name on their entry.

Prussia, as an ambitious state, had its beginning under the influence of Frederick William the Great Elector some three hundred years before World War I. Frederick immediately demonstrated that he was a monarch by abolishing the constitution. Following this he organized a rigorous well-trained army which was used to attack neighboring countries. Success was instantaneous and captured territory began to grow to great proportions. After careful deliberation Berlin was chosen as the capital for the growing empire. Thus precedent was established by use of an aggressive military operation which future rulers of Germany would follow: fight,

conquer, and keep what was taken. And the "Nordmark"—
the symbol of Prussia—was under his control completely.

Thus established, the pattern of Prussianism ran unchecked
until it confronted the free nations in the First World War.
"Could Prussianism conquer democracy?" The maelstrom
that followed provided the answer—but Germany did not believe it. The same question would arise again just 21 years
after World War I—and it would again be answered in the
same way.

Events followed rapidly as East Prussia joined with William's domain and in 1701, Frederick III became the King of
Prussia. Prussianism practices continued to extend the dynasty until by 1800 the ever-growing domain included Posen,
Silesia, Pomerania, and certain provinces of Poland. The major setback experienced came at the hands of Napoleon. But
by 1814, Prussia was able not only to recover most of what
she had lost to him, but gained additional territory as well.

The wave of democracy that swept America in the 1770's
also affected Prussia. In 1848 and 1849, flames of insurrection raged in Baden and Saxony. These fires were brutally
extinguished by the armies of Prussia and the power play
demonstrated so many times in the past continued unchecked. And those in power scanned the maps of Europe for
new fields to conquer.

It was at this time Bismarck came into power. The House
of Hapsburg which ruled Austria had often allied in the past
with the House of Hohenzollern but Bismarck looked upon
any joining of forces as a sign of weakness and he decided to
eliminate Austria as a potential rival. But an excuse to pro-
ceed was needed so an excuse was provided by manufacturing
a dispute over the territory of Schleswig-Holstein. After properly planned agitation, the well-prepared and trained armies
of Prussia overwhelmed both Austria and her sister Bavaria
which had been foolish enough to side with Austria. The end
for Austria came at the battle of Konnigsgratz—it had taken

only seven weeks. The way was clear for further empire building and Bismarck reacted accordingly. First he scanned the maps—but second, he paused to allow his lieutenants to organize internal affairs.

A constitution was adopted giving the House of Hohenzollern and successive rulers autocratic control which would be backed by military power. Stunned by her defeat in the Seven Weeks War, Austria reluctantly came into the confederation. The German states were thus further welded together—at least on the surface—but hatreds had been bred within. For example, for many years after this victory—and the corresponding defeat—it was declared by Austrian statute to be unlawful to fly the German flag in Bavaria.

The restless Bismarck then provoked a fight with France. The territory he had consolidated in the German confederation only fanned the desire for more. The provinces of Alsace-Lorraine were just too tempting and they were taken in due course. The pattern was firmly set: plan long in advance; build an army—wait and when the time was right— strike out vigorously and bring in more territory. The 40 years' peace that followed Bismarck's last action only temporarily stalled the progress of a pattern now well established. In spite of peace, building a great army and navy and Prussianization of the people of Germany was firsthand business and it continued. "The German people were made the docile tools of the Prussian Dynasty, serviceable for the later execution of its maturing plans."[30] The stage had carefully been set for the First World War. But it should be acknowledged that the rulers of Germany could not have believed—at this time in history—that they were wrong.

A new, rigorous period of training for future conquest began. The youth of the nation were told both in schools and churches that God had chosen Germany to rule the world. The Kaiser, with the army as an effective spokesman, provided a new voice for the people of Germany to follow. And

the voice announced nationwide a series of events that led to
the fatal day when Germany would once more use military
power to force its boundaries outward. One who viewed
these events at the time may have concluded that they had
been both accidental and unrelated. But observed histori-
cally, it seems obvious that the events were both carefully
thought out and expertly timed to achieve planned objec-
tives.

Kaiser Wilhelm II became impatient to unsheath the German sword. He was ready—in the Prussian style—to slash out
at those who did not understand that they would be better
off within the German confederation than without. Maps
printed in Germany during these years illustrate the planning
that had been carried out. On these maps Germany was in-
variably shown as encompassing a territory larger than that
which it lawfully possessed. Even South America and Argentina were within the proposed realm. This early ambition of
territory to take may explain why fugitive Nazi officers of
another decade would seek refuge in this part of the world.

Through efforts of the Kaiser, Germany finally received a
concession from Turkey allowing Germany to construct the
Bagdad railway thus creating an opening through the Balkans.
But the Balkan War and the defeat of Turkey deprived Germany of this exit and the Bagdad corridor was closed.

The territory that had made up the named German right-
of-way became Serbian land. Serbia—with good reason—was
antagonistic toward Vienna and Berlin. Diplomatic maneu-
vers were no longer possible so Prussia looked to precedent in
deciding how to chart its new course. The answer was simple:
force. But as before an excuse was needed. A critical day in
June, 1914 provided the answer requiring the assassination
of two persons. On Sunday, June 28, the Archduke Francis
Ferdinand, heir to the Austrian-Hungarian throne, and his
wife, the Duchess of Hohenberg, arrived at the Bosnian capital of Serajevo. The citizens of Bosnia had demonstrated

great unrest prompting the visit of state. Within minutes after their arrival a 21-year-old youth named Gabrinovics hurled a bomb at the auto in which the royal figures were riding. None of those in the party were harmed by the explosion but the Archduke was beside himself with indignation—and fear. As the party proceeded south from the town hall, Gavrilo Prinzip stepped into the street and fired two fatal shots into the Archduke's auto. The Duchess was fatally wounded by the first one and the Archduke died almost instantly with a severed jugular vein from the second one.

The world was shaken by the tragedy and it was obvious that graver trouble was ahead. Germany issued a detailed ultimatum to Serbia, demanding a reply within two days which was unreasonable under the circumstances. When the demands were made public it seemed obvious that Serbia would not meet them. But to the amazement of the world, Serbia accepted the eleven demands without major alteration. But in spite of this the Austrian minister left Belgrade without reading the reply which had been sent promptly. This occurred at 5:45 P. M. on July 15, 1914. Diplomatic relations between the nations involved were thus severed without notice or reason.

Conciliatory words were interposed by Great Britain but these were rejected. Austria mobilized her armies and on July 28 war was declared against Serbia. The same day the Kaiser mobilized his great navy—in spite of the fact that there had yet been no threat by anyone directed toward Germany. On July 29, Belgrade was shelled by Austrian artillery from the north side of the Danube. General mobilization of the German army was ordered on July 30. On August 1, Germany declared war against Russia and on this day a German patrol crossed the French border at Cirey. Two days later on August 3, Germany demanded that Belgium provide her citizens free passage across the nation. Upon refusal of this demand Germany promptly declared war on Belgium. In the afternoon of the same day German troops entered the Belgium town of Arion. At midnight at Trafalgar Square in London it was announced that Great Britain and Germany were at war.

The stage, so carefully set, was ready for the terrible show that followed. And once more Germany reached out to expand its great territory at the expense of others. The First World War was under way. The price of victory for the Allies and defeat for Germany is told best in the lives of those who paid the biggest price. The United States lost 73,000 persons; the British Empire, 975,000; France, 1,500,000 and Germany, 2,750,000. The total battle deaths of all nations that engaged in combat exceeded 11,000,000 persons. More than 33,000,000 suffered battle wounds. The price of victory—and defeat—had been much too high.

As time and events passed the "Nordmark" of Frederick's time had been replaced by a new name: "The Mark of Brandenburg." Naming their racing balloon was an easy task for the Chemnitz Aero Club. Why not choose a name that represented over three hundred years of aggression—and conquering? Why not send forth a balloon entry that carried the name of the conqueror? Armed with this appropriate name, the construction of the new balloon and the assembly of its equipment moved forward at top speed.

BALLOONS AND WAR

Those who lived in the Land of Brandenburg in the Twenties had a feeling of closeness to lighter-than-air flying. This was principally due to the ballooning activity that had prevailed there in prior years. In peacetime, Germans flew in balloon races and tried to establish records. In war, they used balloons to bomb enemy cities. The German Treaty of Peace, as drafted by the victorious allies, demonstrates that the allies' fear of German balloons was enough to include the following provisions:

> *Air*—The armed forces of Germany must not include any military or naval air forces except for not over 100 unarmed seaplanes to be retained till Oct. 1 to search for submarine mines. No dirigibles shall be kept. The entire air personnel is to be demobilized within two months, except for 1,000 officers and men retained till October.
>
> No aviation grounds or dirigible sheds are to be allowed within 150 kilometers of the Rhine or the eastern or southern frontiers, existing installations within these limits to be destroyed.
>
> The manufacture of aircraft and parts of aircraft is forbidden for six months. All military and naval aeronautical material under a most exhaustive definition must be surrendered within three months, except for the 100 seaplanes already specified.[31]

One person more than any other, deserves the credit for the lighter-than-air success of Germany. He was a German named Zeppelin. This name became the "sabre" that the German General Staff rattled at Great Britain prior to World War I. If England was foolish enough to enter the war, London would be reduced to rubble by the great airships of Zeppelin.

The esteem in which the man found himself is directly traceable to the American Civil War—a curious fact of history.

The United States Air Force had its unceremonious beginning in the form of The United States Balloon Corps. Professor Thaddeus Lowe had been persistent about the use of the balloon in warfare and President Lincoln agreed to give him a chance. At first Lowe worked with one balloon and a mobile hydrogen producing unit. This unit was made up of a wooden tank in which nails, horseshoes, scrap metal and sulphuric acid could be mixed. Mounted on a wagon, the equipment was taken to the site where an ascension was desired.

The sulphuric acid reacted with the metal within the tar-sealed wooden box to produce hydrogen: a gas lighter than air—and extremely volatile. Hydrogen had been discovered in 1766 by Henry Cavendish (1731-1810) of the United Kingdom. It is listed as No. 1 on the Atomic scale and carries the symbol "H". The word is derived from the Greek "hydro" or water. One thousand cubic feet of hydrogen of 98% purity will lift 78.6 pounds at 20° Fahrenheit if the air is dense enough to support 32 inches of mercury in an inverted glass tube. As the temperature drops the lifting power decreases. It was this gas that placed one branch of the American Army into the skies for the first time.

Professor Lowe dodged cannon shell and Minie balls fired by soldiers for *both* the North and South. (A large gasbag within rifle shot was just too tempting to infantrymen—and it apparently made no difference if the balloon belonged to friend or foe.) Lowe was soon called "the most shot at man of the war." He made many important and heroic flights in combat constantly seeking information from the air about Confederate movements. But the eyes of the army had always been the cavalry—not a gasbag overhead that contained a telegraph operator who tapped out messages of troop movements. For this reason, the many reports filed by Lowe were ignored by the Union officers and the value of aerial reports was lost to the war effort.

It was the custom of warring armies then to invite military men to join the troops in the field in order to gain firsthand combat experience—a sort of apprenticeship arrangement. And a young Prussian officer had been invited to serve with Lowe during his combat flights. His name? Count Von Zeppelin.

Zeppelin gained firsthand experience by making many ascensions with Lowe during the Civil War. He served as an observer and helped plot Confederate gun positions and troop movements. Zeppelin returned to Germany fully convinced of the value of air observation. While the American officers had ignored the reports of Lowe, German officers eagerly accepted the reports of Von Zeppelin. When the Franco-Prussian War began some five years after the close of the American Civil War, Zeppelin commanded the Prussian Balloon Observation Corps as might have been expected. France was ultimately defeated and Europe had 40 years of peace: a time to plan for a new war. Von Zeppelin used the time to work on his balloons. He developed the largest airships in the world near his estate at Friedrichshafen. He theorized that if a lighter-than-air craft was to have reasonable speed for military use the round shape must give way to a long, cigar-shaped craft.

The first product of his research and construction was the *LZ-I* which was 420 feet long. By the turn of the century, the aging Von Zeppelin was running the Deutche Luftchiffart A.G., the world's first passenger airline. This was remarkable in view of the fact that man had yet to make a successful flight in heavier-than-air craft. By the time World War I broke out, Zeppelin's airline had carried 34,230 passengers a total of 144,000 miles without a fatality. His ships were manned by careful, well-trained men who took pride in what they were doing.

At the outbreak of war the German High Command confiscated Zeppelin's stock which consisted of shops, hangars, and seven true Zeppelins or dirigibles. These were so named for the fact that they were "steerable" by rudders and powered by motors as contrasted with free-flight balloons which were not. For the first time in history someone suggested using dirigibles for bombing purposes.

The potential bombing of London was a real threat to the English people and the Berlin papers called for the bombing almost daily. In self defense, the British sent Flight Lieutenant Marix on a night attack on the Zeppelin sheds at Dusseldorf with some success since he destroyed one airship. A later flight of British planes flamed another Zeppelin in its hangar. London had yet to be bombed.

The first Zeppelin raid of London came in the early part of 1915. A dirigible commanded by a Captain Linnarz headed for London with a small load of bombs. The craft made it to Southend, finally dropping its incendiaries in the general direction of the *H.M.S. Edward.* No hits were scored. The gunners on the ship returned the fire but they also missed. Within one month Linnarz returned to London and dropped enough bombs to kill seven civilians.

On the night of May 17, 1915, one of the strangest events of the war occurred—and a Zeppelin was involved. For some 40 minutes the city of Calais on the French coast was under mysterious fire that was both accurate and destructive. Searchlights frantically scanned the air expecting to find a Zeppelin overhead—none was there. Yet the bombs fell with great accuracy, moving from target to target. The "Ghost" finally departed never to return. The mystery was not solved until after the war. The officers of the *LZ-XII* had constructed a cable car in which a man with phone communication could be lowered more than a mile below the Zeppelin. Baron Max von Gemmingen rode the cable car over Calais while the main craft remained well above the overcast. He had whispered instructions to Captain Ernst Lehmann who commanded the Zeppelin above. The pattern of the bombs was thus accurately moved about the city doing great damage. While the searchlights moved back and forth in the clouds above, the observer rode just over their heads in the cable car. In spite of its success this was the only time that the cable car was used during the war.

The *LZ-XII* was lost later in the war over the North Sea, but Lehmann survived. Nineteen years after the Armistice, the Zeppelin *Von Hindenburg* burst into flames over Lakehurst, New Jersey, killing 35 passengers—one of the dead was Captain Ernst Lehmann.

A few nights after the Calais raid, London was again threatened by a Zeppelin. This time it was the *LZ-XXXVII*, some 521 feet in length and filled with 950,000 cubic feet of explosive hydrogen. Commanded by Captain von de Haegen, the ship carried a group of officers and other German officials who went along for the ride. As the craft crossed the English Channel, it was spotted by Regiland Warneford, flying for the Royal Navy. Shadowing the giant ship, Warneford determined that its line of flight would take it to London. Armed with a 30-30 caliber carbine and a few hand bombs, the young flyer attacked. He immediately came under the fire of several appropriately mounted machine guns. The few shots that Warneford fired showed no effect at all. A bullet hole in the thin skin of a Zeppelin allowed little gas to escape.

Suddenly the captain of the Zeppelin dropped water ballast and moved higher into the atmosphere. The small aircraft was above its service limit, the Morane engine straining at its maximum. With a last burst of power the engine lifted the small plane above the Zeppelin and the young officer was suddenly flying down the back of the giant below. Warneford immediately dropped his small hand bombs with disastrous results for the Zeppelin—and almost for him. The explosion that followed threw his small plane out of control. Tossed violently through the black skies now brilliant with the intense light of flaming hydrogen, Warneford made a dead-stick landing behind German lines. The lieutenant made quick repairs to his engine and returned home to tell fellow pilots that the Zeppelins could be stopped. In the meantime, the remains of the dying *LZ-XXXVII* fell on a convent near Ghent killing one nun outright. Several died later from burns. Most of the crew and passengers died in the flames although one man escaped death after a fall of several thousand feet. Warneford was awarded the Victoria Cross for being the first man to down a Zeppelin in air-to-air combat.

The first dirigible victim of machine gun fire was the *SL 11 Shutte-Lanz*, often mistaken for a Zeppelin because of its similar shape. During the night of September 2, 1916, this craft swept over England bound for London. Lieutenant W. Leefe-Robinson, flying night patrol in a BE2, sighted the ship outlined against searchlight beams. He immediately attacked pouring explosive bullets into the ship. Nothing happened at first. Suddenly the huge craft glowed from within like an open-hearth furnace. As flames burst through its sides the ship rocketed from the sky like a flaming torch. Leefe-Robinson also received the Victoria Cross.

By the end of 1916, the defending airplanes of Great Britain and other nations had destroyed the Zeppelin threat. A few Zeppelin raids continued during 1917 but were scattered and ineffective. A total of 5,806 bombs were dropped by Zeppelins during the war killing 557 persons.

The silver balloons were too easy to burst and the Kaiser replaced them with the huge long-range Goatha bombers which were more effective although not much so. The threat of the destruction of London would have to wait for another war.

The balloon was used most effectively during the war for observation purposes. Also it was the most reliable source for confirmation of the kills of conventional aircraft. By the time the war ended, the Germans had attacked 87 U. S. balloons and destroyed 47. The United States crews had made 5,866 ascensions clocking up 6,365 hours in the air. A total of 939 artillery adjustments were made from balloons with each adjustment including all shells fired after the adjustment. The effectiveness and damage caused by these corrections would be impossible to estimate—but it must have been considerable.

THE RACE BEGINS

Even though the balloon came down after 24 or 36 hours, it might land in a wilderness several days journey on foot to the nearest building.[32]

At his weather station at Ford Airport, Mr. Andrus continued his briefing up to the last minute because weather conditions never remain stable for any long period of time. His forefinger moved across a large weather map of the Eastern United States as he traced an estimated flight pattern across Michigan River, into Canada, down Lake Erie to Cleveland, past Pittsburgh, across West Virginia, Virginia, North Carolina, South Carolina and south to Florida. It would be a record flight if any contestants could fly this route to its end.

Near the balloon site a platform had been constructed of pine timbers decked with pine planks. The only son of Henry Ford, Edsel, stepped to the platform. A young man handed him the white starting flag, staffed on a six-foot pole. Raising the flag, Edsel held it motionless as a gentle wind ruffled his dark hair. An official down the field hand-signaled to Ed Hill, pilot of the pilot balloon. When an airplane went up, people would shout and cheer but this was not so with a balloon ascension. A feeling of awe comes over a person at a balloon ascension. Maybe it is the majesty of the thing. An ascension seems to awaken some ancient and primitive instinct in man—an instinct that calls for escape. A wave of silence swept across Ford Airport. The aide shouted, "Go," and the call was heard across the entire field.

At the site of Hill's balloon an aide assisted him into the gondola. Ballast bags were quickly released and dropped to the ground. Two aides placed their full weight on each side of the basket as a third dropped a final ballast bag. Enough ballast had been removed. A hand dropped: The two men jumped from the basket and Hill was airborne. Pushed by a gentle breeze in the direction of the River Rouge Ford Plant, the pilot balloon was flying. The race was ready to start.

The *Brandenburg* was now fully inflated but the gas line was still attached to the appendix. Lieutenant Frobel completed his check of the equipment and then slipped the strap of a small satchel around his shoulder. Made of brown canvas with brass clasps, the bag was the crew's survival kit. It contained first-aid gear, fishing equipment—and an automatic pistol. The colors of Germany in the form of a large silk banner had been fastened around the basket. (See Figure 15.) Its purpose was to aid others in identification of the craft as it flew in the race. Stowed in the rigging above the load ring was a small rubber boat with a set of oars. (See Figure 9A.) The possibility of falling into Lake Erie was too real. Furlined suits, sufficient for Arctic use to protect the flyers from both the sun and cold, and other clothes had been packed in waterproof packs. (See Figure 16G.) In addition, food and iron rations had been carefully packed in waterproof containers. At one side of the basket were two small oxygen bottles (see Figure 9B) for use at higher altitudes. Strapped on the outside of the basket was a small handsaw. (See Figure 9G.) The need for this item did not seem apparent at the time but later became critical. Bertram stepped into the basket joining Frobel as their ground aides stood by. The canvas gas line was still attached to the valve of the *Brandenburg*—a serious and almost fatal mistake.

Edsel Ford, by then bareheaded, raised the white flag and dropped it with a sharp snap across the front of the officials' platform. It was 4:00 P. M. and the race was officially under way. The program stated that the entries would lift off at five-minute intervals. A mass lift-off could cause disaster and the race officials would not permit such a risk.

The *Munster* was the first of the entries to leave the ground and it lifted off smoothly spewing sand from a damaged ballast bag. Eimenacher waved and smiled to the throngs that had practically made it impossible to remove excess ballast. Eimenacher, wearing a heavy beard, was a veteran of many races and he almost won this one. The American entries followed with the *American Business Club* lifting off second, followed by the *Detroit*. The *Brandenburg* was airborne sixth but only after difficulties.

> The takeoff was marred by bad luck. As the starting gun sounded the balloon was let go without the filling device being removed and the departure lines were torn. Since the danger existed that the balloon (as tied down at the takeoff) would blow up, we had to start at once to close valves until after many efforts we succeeded in opening the filling device somewhat at about 600 meters.[34]

The last entry to leave was the *Blanchard* of France. Its pilot, Charles Dolifus, and his aide, George Carmier, followed a flight pattern almost identical to that of the *Brandenburg*. The Frenchmen fared a little better in the end however. Andrus predicted the wind blowing the balloons southeast would hold steady for 24 to 48 hours. He stated, "Carried on a steady wind which ought to prevail for them throughout the flight, they should have no trouble at all."

The *Associated Press* reported: "As each bag was released and swung gracefully into the cloudless sky, a band struck up the national anthem of the nation it represented."[35] The bands continued to play as the last entry faded into the distance. Some enthusiastic spectators had followed the entries in autos as the balloons left Ford Airport. Others soon tired of looking skyward and gradually turned their attention elsewhere.

As was expected, the first entry to be eliminated from the race was the smaller *Helvetia* piloted by Ernest Maag, a mechanical engineer, native of Zurich and a lieutenant in the Swiss Army. Maag was sponsored by the Swiss Aero Club. His craft was forced down July 1, at about 1:30 P. M. on Harter Hill, 11 miles south of Fairmont, West Virginia. The location was about one mile west of Bingamon, West Virginia. He had lifted off at Detroit at 4:30 P. M. the previous day. Just prior to the force-down he had been flying at 4,500 feet and was unaware of his location. Lack of ballast and loss of the services of his aide who had been forced to stay behind in Detroit contributed to his elimination. The *Helvetia* had bounced off of several hills before residents in the area of Harter Hill came to its aid. They eventually grounded the craft by grasping ropes thrown down by the balloonist and over a dozen men assisted in bringing the balloon to a safe rest. Among the first men to reach the craft were Harvey Talkington and Gale Lipson of Worthington, Thomas Robey of Bingamon and R. M. Moran of Shinnston. Later, Talkington drove Maag around the town of Fairmont prior to the latter's departure for Detroit. Lieutenant Maag stated that the uncertainty of the finish of a balloon flight was the reason that the sport was of such great interest to him.

The *Helvetia* had been carried into Canada at the outset of the race and was blown across Lake Erie. Maag arrived over Cleveland at about 11 o'clock Saturday night. The *Helvetia* arrived over Fairmont at about 11:00 A. M., July 1. Drifting further south, it landed at Harter Hill.

The beauty of West Virginia made an impression upon Maag. He stated: "This state is surprisingly like Switzerland both in topography and beauty. The hills and the country remind me very much of home." After careful packing, the *Helvetia* was shipped to Detroit by train. Lieutenant Maag followed by passenger train. Fortunately, the balloon and all equipment survived without injury—as did the flyer.

The next balloon down was the pilot ship. Ed Hill and Jack Engle were forced to earth near Durbin, West Virginia, a short time after the *Helvetia.* This left nine balloons in the race. All but two had been officially accounted for.

Early on the morning of July 1, many persons in Fairmont (a city of about 20,000 located 88 miles south of Pittsburgh) were treated to an unusual air show. The first of two lighter-than-air crafts was sighted at about 8:00 A. M., moving south at 8,000 feet. The other was close behind. Lieutenant L. H. (Scotty) Scott of Marietta, Ohio, had been temporarily stationed at the Arnettsville, West Virginia, airfield. He immediately took off and attempted to fly as close to the balloons as possible in order to identify them. His plane would not climb to the altitude of 8,000 feet but he came close enough to the lower balloon to read the large words on the side of the silk bag. The *American Business Club* entry was located.

After landing to refuel, Lieutenant Scott attempted to identify the second balloon which was at 10,000 feet. Scott was unable to make a positive identification but he reported that it was a German balloon. It was thought that the *Brandenburg* had been sighted but this was an error. The ship over Fairmont was the *Bremen.* At the time, the *Brandenburg* was over Salem, Ohio, some 90 air miles to the northwest. The balloons were being pushed by different air currents.

A change in weather conditions caused the force-down of the next two balloons. The *American Business Club* went down at Stuarts Draft, Virginia, and the *Argentina* at Millboro, Virginia.

A few minutes prior to starting time, the flyers had been warned to keep their crafts at less than 5,000 feet to avoid sluggish winds predicted over parts of Pennsylvania. The downing of the *American Business Club*—a balloon of 80,000 cubic foot capacity—after only 300 miles in the air, led race officials at Detroit to predict that none of the balloons would

come near the previous year's record. Ed Hill, assisted by
Albert Schlosser, had flown 800 miles in 1927.

Karl Betts of Detroit, in charge of the race, predicted on
July 1 that the race would probably end the following day
with little chance of any entry getting to Florida. However,
he felt that some entries might reach the Carolinas and possibly Georgia.

By the close of Sunday, July 1, 1928, several other balloons were reported down. The *Wallonie* was down near Bev-
erly, West Virginia; the *Detroit*, down at Cass, West Virginia;
and the *Lafayette*, down safely near Elk Hill, West Virginia.
At 9:00 A. M., the *Bremen* carrying its father-son team came
down at 10:00 A. M. near Chase City, Virginia, and at 2:00
P. M. the *Denmark* landed on a farm northwest of Roanoke.

A news release of July 3 reported that the U. S. Army
balloon was down after traveling 460.9 miles. The German
Bremen had landed one mile behind. The French balloon
Blanchard was down 13 miles from the *Bremen.* The Army
balloon came down three miles southeast of Kendridge, Lun-
enburg County, Virginia; the *Bremen*, three miles south of
Chase City, Mecklenburg County. The *Blanchard* was down
four miles northeast of Walnut Cove, North Carolina, on the
banks of the Dan River. As later determined by the Geologi
cal Survey for the Aeronautic Association, the three balloons
in the order listed were the first, second, and third winners.
The *Brandenburg* was missing.

FLYING FREE

*Moses sent them to . . . the land of Canaan,
and said to them, "Go up into . . . the hill country, and see what the land is, and whether the
people who dwell in it are strong or weak,
whether they are few or many, and whether the
land that they dwell in is good or bad, and
whether the cities that they dwell in are camps
or strongholds and whether the land is rich or
poor, and whether there is wood in it or not."*[36]

The initial difficulties of liftoff overcome the *Brandenburg*
rose to an altitude of 1,750 meters. The craft moved in the
same general path of those before it . . . toward Windsor,
Canada. From Ford Airport the flight pattern was across Melvindale and over Lincoln Park. To the left of the *Brandenburg* sprawled the giant Ford plant on the bank of the River
Rouge and in proximity to the airport. Crossing West Jefferson Street the free-flying balloon edged over the Detroit
River, dropping sharply because of the cool moisture rising
from the river on the warm summer day. (See Figure 2.) The
international border between the United States and Canada
was crossed in the middle of the river. Swaying from side to
side gently, the *Brandenburg* was over Ojibway, Ontario,
drifting away from Windsor and heading southeast.

The flight across Canada was uneventful. As night neared,
the airship was carried by a firm wind in the general path of
Canard River and Cedar Creek. The flight was going well and
the flyers had every reason to believe they could win the
race. The ship left the landfall of Canada at the approximate
location of Kingsville. The dangerous flight over Lake Erie
had begun.

Some 60 miles of open water was ahead of them but if the

wind held steady, they would make landfall again at or near
Cleveland, Ohio. The anticipated flight over Lake Erie
prompted the crew to carry the rubber lifeboat. They might
not be lucky enough to come down on an island as the *Brandenburg* had the year before. The dial on Frobel's watch read
9:30 P. M. The shimmering summer sun slid down the water
line to the west. Weird shadows were cast across their craft as
the water darkened below. The sun rays still shined on the
cotton bag above them.

As night closed in, the maps became hard to read. Free
flyers must always be concerned about orientation because a
sudden shift of wind might take them on some accidental
course. In the flight at hand the prospect of flying toward the
North Pole was possible. Worse yet the flight might extend
due east and over the Atlantic. Flying without navigational
aids and in darkness obviously left much to be desired.

As darkness deepened both men had time to meditate.
Reflecting upon the flight they agreed that if victorious they
would help restore confidence—in some measure—to their defeated nation. This provided them with a new feeling of importance. To some degree they were risking their lives by
flying in a cotton fabric craft. But the risk was worth it—if
they would either win or make a good showing. They wanted
that badly.

The year 1928 had been a confusing one for the two Germans. They were military men and could not fully compre-
hend the changes taking place in the unsettled world below.
Both were from Chemnitz, Germany, but neither could fore-
see the day when their nation would be broken into parcels;
or the day when their hometown would be renamed "Karl-
Marx-Stadt." (Chemnitz had a population of 295,160 persons
as of December 31, 1965. Occupied by the Russians in 1945
the population was 82 percent Protestant and 11 percent
(plus) Catholic. The parcel taken by the Russians encompassed 41,661 square miles including East Berlin. The land of

Brandenburg would be placed to the acid test and the people there would suffer terribly.) But now it was dark and a firm wind was with them. Tomorrow, victory . . . perhaps.

Midnight passed . . . it was July 1. On the morrow universal suffrage for the women of England became a fact. Owen W. Richardson of the United Kingdom won the Nobel Prize in physics. The 1928 Nobel Prize for medicine went to Charles J. H. Nicholle of France and the prize for chemistry went to a German, Windaus. It was a good omen. Thomas Mann helped bring Germany back to the front in the coming year by winning the prize in literature. Germans could win— and Bertram and Frobel were determined to do so.

Bertram mentioned that in the previous year the anthropologist Bohlin at Choukoutien, near Peking, China, had discovered a tooth of the Pithecanthropus Pekinensis, of the lower Paleolithic period dating about 400,000 B.C. "Strange find," said the German captain—and a strange thought for a balloonist in an international race. (In the coming year the anthropologist Garrod, near Mount Carmel, Israel, found parts of 16 skeletons of the Neanderthaloid Man of the Middle Paleolithic or Mousterian period of 120,000 B.C.)

Startled by a sudden flash of summer heat lightning, the flyers were aware once more of their position over the water below. It had been a night to dream—if only for a few seconds. Under them was the 12th largest lake in the world. Covering 9,930 square miles, the lake was 241 miles long, 210 feet deep maximum with an average depth of 60 feet. It was no place for a balloon to land. The lake was a mere 572 feet above sea level. Bertram knew this and was counting on saving all gas and ballast possible to gain altitude for the coming day. It was risky but worth it. The lieutenant remarked in German that the Battle of Lake Erie (September 10, 1813) had been fought somewhere below them. His voice trailed off into the night. The captain asked him what he had said, as he carefully dribbled a handful of sand over

the side. The continually cooling air prompted Bertram to do
this in order to gain slight altitude. Several ballast bags at the
top edge of the basket had been opened for this reason. The
lieutenant did not answer.

Six hours of moonless, starless darkness passed. The blackness below had been broken only occasionally by twinkling
lights of coal barges crossing the lake. On the horizon ahead
small blinking lights of a city were spotted. Landfall would
be reached in several minutes and it suddenly became apparent to the flyers that their craft was at an extremely low
altitude. The coolness of the night had caused this. Until they
had reference points they were unable to accurately judge
their height. The sounds of the lake seemed deceptively far
away. The craft was flying for Cleveland.

CLEVELAND

A modern-day drive from Richfield, Ohio, to Cleveland is a pleasant experience. Route 21 intersects with Exit No. 11 of the Ohio Turnpike as the four-lane highway points due north. Fabulous restaurants and roadside attractions dot the highway as one passes through Broadview Heights. The community of Independence follows quickly as some 18 miles drop behind. Crossing the Cuyahoga River, a smoky approach to Cleveland is encountered. To the left rise the skyscrapers in the center of the city. The road rolls to the right under several overpasses then back to the left and onto Shoredrive. Across the drive is the runway of a shorefront airport occupied by a four-engine piston-driven plane grinding its way into the foggy evening. Further out the waves of Lake Erie clip onto the shores beneath the asphalt pads of the airport. Six lanes run parallel with the runway on the left as furnaces in a light company building add air pollution by pouring black smoke into the sky.

An exit to the right leads to Howard Johnson's motel—a skyscraper in its own right that provides a startling view of Lake Erie, the airport, the city—and the approach run of the *Brandenburg*. Another right turn leads into the parking lot of a fence-enclosed factory—closed for the weekend. A combination of fog, rain and moisture from the Lake, mixed with smoke and fog from the city, makes picture taking difficult. Moving closer to the lake by another road, a better location is found. A large stone wall juts upward as water spouts several feet from a nearby storm drain. A slight clearing of the rain-laden sky allows a reasonable photo to be made of the approximate location of the Cleveland landfall of the German flyers. (See Figure 17.)

Based upon information available at this time, the *Brandenburg* flew over Cleveland between the power company and Cleveland Stadium. As one stands today looking across the endlessness of the Lake, it is almost possible to imagine the excitement that must have been experienced by the few who witnessed the approach of the German airship. The giant size of the 85,000 cubic foot balloon coupled with the fact that it was very low, must have created a mild sensation. But to relive an experience such as this is impossible today. A four-engine jet overhead crosses the path of the German airship and the whole matter dissolves into an event of four decades ago. The flight of the *Brandenburg* becomes a small sentence in the chapter of the year in which it occurred. The trail left by a racing balloon is such that it can be followed only within the imagination—and the trail quickly dissolves into the insignificance of time.

The *Brandenburg* made Cleveland landfall at about 12:50 A. M. The racing ship had covered 100 air miles in approximately seven hours: an average of 14.4 miles per hour. Speed in a racing balloon usually averages slow because at times the balloon comes to a complete stop.

Crossing Summit Avenue, the flyers moved past City Hall which was close to their right. Summit Avenue passed below with Euclid Avenue ahead. The southeasterly pattern continued as Prospect Avenue slipped beneath them. They were flying so low that the slow rumble of the late traffic below jingled in the flyers' ears. The lights in houses and office buildings blinked and twinkled at them as they flew by. Some of the lights of office buildings were above them due to their low altitude and cleanup ladies scrubbed marble floors on their Saturday night chores.

The flyers were approximately 20 meters above the rooftops of the store buildings and surrounding dwelling houses of the sprawling, industrial city. The center of Cleveland was sliding to their right as the lieutenant examined their map by the yellow glow of his flashlight. The conservative use of ballast over the lake had been a gamble—but it had paid off by 19 meters!

Parked on a small crest at Cleveland Heights, a young man and his date suddenly spotted the huge round shape silhouetted against the dark sky. Overcoming their initial shock of this unexpected confrontation, they called to the men in the basket close above. After identification, the captain oriented the ship in reference to the city.

Now followed the beginning of a parade that swelled to considerable proportions within ten minutes. Turning their car quickly, the young couple began blowing their horn and zigzagging through the streets as they followed the airship above. Others fell in behind in autos as well as on motorcycles and the din increased as they shouted and pointed their way through the suburbs of Cleveland.

Awakened by the approaching cavalcade of horns, lights and shouting people, many sleepy inhabitants scrambled for the family car. Several less enthusiastic observers called to the flyers as they drifted past iron-railed balconies.

The parade continued to grow as more and more of the followers became convinced that the ship would touch down soon. Several of those below carried hip flasks—and tossed them from one car to another as they passed each other. This was as good a reason to celebrate as any other—and who knew when the event would be repeated?

A police substation had been alerted. Was it a union riot or a plain old insurrection that flared in the middle of the city? Two officers were dispatched to investigate—and they promptly set up a roadblock at an intersection directly in front of the lead cars in the strangest parade in the history of Cleveland.

Quickly orienting themselves to the situation, the officers switched on the whirling red light on the inside of their front windshield—and did the only reasonable thing to do under the circumstances. They led the parade!

Time and again from the caravan below, came the demand: "Come down or give us a souvenir."[37] Somewhat disturbed by the proportions of the jumble of humanity following them, the two Germans dropped the one thing they could spare—sand—and empty ballast bags. "Unfortunately we had only empty ballast sacks which we also gladly threw down," reported the captain in his written account of the flight. The raining sand decreased the weight of the German airship and altitude was gained immediately. The equilibrium point was above and they headed for it. The long line of car lights faded in the haze of the night. The sounds below softened as the gentle whisper of the night wind shoved the flyers southward. The noisy encounter soon became only a few sentences in the captain's record. But a strange encounter it had been. Clouds building to the front attracted their attention and Cleveland, and its fun-loving inhabitants, disappeared into the closing blackness below.

By 1:30 A. M., the *Brandenburg* was flying at 1,500 meters and still rising. A small amount of gas was valved as the flyers tried to determine if the flight pattern was still in a southerly direction. Based upon prior experience the captain expressed concern about the weather. The coolness of the night coupled with the overcast and shifting haze, prompted him to alert his aide. "Prepare to drop ballast if I give the word." Reasoning that the easiest ballast to drop was still slung to the outside of the basket, Frobel unsheathed the staghorn-handled hunting knife that he carried on his belt. It would be a simple matter to slash the bags open or clip the tie ropes. Each severed rope would dispatch 25 pounds of sand into the darkness below. The possibility of injury to others was remote in farm country over which they flew. Bulk sand, however, was never to be dropped except in an extreme emergency.

Suddenly the *Brandenburg* was struck by a strong vertical squall which was accompanied by a low-pressure area. The hunch of the captain had been correct. The craft began a slanting, violent, sliding rush toward the earth. Quickly Frobel clipped ballast bags from the side of the basket where he was standing and the captain dumped sand from several bags on the floor of the basket. The slide continued and for the first time in the flight the flyers feared for their lives.

The quick reaction by both flyers to the emergency checked the rapid descent and the gondola never touched the ground. However, because of the momentum generated by the rapid 45-degree angle slide, the basket violently crashed into the top of a small clump of trees. Emerging from the crisis, the balloon lifted slightly at the last possible second preventing contact with the earth.

Flying on a level line for several seconds the captain recalled later that they had been so low that it looked as though they were walking along the ground. The low-pressure area behind, precious altitude was regained and once more the ship was relatively safe. Inexperience could have cost the lives of both flyers in this crisis.

The captain remembered later that they had flown almost even with the dual doors of a large dark red barn. The lightning rods across its peak seemed like needles looking for a balloon to burst. Fortunately, the flight pattern was not obstructed by any solid objects. The balance of the night proved to be uneventful—although very cold. The heavy furlined flying suits were placed to welcome use.

Sufficient altitude was attained to assure the flyers that the recent emergency would not be repeated the next morning. A strange darkness once more enveloped the land of Ohio, slipping by below. Orientation was not possible until some identifiable objects could be seen. None were available for almost three hours. Frobel suggested that a cigarette would calm his slightly shattered nerves. The captain agreed.

(Both enjoyed American cigarettes.) But they knew that a cigarette was a luxury denied to them while aloft. Neither was foolish enough to light a match so close to 85,000 cubic feet of illuminating gas. Such errors are reserved for fools.

The flight continued in a southeasterly direction. The flight had taken them over Mayfield Heights, close to the birthplace of James A. Garfield located near Chagrin Falls, and down the general direction of Route 422. Crossing the Cuyahoga River near Hiram at the intersection of Routes 700 and 305, the flight continued to Garrettsville, across the present location of the Ohio Turnpike to the town of Windham on Route 303.

Morning "nautical twilight" began at about 4:00 A. M. This is the time of the morning when military men in combat zones break from their sleep and prepare weapons and machines for possible attack. Located between the deep slumber of troubled men and the first light of day, the beginning of morning nautical twilight provides a psychological advantage to an attacking force. Both flyers were alert due to combat training designed to overcome such advantage.

The first sun of July prepared to top the horizon to the east. As the hour wore on the first rays struck the very top of the balloon which was then at 1,550 meters—while the darkness was still complete in the basket. The brilliance of the sun moved down and enveloped the 85,000 cubic feet of gas causing it to expand. This expansion lifted the ship another 500 feet within 10 minutes.

By 5:30, the *Brandenburg* was sighted by a few early risers in the small Ohio town to the northeast of the German airship.

NEWTON FALLS

In 1928, the *Newton Falls Herald* (a weekly newspaper) was managed by A. H. Bowker. The June issue, Volume 47, No. 23, reported that the Kiwanis play, *The Arrival of Kitty*, was well attended. The issue stated that a park beautification program was under way in the nearby park. Consisting of good acreage of level land the park was popular with the townsfolk. The paper reported good news from Seward, Alaska. Five flyers, not heard of for a month, were found safe about 150 miles from Point Barrow although they had suffered considerably from the cold and exposure. The *Herald* further reported the amount collected per car for taxes in 1927 was $19.44 in Ohio, $27.28 in Pennsylvania, and $32.21 in West Virginia. (Mountain State motorists were paying a heavier tax toll than their immediate neighbors to the north and west.) By June 14, the nomination of Hoover as the Republican candidate for President had been assured. And other news was reported.

The time limit for servicemen to apply for the "federal bonus" had been extended from January, 1928, to January 2, 1930. The Trumbull County Chapter of the American Red Cross had the blanks to be filled out by the veterans who were eligible. A worried mother was quoted as saying: "We had to close the saloons to save our boys. Now we will have to close our gas stations to save our girls."[38] An interesting declaration, it was typical of the times.

Al Bowker was running for County Commissioner. "Twenty years' experience in newspaperwork" was his platform. Gas consumption for 1927 was reported at 771,000,000 gallons in Ohio; 684,000,000 in Pennsylvania and 593,000,000 gallons in Michigan. "Walhoffs" at 120 East Market Street in nearby Warren offered 100 percent all wool suits at $22.50. W. C. Liber and Son at South Canal Street, Newton Falls, was offering the Whippett "Sir," America's new light car in a sedan, at $695.

The A&P stores advertised hamburger at 20 cents per pound; Lifebuoy soap at three bars for 19 cents and a "good broom" at 43 cents. A nearby competitor, Kroger, offered hams at 23 cents a pound and 15 pounds of U. S. No. 1 Cobbler potatoes for 35 cents. A round trip from Newton Falls to Atlantic City was advertised at $18.69, prompting a resident to remark: "The shorter skirt came with the shorter working day and longer playing night." The Trumbull Savings and Loan Company, at Warren and Girard Streets, offered 5 percent on savings deposits. On June 21, a flock of sheep owned by L. S. Cover & Son were attacked by two black and tan dogs. A total of 20 sheep were killed. The lawmakers considered legislation to control such events and provide compensation to the person who sustained such loss. Reading deeper into the newspaper, the reader of 1928 probably became more absorbed.

"Will Lindbergh soon be forgotten?" someone asked. The *Spirit of St. Louis* was resting silently and majestically in the Smithsonian Institution. Someone suggested that this fact would make us ". . . feel a little like some of the millions of 'Spirits of Detroit' that are still knocking around in Ohio."[39] And there were contests in 1928 also.

Herald's "have trade" contest was under way with a first prize of $50 in gold. The Ohio State University roster for 1927-28 carried 13,925 full-time students and it would increase considerably in the years to come. This was a large enrollment compared to other universities. A scientist reported that there was little danger from lightning flashes. (Apparently he excluded free-flight balloons from his statement or he had not heard of the tragedy that occurred in the elimination races at Pittsburgh.) At the Newton Falls fair-grounds the largest religious meeting in the history of Trumbull County was under way. Visitors streamed into town through Newton Falls' covered bridge. Erected in 1831, the bridge served the community for 97 years and would do so for years in the future. Constructed out of hand-hewn wood beams, the gable roof protected the bridge from the elements. A walkway for pedestrians was added on one side and this, too, was covered by a slanting roof. (See Figure 18.)

The *Newton Falls Herald*, Thursday, July 5, 1928, reported the following story:

> Balloon is sighted over Lake Milton just south of Newton Falls, Ohio . . . A balloon, apparently one of the 13 which left Detroit Saturday in the James Gordon Bennett International Balloon Race, was sighted drifting over Lake Milton between 5 and 5:30 a.m. Sunday. The big gas bag seemed to hang stationary over the lake for a few minutes and then slowly moved southward. The balloon was so high up that it looked like a big orange.[40] It was too high for anyone to be able to make out its name.
>
> E. H. Roth vouched for this report as all early risers here saw the big gas bag creeping over the south of Newton Falls between 5:00 a.m. and 6:00 a.m. Sunday morning.

In the basket of the balloon mentioned in the news item, two flyers were busily engaged orienting themselves. The town below was too small to be Warren, Ohio. Using dead reckoning the lieutenant suggested that they were over Ravenna, Drakesburg, Braceville or Newton Falls. The lack of wind caused their ship to hang motionless providing them a good chance to scan the countryside below. The air was clean and still. While a slight haze spotted the countryside in patches their view was unobstructed.

The town below had very wide streets. (See Figure 19.) The few parked cars were slant-parked against the curbs. Two

main streets intersected and tapered off into the distance.
One led to the covered bridge and then turned south.

To their left was a huge fairground and railroad cars at a
siding were loaded with bright-colored equipment. This was
the A. C. Club Grounds and tomorrow, July 2, the Ketrow
Brothers Traveling Animal Show opened. Small fry paid
twenty-five cents to gain entrance and their parents fifty
cents. The religious meeting continued as a side attraction.

(In later years citizens of Newton Falls would boast that
their people worked for such companies as North American
Rockwell, Falls Steel Tube and Manufacturing, Luxaire Cush-
ion, Ohio Structural Steel, Gilliam Packaging and Republic
Steel. Founded in 1806, Newton Falls had a long industrial
history ahead of it. Today straight train tracks traverse the
huge park. Picnic shelters are neatly maintained with concrete floors to serve those who frequent the park on evenings,
holidays and each Sunday. Young boys make perpetual use
of the basketball courts there—and none of them know of the
German airship that once flew overhead.)

A gentle breeze began to push the ship south. The sharp
rays of the morning sun flooded the basket forcing the flyers
to pull the sunshades of their military hats low over their
eyes. Looking south, Frobel spotted a heavy mist rising about
five miles away. Military training told him that this indicated
a large body of water. The morning sun striking the cool air
above water caused evaporation and the resulting mist. He
had watched this type of mist many an early morning on the
decimated battlefields of France. Referring once more to his
map, the lieutenant concluded that the body of water ahead
was Lake Milton, thus identifying the town passing on the
left and rear as Newton Falls. The captain quickly confirmed
the location by spotting a huge yellow lettered sign painted
on a barn slightly west of their position. The large letters,
sideways to them, read "Newton Falls." Glancing to Cleveland on the map the flight pattern was clearly established.

They were heading south on a course about 20 degrees east at 3,600 meters altitude. Providing the weather remained clear they would be able to trace their flight pattern accurately on their map. At this altitude a map looks very much like the earth below. The roads, lakes and towns were easy to identify. Their map was accurate and they both knew how to read it.

(Mrs. Lena Lyman, Quarry Street, who is writing a history of Newton Falls, recalls that there was a yellow roof marking on the barn of the "Old Mason Farm" located just south of town. She further recalls that a "barnstormer" crash-landed there about 1928, but does not have details.)

Releasing a small "pilot" balloon (see Figure 9D), the flyers discovered a strong southeasterly wind above them some 500 feet. The growing heat, plus the discharge of a small amount of ballast, permitted them to rise gently into the stronger wind. Their trip south continued at a faster pace.

Eating breakfast in the gondola of a free-flying balloon at 6:00 A. M. high over the giant "Buckeye State" is an event that has been experienced by few men. Dry crackers with jam from their food roll and cold coffee from an aluminum can (See Figure 9E) provided the main fare. Heavy eating in free flight is not a good idea since air sickness often comes to even the most experienced.

The captain's log reports that both flyers took time to write brief letters to their families. Sealed in pre-addressed envelopes, these were dropped over from the craft in a small, handmade parachute. With these letters was a request in English that they be posted at Newton Falls. (It is not known if these were found and mailed and the newspaper accounts of the flight are silent on this small event.)

Crossing the small northern end of Lake Milton the ship flew almost directly south down Route 534. An occasional auto, raising dust in the distance, skidded to a stop in the middle of the road as driver and occupants piled out to watch the flight of the *Brandenburg*. Some waved and all stared as the huge craft passed overhead.

Approaching an intersection of an east-west highway, Frobel remarked that the small community below was "Berlin Center," an appropriate notation to make in their flight log, carefully kept by the captain. To the left of the intersection was a log cabin motor court constructed the year before. (The word "motel" would be coined in coming years but Henry Ford would lay claim to the first: the Dearborn Inn near Ford Airport.) The Blue Ridge Tavern, the motor court the Germans saw below served those who crossed the straight open countryside in the eastern section of Ohio.

The ship continued across the dark brown fields and small groups of second growth timber. The land had a strange flatness; almost as though it was not flat at all. Broken by small hills the land contained friendly people who spoke with a slight accent. Straight roads ran in all directions and were easily located on the flyers' maps.

Farmhouses dotted the centers of the scattered fields, some surrounded by barbed wire. Pine trees lined the dirt roads and provided shade for the persons who walked along them. Many of the large barns were red and some were badly in need of paint. Wide places in the roads provided stopping places for the Fords and Chevrolets that traveled the land. Elms of about four-inch diameter growth lined some of the roads below. Large dual silos accompanied the red barns and had circular roofs of aged wooden shingles. Some of the dark green fields contained last year's cornstalks—some type of soil conservation. A few of the barns had tin roofs and most had four or more white glass lightning rods tipped with copper spikes. A few of the large barns had curved roofs but most were gabled. The lightning rods pointing skyward were spaced about ten feet apart. These were designed to dissipate into the earth any electrical energy by means of ground wires. Series of wood louvers lined the sides of the barns and permitted air to circulate freely around the straw and hay stored within.

The houses had slate roofs and some were surrounded by low marshy swampland unsuited for farming. They had large overhangs and carved decorations around the eaves. Most were painted white. Slanting doors leading to storm shelters were witness to the heavy winds that prevailed in this state: winds that brought death to the *Shenandoah*—the airship that crashed in 1925 near Ava, Ohio.

Black and yellow "Mail Pouch" signs were observed on some buildings. The flyers later inquired what "Mail Pouch" was. Crossing Beaver Creek, the Germans observed a series of long, low yellow buildings with an oval track close by. A horse farm no doubt. Silos that accompanied the barns had tops that looked like inflated balloons. Below, large letters painted on the roof of a hangar identified Salem Air Park. A town or city was just ahead. Brilliant reflected sunlight shimmered from the panes of a greenhouse and caused temporary inconvenience to the flyers who were scanning the view of the approaching town. Crossing the Columbiana County line at the city limits of Salem, Ohio, the *Brandenburg* flew straight across the center of town. (See Figure 20.)

SALEM

The time was 6:55 A. M. The date: July 1, 1928. The ship had covered approximately 60 air miles since the Cleveland landfall: an average of ten miles per hour. The brilliant morning sun glowed against the yellow folds of the gasbag giving an appearance to ground observers of stripes running from top to bottom of the balloon.

The main street of Salem was at right angles to the flight pattern and the town was crossed in five minutes. Far below to the left was the long low building that housed *The Salem News*. The July 2 issue reported that five balloons were still known to be in the race. "The record appears safe due to mild winds over the east and south." The passage of four gasbags over the county on Sunday, July 1, was also reported. Others were riding the same airstream.

Bob Blake, who works for *The Salem News*, is closely associated with Ed Ferko, the health inspector of the city of Salem. These men are currently working on books that involve the German Imperial Air Force in the First World War as well as reconstruction problems of the German people following World War II. Thus, research into the flight of the *Brandenburg* uncovered another connection between the flight line and the nation of Germany.

Germans were in the news in 1928 in other matters. *The Salem News* reported that at Palmnicken, Germany, the hunt for "Prussian gold" was under way. The whole village was digging for amber while 800 persons worked at the plant where it was processed. The ancient Phoenicians traded for amber on the Baltic Coast centuries before—and the demand was still great. Out of an annual excavation of three million cubic meters of soil, a yield of a 125,000-pound crop was expected.

Another 1928 story in the Berlin newspaper, *Neue Berliner Zeitung*, reported:

> German waiters again will work in England. They will work in English hotels and restaurants for the first time since the war. Four Germans have left Germany for England and others will follow. Before the war 40 percent of the waiters in English establishments were German. They are expected to start at $30 to $35 per week.[41]

Leaving rows of party-walled red brick buildings behind the flight continued south. At the southern edge of town a large farmhouse and barn with white and orange tiled roofs caught the captain's eye. Keen, military-oriented eyesight enabled him to count eight white-glass cylindered copper-pointed lightning rods. The fenced fields that surrounded the central building encompassed more than 200 acres in his estimation. It was an estate fit for a German prince.

At the junction of Route 344, just beyond the very small village of Franklin Square, a small hilly range was encountered. Traversing this range at right angles to the *Brandenburg's* flight line was a depression caused by the meanders of Little Beaver Creek. A slight low-pressure area was encountered but the effect upon the ship was minimal. In the distance a black mountain range was coming into view across the plowed fields which were striped with fertile green areas. The Ohio crossing was almost complete.

The time was 8:10 as they reached the outskirts of another Ohio town. At 3,180 meters, identification by visual means was impossible. However, the Germans knew their position because the flight from Salem had paralleled Route 45. The town below was Lisbon, Ohio. (See Figure 21.)

A large red brick building on the square in the center of

town stood out plainly. Topped by a white four-clock steeple with statue on top, the building was the courthouse.

Once again the flyers dropped messages by parachute. This
time the messages were handwritten on Form 1512 of the
Western Union Telegraph Company. (Headed by Newcomb
Carlton as president and George W. E. Atkins as first vice-
president, Western Union had a bright future. Far-reaching
advances into the field of computer sciences as applied to
business operations would be made in the coming years.)
Pre-addressed to *The Detroit News* with "Press Rates Col-
lect," the messages drifted lazily to the earth. From information available the telegrams were either not found or were
kept by a finder as a souvenir. Word of the location of the
Brandenburg never reached Detroit by this means. An un-
finished telegram was found later in Bertram's papers and is
representative of those carried on the flight. Race officials
did not learn the location of the *Brandenburg* for another
48 hours.

Checking their map once again the flyers estimated that
they were close to Morgan's Surrender Monument near the
little town of West Point, Ohio. In about 20 minutes the
crossing of the state was completed. (Ohio, with an area of
41,222 square miles, is the 35th state in size. Admitted to the
Union on March 1, 1803, as the 17th state its capitol was
constructed in Columbus. The gray limestone columned
structure in Greek style occupies a 10-acre park in the center
of the capital city. Ohio was inhabited first by Archaic men
from Asia about 5,000 B.C., and became famous because of
the Hopewell Indians—the Mound Builders of 600 B.C. to
A.D. 1500. Originally claimed by France and Britain, Ohio
was ceded to the British by the Treaty of 1763. The defeat of
the Indians followed at the Battle of Fallen Timbers, August 20, 1794, and the Treaty of Greenville was executed on
August 3, 1795. The Ohio Constitution was adopted in 1851.
The state is famous for manufacturing of machinery, rubber

processing and agriculture. Chief modern points of interest include Mound City Group National Monument, Kelley's Island, Cedar Swamp and others. It was this land that the Germans crossed.)

Below, the level earth of Columbiana County gave way to increasing ridges and low mountains. Small streams formed from rivulets from the flat land, joined into larger streams flowing near industrial complexes, past cupola-topped barns as the flyers approached the Ohio River.

The warm, pleasant summer morning changed abruptly. By 9:00 A. M. the captain's log records that the weather was taking a turn for the worse.

SOUTH OVER PITTSBURGH

It was mid-summer. Two men in a balloon floated through the air several hundred feet below and about ten miles away from the danger area. Here the stars still winked overhead but the two airmen peered off into the distance, where mountains of clouds, blacker than the ocean of night, were fanned by the yellow lightning, and where the flashes were answered by long rumbles that awoke memories of heavy guns laying down a nervous barrage.[42]

The peaks of the cloud mountains began curling up and damping out the stars; the fan flashes of lightning became vivid tricklings which set off terrible salvos of thunder. But the balloon bore on.[43]

The sun was blacked out by clouds and the sky grew dark in the distance. The sudden cooling of the gas caused the *Brandenburg* to drop sharply toward the earth as the two flyers busied themselves sacrificing ballast in an effort to climb above the bad weather building before them. The Ohio River flowing by East Liverpool was seen through breaks in the clouds. (See Figure 22.) It occurred to Bertram that the Ohio resembled the Rhine in his native Germany, although the Rhine was wider in places. The twists and turns of the beautiful river below carried its water from Pittsburgh, the point of its origin, to the Gulf of Mexico. (The Ohio River lies within the boundary of the State of West Virginia but Ohio retained the name given to this river of steamboats, gamblers and river pirates of long ago.)

The hills rolled upward from the edge of the Ohio where it whipped onto rocky but level strips of ground along its banks. And the airmen were busy considering the various factors involved in their flight. In less than 25 minutes, their airship touched three states.

From the Ohio side of the river near a toll bridge, the ship flew directly over Chester, West Virginia, the companion city of East Liverpool—although separated by the mighty river. From Chester the flight continued in a southeast direction across the tip of the Mountain State—West Virginia—into the Keystone State of Pennsylvania. The brief visit to West Virginia was renewed before the day ended.

By 11:50 A. M. the *Brandenburg* had climbed to 4,100 meters and orientation was possible only through holes and breaks in the clouds beneath. Pittsburgh was spotted through one of the breaks and the two Germans saw for the first (and last) time the skyscraper city enveloped in black clouds of coal smoke that bellowed from countless furnaces and stoves. Pittsburgh of 1928 was a smoke-strewn spectacle—but seeing it from the extreme altitude at which the *Brandenburg* flew, created an impression that lasted a lifetime.

The skyscraper city and its environs spread across the hills and valleys below as far as the Germans could see. The buildings were soot-covered to an almost dead black. The flyers saw the central part of the city outlined sharply against light reflected from two rivers that held the center of town in a grip on both sides. These two rivers converged at the "point" of Pittsburgh and formed a third. First, the Monongahela River flowed from the south almost due north—one of few rivers in the world that did, and does so. Fed by tributaries, rivulets and streams from West Virginia, the "river of falling banks" flowed down the south side of the triangle-shaped real estate below. From the north came the Allegheny River winding its way across the northeastern section of Pennsylvania, passing down the north side of Pittsburgh's triangle. Joining at the point of the city, the two rivers flowed then (and flow now) northwest then south, forming the famous Ohio River.

A focal point of American history was below the German flyers. A mighty fort once occupied the large arrowhead-shaped piece of land below. (And George Washington almost lost his life while falling into the icy Allegheny River close to the foot of what is now 33rd Street of Pittsburgh.) Since the captain was in the iron and steel business in Chemnitz, he had the greatest respect for the industries that crawled into the horizon in all directions below. Planning with others to establish American connections in the steel industry, Pittsburgh was a name often mentioned by his associates. Frustrated by the First World War, their plans were completely abandoned by the time of the Second World War. (Flying free that July day over the land of democracy and so close to the "Gateway to the American West" below, Bertram, in his wildest dreams could not have predicted what the future held for him. The lieutenant would be spared the agonies of the captain by the intervention of an early death. The captain would live to experience a fate almost worse than death itself in just 20 years. There would be little time in his future for a normal, productive life in the steel and iron industry.)

Running parallel with the Allegheny River and across the "point" to the Monongahela River, were long, low soot-covered industrial buildings, tenement houses and junkyards. The coal smoke from the surrounding mills, coupled with discharge from thousands of furnaces and stoves in the center of town, earned for Pittsburgh the name of the "Smoky City." Nestled among the maze of dirty buildings, railroad tracks, bridge approaches, railroad sidings, junkyards and refuse—not to be seen from the air—was the last remaining remnant of once proud Fort Pitt that stood here at the "Forks of the Ohio." Crisscrossed by bridge abutments, roads, and train tracks, the fort had methodically been overrun by compounded efforts of generations in their ceaseless struggle for "a share of the profits" and a place to live.

The redoubt, or blockhouse, had not been constructed at

the time General Stanwix erected Fort Pitt in 1759-1760 and the reason was simple. Originally the fort had been designed to be surrounded by a moat to prevent those on the attack from gaining direct access to its outer walls. At the time of Pontiac's War in 1763, a Colonel Boquet traveled to the fort in Pittsburgh. Finding the moat dry because of low river water, he constructed the blockhouse to enable musketmen to command the dry moats with small-arms fire. The little redoubt was five-sided and had two floors with rifle openings on all sides. Two underground passages connected it with the main fort and the Monongahela River.

The land containing the blockhouse had been inherited by Mrs. Mary E. Schenely from her mother, Mary Croghan, in 1827, and she made a gift of it to the Allegheny County Daughters of the American Revolution on April 1, 1894. At that time the blockhouse served as a part of a larger dwelling house. This fact probably contributed, as much as any other, to its ultimate salvation. With the deed conveying the property, went a parcel of land measuring 100 feet by 90 feet together with a right-of-way, or easement, to Penn Avenue, measuring 20 feet by 90 feet.

With the land containing the blockhouse covered with tumbledown tenement houses, the DAR began the job of moving families, tearing down firetraps and clearing real estate. The expensive, time-consuming job continued at a snail's pace with constant frustration and some failures. However, fired by the determination of women in a new revolution, the project began to make noticeable headway. By 1908, the manmade jungle had been pushed back far enough that the decay and century-long deterioration was checked. A plaque of brass was set in concrete at the main entrance of the blockhouse. This scrolled plate read simply: "The Site of Fort Pitt Built 1759-1761. Visited by George Washington 1753-1758-1770." These early and courageous ladies of Allegheny County could not imagine what the future held for not only the blockhouse that they saved, but for the entire point of Pittsburgh. The Pittsburgh that the Germans saw and the magnificent city that others would see another day were as different as bright day against a dark night. The Germans viewed Pittsburgh as it was then as their flight continued.

The flight pattern carried the *Brandenburg* across the Pennsylvania railroad shops on the north side at California Avenue, straight down Galveston Avenue and across the Manchester Bridge. Crossing the point of Pittsburgh, the flyers passed over the first blast furnace erected in the city. Constructed in 1859 it was too insignificant to be noticed from their altitude.

Stratocumulus clouds closed beneath the German airmen. Whitish with gray patches the clouds showed dark spots with rounded masses and rolls which were in the process of merging. Near where they were flying they witnessed a rare form of lightning called a Flachenblitz.[44] This was lightning that struck upward and ended in clear air. The Germans knew that meant the cloud structure was changing to cumulonimbus. Suffering no harm by the freak of nature, the *Brandenburg* continued south.

The captain's log was silent for one hour and twenty minutes after the Pittsburgh sighting. As a result of building winds the ship moved south at an increasing rate of speed. The airmen probably passed over Dormont, south to Bethel Park, down to New Eagle on the Monongahela River, past Charleroi, Speers, Brownsville and then south in the direction of Uniontown. This is only a guess based upon the final flight pattern; but it should be reasonably accurate. The narrative of the captain graphically describes what followed: "At 1:10 in the afternoon we were at 4,400 meters over a solid cloud deck. Over us beamed blue skies and burning heat of the sun so that we had to put on our fur coats for protection. Under us raged the lightning. The cloud formation was like one that

one is only used to seeing in Switzerland on high mountains."
Behind and likewise over the clouds were three further balloons: the American, the Belgian and one of the French balloons.

The precise path of the *Brandenburg* from Pittsburgh to
Davis, West Virginia, will probably never be established. With
several balloons following the same general path, coupled
with multiple reports of those who sighted balloons, accuracy
from ground reports is impossible. The account left by Captain Bertram is silent on this phase of the flight and leads to
the conclusion that since they were above the clouds they in
fact did not know where they were on this part of the trip.
The sighting at Fairmont, West Virginia, earlier in the day of
July 1, led race officials to believe that the balloon at 8,000
feet was the *Brandenburg*. The timing of this sighting was
wrong when checked against Bertram's account.

Mrs. John E. Goodwin of 636 Madison Avenue, Morgantown, West Virginia, vividly remembers a balloon passing over
Forest Avenue in Morgantown, West Virginia, on July 1,
1928. Recalling the bright silver bag with attached gondola
she relates that the sighting caused her concern and worry for
the safety of the flyers that lasted for some time thereafter.
Others who saw these balloons for the first time were affected in a similar fashion. The age of spectaculars carried
with it soul-reaching compassion from certain members of
society. The ship sighted was *Army Entry No. 1* and its captain was William E. Kepner.

About 2:50 P. M. the *Brandenburg* crossed the famous
Mason-Dixon Line: The line that separates the North from
the South. The flyers were flying in "rebel territory." From
the Mason-Dixon Line the flight pattern probably crossed the
following West Virginia towns: Pursglove, Masontown, Reeds-
ville, Kingwood, Rowlesburg (now flying across Preston
County), to Horse Shoe Run. Ahead was the border of Tucker County, West Virginia, near Lead Mine and slightly east of

Backbone Mountain. With an elevation of 3,360 feet this mountain is the highest point in neighboring Maryland. Mountains soon entered the story of the flight of the *Brandenburg.*

Aviators traditionally regard mountains with concern and respect. While mountains are useful for skiing and mountain climbing they may be fatal to the careless flyer. Flat land and mountains are two different things to an aviator or a balloonist. Mountains create rapids in the air and cause constant changes in the pattern of flight of both balloons and airplanes.

Low atmospheric density near mountains causes part of the problem. At first turbulence gives the impression that mountains have more than their share of air. But the opposite is the truth. The higher one goes the less air there is. In addition mountains are also deceptive. Depth perception of a flyer approaching mountains is often out of line with the facts.

In British Columbia flyers have developed rules for flying over mountains. Two of the rules provide some idea of the problems involved in mountain flying. First, trips should be made early in the morning since air generally grows worse after 10:00 A. M. but improves after 4:00 P. M. Second, ridges should be approached at an angle so that a turn away may be made if a downdraft is encountered. After crossing a ridge the flyer should move directly away from it.

In a free-flight balloon, both of these rules would be followed if it were possible. But the horizontal flight of a free balloon cannot be controlled. The depth perception problem caused two German flyers to believe they were high enough to clear a West Virginia mountain, only to find that they were wrong. After crossing one mountain they saw another ahead. At this point they encountered a low-pressure area and began a slide toward earth. They would not be able to regain enough altitude in the thin air to clear the impressive range of mountains that faced them. Confronted with this situation a pilot of a motor-driven plane would simply bank away from the mountains to avoid the low-pressure area. But the *Brandenburg* was committed; its flight pattern was fixed, and the obstacles ahead were immovable. Its fate was sealed.

The German airship flying in visibility zero weather, completed its passage of Preston County, West Virginia. The ship started its run into Tucker County at an altitude of 3,500 feet passing within 1,000 feet of the Fairfax Stone. (The stone marks the headwaters of the Potomac where the West Virginia-Maryland border joins the intersection of Preston County, West Virginia, and Grant County, Maryland, and was a corner of the vast estate of Lord Fairfax. The original line, established in 1736, was checked in 1746 by a survey party on which Peter Jefferson was engaged. His son, Thomas, became president of the United States.)

TUCKER COUNTY, WEST VIRGINIA

The Upland Section of the Alleghenies embrace the high mountains and flat ranges of Tucker, Preston, Randolph, Webster, Nicholas, Pocahontas and Greenbrier Counties. The mountains range from 4,860 feet at Spruce Knob, the highest point in West Virginia, to varying levels of elevation below this peak in the sky. Many of the mountains and plateaus exceed 4,000 feet in height.[45] *Not a paradise for free-flight balloonists, it is a paradise for others.*

Tucker County, West Virginia, was named for Henry Saint George Tucker and is located in the northeastern portion of West Virginia (excluding its eastern panhandle). Occupied by the "friendliest people in America," the county is rectangular in shape, contains 421.67 square miles and ranks 28th in size of the 55 counties of the state.

Being part of an ancient plateau, evidence of violent geological disturbances is found everywhere. A large part of the terrain is made up of rugged surface rocks too large for any human to budge. Prominent features of the county include the steep mountain slopes. The valleys (one being world famous) were formed by structural disturbances coupled with century-old erosion of the softer materials. Reddish brown soil covers the earth between the boulders and the subsoil is also reddish brown. The land is well suited for growing oats, corn, wheat and other products, except at higher altitudes.

The most productive farms in Tucker County are covered by what is known as "Moshannon Loam." One of the best farming areas in the county is "Holly Meadows"—a region covered with the rich, productive soil. Other loams lend

themselves to the raising of hay or development of grassland
and pasture. Since much of Tucker County is not suitable for
agriculture a large portion is now owned by the United States
Government.

In the high plateau region where Thomas and Davis are
located, frosts have occurred in every month of the year. The
climate is healthful; the characteristic being derived from the
high mountains that dominate the terrain. Tucker County is
one area of the earth where malaria cannot exist because of
year-round low temperatures. Killing frosts have occurred as
late as June 11 and as early as September 19. The growing
season in the Canaan Valley is usually two weeks shorter than
at Parsons. In this high region, potatoes, oats, buckwheat and
grass grow well during the cooler season. However, the
growing season is not long enough for corn.

Two natural resources attracted exploiters to the county—
coal and timber and both were king until depleted. Coal was
first discovered in Tucker County around 1835 in the Sugar-
lands area. Later coal was found on Backbone Mountain on
its eastern side. A "coal rush" resulted and production aver-
aged over a million tons annually during the first 20 years of
the Twentieth Century. (See Figure 23.) But timbering was
the star of the show.

Rebecca Harding Davis (mother of Richard Harding Davis)
visited Tucker County in 1879, accompanied by Charles Graham. Graham was an accomplished artist and Davis a distinguished novelist. "Judge" Hixley (known as a duelist before
the Civil War) made an accurate prediction to her when he
said:

> The Wilderness comprises seven hundred square miles
> of Virgin forests, which will be a mine of wealth in
> timber some day, when it is opened up by a railway.[46]

The county was desperately in need of a railroad and the
Potomac and Piedmont Coal and Railroad Company was

organized in 1866 to fill the need. The initial corporation came to little however, even though Henry Gassaway Davis, U. S. Senator from West Virginia, lent his reputation to the venture. Later the corporation changed its name to the West Virginia Central and Pittsburgh Railway Company. The railroad finally reached Davis, West Virginia, in 1884 and played a major role in the destruction of virgin forests on the mountains in the area.

Branches of the railway were then extended to the neighboring towns of Thomas and Parsons and a web of steel closed about the giant trees on the hillsides. The instrument to carry the giants away once felled, was in place: The instruments of destruction, men and their saws, were close behind.

In older days lumbering had been confined to those slopes from which timber could be moved easily to the Cheat River and then floated out. Trains took the place of the river—and webs of iron reached into the depths of the state connecting major cities to nationwide markets.

The first sawmill west of the Alleghenies was constructed in Tucker County in 1776, the year of American Independence. It was located near the small town of St. George and the material for the mill had been transported from Moorefield, Hardy County, 75 miles away.[47]

The largest lumber mill in the history of the county opened at Davis in 1884 and operated until the destruction was complete in 1924. A total of almost 900 million feet of lumber was produced by this single mill in its 38 years of operation.

In the prime timbering days stands of virgin timber produced 80,000 to 100,000 board feet per acre.[48] "A yellow-poplar cut by the Otter Creek Boom and Lumber Company at Hendricks, Tucker County, completely filled a log train. It contained 12,496 board feet."[49]

In earlier years the county abounded with game of all sorts

and plentiful fish. Three elk were killed near the site of Davis as late as 1843.

Although hunters, fishermen, trappers and explorers probably visited the Canaan Valley in the last years of the 18th and the first years of the 19th Century, it was not until the 1840's and early 1850's that the area was afforded even an infinitely small degree of accessibility. By then the Commonwealth of Virginia's "Northwestern Road" connecting Winchester and Parkersburg had been completed through what is now the village of Gormania, West Virginia, and, at about the same time, the Baltimore and Ohio Railroad was pushed westward as far as the present city of Oakland, Maryland. The "Maryland Glades," that area around Oakland and around the head waters of the Potomac River, attracted many visitors and soon the wild and virtually unexplored Canaan began to beckon to the more venturesome.[50]

It was into this natural wonderland that the German airship moved deeper. . . . Crossing Pendleton Creek at about 4:00 P. M., the flyers were keenly aware of the rapid rise of the mountains under them as the clouds cleared and visibility increased. Topping a mountain they saw a small town spread out on a flat plateau about one-half mile to the front. The mountain under them crested at 3,250 feet. The plateau of the town was at 3,085 feet thus giving them a sudden—and welcomed—edge in altitude. But about four miles to the front, both flyers saw mountain ranges much higher than the altitude at which they were flying. Ballast was again discharged as they made the approach run over the center of Davis. Certain residents of the small community experienced a brief "sand shower." Bulk ballast was not discharged because of the danger to those below. (See Figure 24.)

The mountain town below was unique for many reasons. The Germans visited there briefly but did not have an opportunity to learn in detail the background and nature of the town and its people. They crossed Davis much like a speck of sand crosses a lost diamond lying on a beach in a windstorm. But one thing was for certain: The town below was a gem for many reasons.

DAVIS
THE GEM CITY OF THE ALLEGHENIES

She hangs upon the cheek of night
Like a rich jewel in an Ethiope's ear.
Shakespeare, *Romeo and Juliet*
1,5

The Tucker County Republican, Davis Industrial Edition, reported in 1895, "One decade ago the plot of ground which is now occupied by the rigorous town of Davis was a dense and howling wilderness, known only to the speculator, the hunter and the roaming wild beast."[51]

On March 14, 1884, Colonel Robert Ward Eastham gave the "go" signal to his crew of timbermen who cleared a wagon road from Davis to the Canaan Valley. At first, the best the men could furnish was a mere bridle path because of the density of the woods in which they struggled. The path was later developed into a fair wagon road.

After the town site was cleared the first train made its appearance on November 1, 1884. Surveyors laid out lots and streets and William, Thomas and Henry were the names given to the first wide avenues. Eastham purchased a parcel of land near the mouth of Beaver Creek at the Blackwater River and, using logs, constructed the first house in Davis. Stores, houses and other buildings followed. The town was named for Henry Gassaway Davis.

With the expansion came the merchants: O. S. Wilson & Bros., J. N. Oliver, Ash & Lashley and J. N. Robinson to name a few. Following quickly came the tanneries, the lumber companies—and some saloons. (See Figure 25.) Schools, a fire department, a city government (A. C. Finley was the first mayor), free postal delivery, clear streets and alleys—and even a park followed.

An early business in Davis was a hotel venture. Owned initially by the West Virginia C.&P. Railroad, the "Blackwater Hotel" was leased to H. N. Worden. Operated by Worden and his son Harry, the hotel was one of the most popular in the state. Its 40 rooms were constantly occupied by West Virginians—as well as persons from all over America. (See Figure 26.) The landmark was replaced by a modern building.

The inhabitants of Tucker County—and Davis—were the subject of many "tall tales" and folklore. While some had been true, most were exaggerated. For example, in one of his minor tales Edgar Allan Poe made reference to the mountains of western Virginia, inhabited by ". . . fierce and uncouth races of men."[52] The curiosity aroused by what Poe wrote inspired some to go see this race of men—and most who did came armed. Visitors usually traveled by way of U. S. Route 50. This famous route had been engineered by Colonel Claudius Crozet, a former military officer under Napoleon. Crozet performed his work for the State of Virginia, which until June 20, 1863, owned the land surrounding Davis. On that day West Virginia became the 35th state of the Union.

When visited by the Germans, Davis had a population of about 1,700 persons. This dropped to less than 900 by 1969. According to the Bureau of the Census, Davis' population was as follows: In 1890 the town had 918 persons; by 1900 feverish timbering activity increased the population to 2,391; in 1910 it reached a peak of 2,615. By the end of World War I the population dropped to 2,491 and after the crash of 1929, it had taken another drastic drop to 1,656 persons. By 1960, the census showed 894 persons living there.

As the timber was stripped from the mountains; as the coal was produced and as new methods of tanning were devised, the number of jobs decreased. The economy of the area—like a balloon in a low-pressure area—started downhill. By 1928 the timbermen had moved on; the trains seldom came to town and the population had declined substantially. The town became a "former boom town"; the death knell had been sounded—at least some so believed.

Today as one drives up Route 219 on the approach to Thomas, West Virginia, (the sister city of Davis) a strangeness crosses the mind. The air becomes lighter as the road lifts into the sky. A feeling of caution prevails when the journey is made for the first time. About four miles from Thomas, a roadside overlook provides a breathtaking view of the valleys and mountains near Thomas and Davis. Across countless ridges are seen unbelievably beautiful hills of the state seated thousands of feet below the overlook. High flying clouds often drift below the visitor.

As the drive to Thomas continues, small stands of small timber fade until there is the realization that the timber is gone. Underbrush is everywhere but tall timber is nowhere to be seen.

After passing through Thomas, the rise into the sky continues until the town of Davis comes into view across gentle rolling knolls covered by green underbrush. (See Figure 27.) The lack of standing timber bears witness to the effectiveness—and destructiveness—of timbermen of other days. One suddenly feels that the top of the world has been reached—yet mountains rear higher in the distance.

In Davis, church steeples rise above white frame houses as the townspeople go about their business. Children play on the sidewalks and older men gather at the drug store in the center of the town. A holdover from the timbering days, the store contains beautiful oak shelves which have gentle swirls and scrolls, pointed up by other decorations, artfully carved into the wood. The timbering days seem present on a visit there.

Further down the main street is the Mountain State Historical and Natural Museum. Owned and operated by Joseph McCleary, his charming wife, Betty, and daughter, Betty Jo, this private operation houses more than 20,000 items of historical interest. Starting in a saloon and bowling alley of yesteryear, the enterprising family created a unique business. "We live and breathe museum," and it is obvious to the visitor that they do.

The main attraction at the museum is the Crystal Bar Room—a reconstructed turn-of-the-century saloon. "The bar is an ornate hand-carved quarter oak masterpiece, with a glitter all of its own."[53] It was once part of the Blackwater Hotel (1885-1921), the social center of Davis. Massive oak columns support curved beams above and the bar is amazing to behold. Artfully carved designs decorate the edges and huge mirrors reflect the faint light from red chandeliers. Stained glass oval inlays are surrounded by ornate oak frames that hold them in place. The bar top is highly polished and yet reflects the wear imposed upon it by several generations of guests.

It has been named the Crystal Bar Room because its decor includes copies of the original crystal chandeliers from the hotel and it is with touches like this that the McClearys hope to recapture the ebullient atmosphere of the boom days when robust, jovial lumberjacks would come to town to relax.[54]

The Saint John Lutheran Church at Davis is located at Third Street and Henry Avenue. The church is of frame construction and has a high gabled roof. At the entrance is a steepled tower that rises above the surrounding buildings. Atop this steeple is a large cross that faces north and south. As one leaves the center of Davis and drives up Third Street past the church, a small rise is encountered. At the top of the rise, a view of the entire town is available. (See Figure 28.) Southeast from here, the Canaan Mountain range rears its

back like some ancient beast crawling across the distant land-
scape. The view from the rise gives one a fair idea of what the
German flyers saw as they flew over Davis.

In 1928, the ceiling beams within the Lutheran Church
were 80 feet long and carved from solid timber: convincing
evidence of the majestic virgin timber that once covered the
mountainsides nearby. To duplicate this span today with timber would require lamination of a series of smaller pieces
glued under high pressure. "Mother Nature" may never have
another opportunity to create trees that provided such
beams. The church played an indirect part in the last tragic
moments of the *Brandenburg.*

And so the town of Davis, West Virginia, basking in the
glory of golden timber days gone by, was host to many persons from many walks of life. Some came out of curiosity to
see the wonders of the town and the mountains surrounding
it. Others came to seek fortunes that sometimes eluded the
seekers. The visitors came by horse and wagon in the early
years and later by automobile, truck, train and bus. A few
visited on foot—and a very few came by air.

On the evening of July 1, 1928, two brothers left their
home in Davis to attend evening services at the Lutheran
Church as had been their custom for many years. J. Stuart
Cooper and James C. Cooper, Jr., recall clearly the first sighting of the *Brandenburg.* It was about 6:30 P. M. when the
first of two balloons was sighted crossing Davis.

Proceeding down Third Street to the church the Coopers
kept their eyes on the brilliant yellow craft above flying a
red, white, black and yellow flag around its basket. As they
reached the church door they saw a second balloon in the
distance moving in the general direction of the first. (It was
later identified as the French *Lafayette.*) The men in the
yellow craft were busy dumping sand over the side. James
Cooper recalls that the yellow balloon was at an altitude of
about 300 feet. J. S. and Jim made some quick calculations.

Their estimates told them that the altitude of the ship was about 700 feet too low to clear Cabin Mountain in the distance. As it turned out, church waited—and so did the future bride of James Cooper; the third young lady who missed her date in Davis that evening.[55] Something had captured the attention of their menfolk and it was awhile before they found out what it was. (See Figure 29.)

Jim and J. Stuart looked at each other; they looked at the church where they attended services each Sunday evening; they reflected upon their other commitments and resolved the matter easily. They jumped into their father's 1926 Dodge coupe and speeded out of town on the heels of two free-flying balloons. They crossed the main road of Davis and headed southeast across the small iron bridge that spanned the Blackwater River. The road took them over the remains of the old Lumber Railway embankment that once carried the log trains from the hills east and south of Davis.

After crossing the old railroad site the Cooper brothers spared little gas as they moved up the slope of Canaan Mountain. They crossed Devil's Run at an elevation of 3,157 feet and the rise continued sharply. In just one mile the altitude had increased to 3,537 feet. Losing sight of the balloons, the Cooper brothers concluded that both were down on Canaan Mountain. The mountain topped at 3,850 feet at the crest in line with the flight of the two ships.

The skies were heavily overcast and a sharp wind whistled back and forth across the ridge throwing leaves, dirt and small branches into and across the flat windshield of their car as visibility dropped sharply. After passing near Bearden Knob to their left (which sits at 3,846 feet) the Coopers skidded to a stop. An anxious look told them that if the balloons were down on Canaan Mountain where they were stopped, it might take hours to find them. If the balloons had crossed the ridge they felt certain that they would not be able to cross Cabin Mountain some five miles away. With this

initial conclusion in mind, the Cooper brothers continued
down the west bank of Canaan Mountain to a vantage point
where a large gap in the trees and underbrush provided an
unobstructed view of the valley floor stretching out before
them. (See Figure 30.) They were at 3,580 feet and the floor
of Canaan Valley, while being on a plateau, was below them
at 3,150 feet. Cabin Mountain rose majestically to 4,275 feet
to their left front. They became eyewitnesses to the death of
the *Brandenburg*—and to the near-death of its occupants.

After the German flyers crossed the small town that slid
erratically to their rear, the weather took a typical July turn
for the worse. Noting that it was 6:35 P. M.,[56] the Germans
had only fleeting glances of the earth as increasing winds
tossed them in all directions through the heavy overcast.
Harsh, biting wind whirled and whistled through their gondola as they dropped ballast in an effort to rise above the
winds that violently increased about them.

A sudden break in the overcast gave them false hope. Two
pairs of military eyes quickly noted that their ship was 250
feet above the ridge and that a vast open space at a much
lower altitude was directly ahead. If the weather had been
clear they would have noted that their altitude was equal
with Bearden Knob just to their left but much lower than the
mountains ahead. They had arrived where they had been
sent: "The Land of Canaan." They were at the edge of Canaan Valley.

Tragedy quickly struck in the form of a vertical thunder-
squall and Bertram noted: "We had to throw out nine sacks
of ballast in a short time so strong were the squalls. With
racing speed we descended under a high mountain slope."

They dropped below Canaan Mountain and crossed the
floor of Canaan Valley as Cabin Mountain waited for them
like a giant snare to the front. The Germans from the far-off
Land of Brandenburg were in the heart of the Land of Canaan—and it reached up for them.

CANAAN VALLEY

The wild and beautiful Canaan Valley, some thirteen miles long, lies at the foot of the mountain bearing the same name. Three to five miles across the valley can be seen the sprawling Cabin Mountains which form the eastern rim of this gigantic cornucopia-shaped trough, watered and drained by the Blackwater River.[57]

The Canaan Valley, located in the eastern part of Tucker County, is a long oval-shaped valley carved out of the Blackwater anticline by the Blackwater and Little Blackwater Rivers. With low smooth hills and wide bottoms, the valley presents a sharp contrast to the steep, rocky mountain slopes which almost entirely surround it. Yet the floor of the valley is at an elevation ranging from 3,100 to 3,250 feet. It is a "valley high in the skies."

. . . The Land of Canaan—a wilderness of broken and rugged mountains, its streams falling through deep clefts, or leaping down in great cataracts to the Cheat that sweeps the base of the Backbone.[58]

The Canaan Valley is located about 12 miles east of Davis. The first view of the 13-mile long depression cradled by giant mountain ranges, leaves one wide-eyed with amazement at the beauty below. A sense of awe and disbelief grips one who looks into the "land of Canaan" for the first time. The first impression changes little with continued visits over a lifetime.

From the air the valley looks like a scooped-out plateau at the top of a child's huge pile of sand at the beach. Canaan Mountain forms the western ridge of the valley. From the forward crest a panorama of beauty, wilderness, civilization and history unfolds below. At Martin Luther Cooper's farm, gentle rolling hills provide massive sled runs that carry children in snowmobiles over the silver sprinkled snow of winter. In both winter and summer fertile green areas color the land below. In the spring and summer the billiard table top meadows provide feeding ground for cattle from the scattered farms. In the fall, the valley and its surrounding ridges explode into riotous colors like a giant air bomb on a Fourth of July evening.

About five miles across the valley a 4,000-foot range of mountains rises majestically and runs the length of the valley—and beyond. This ridge of rolling peaks was unceremoniously, and simply, named for the cabin that nestled at its base for more than a century—Cabin Mountain. Today Cabin Mountain and the surrounding ridges seem virtually barren in the wintertime—another mute witness to an age when the giant timbers were felled. As the virgin growth crashed to the earth, stories of laughter and tragedy of the lives of the timbermen were created in the Land of Canaan. Today, the thick sod and the matted moss hide the tales as though they should never be told. Stories of murder, fighting, drinking, laughter and personal tragedy lie buried there. A few of the stories have been uncovered.

On many occasions John W. (Jack) Preble, Jr., a native of Steubenville, Ohio, visited the beautiful mountains of Tucker and adjoining counties. His interest in cave exploration led to the organization of the National Speleological Society on May 29, 1940, at the Worden Hotel in Davis. During the Second World War he flew with the 376th Bombardment Group (The "Ploesti Raiders") and earned 14 battle stars, the Bronze Star and three Presidential Citations. His charming book, *The Land of Canaan*, was based upon his many visits to West Virginia. In the book he tells "plain tales" about the mountains and the people of the state.

There is the story about Luke—the master distiller—who

upon a misunderstanding brewed a potent whiskey from tomatoes. The "Perfidy of Little Mose Callahan" is told in all of its minor glory. Mose "traveled between dawn and dusk and left no tracks." (Someone once accused Mose of running at Gettysburg. He replied, "Yep—if I hadn't, I would still be up there with the rest of 'em.") And there is the story of how Luke lost his ear trying to tame Ethel Audrey, a wildcat named after Luke's former wife. Preble's experiments with rattlesnakes and blacksnakes to determine if one would kill the other are spelled out in detail. "The Redemption of Black Mike O'Connell" is told in all of its tragedy. This man from the backwoods was so dirty that a simple bath caused his death. The story of the "Salvation of Elijah Rameses Bliss" arose out of efforts to trap a bear. Elijah wanted to "show that bear a thing or two." Instead, Elijah was trapped in his own snare, shot at and treated worse than the lowest skunk. He lived on honey for two days and swore he would touch it (honey) no more.

The Fourth of July visit to Luke's still is unforgettable. A firecracker was jokingly tossed at Luke who in turn tried to lever his Winchester with dough-covered hands. The hanging of Joe Brown by a mob led by drunken Mose Callahan just for the reason of scaring Joe must be mentioned. The capture of Richard Rattlebrain (a gentleman from Virginia) by robbers at the Gandy Sinks is told with precision. And the mystery of Eastham's Riffles remains unsolved as the ghost fisherman casts for his six-pound trout in the hopes of winning a bet made decades ago. They are all there, delightful, sad, colorful stories. Preble left very little else to be told. However, there is one story he did not mention. It is the story of Joseph Graham and his trout and is directly related to the flight of the *Brandenburg*. Uncovered as a part of the research into the flight, the story is now part of the folklore of Tucker County—although probably recorded here for the

first time. The tale involved Joseph C. Graham, Jr.—and his
farm where the Germans crash-landed.

Graham, who was born in Indiana, traveled to God's
Land—the Land of Canaan—where he resolved to live out his
life. The records in the office of the Clerk of the County
Court of Tucker County, at Parsons, show that on May 24,
1898, part of the Graham Farm was conveyed to Mrs. M. A.
Graham, widow of Joseph, Joseph C. Graham, Jr., and Mrs.
Josina Harr. All were heirs of Joseph C. Graham, Sr. (The
deed is on record in the clerk's office in Deed Book 17 at
page 246.) The property was formerly owned by Isaac Freeland, who lent his name to a stream that cascades from between two peaks on Cabin Mountain at the edge of Canaan
Valley. The stream, upon reaching the floor of the valley,
splits into two branches. The left branch cut deep grooves
into the valley floor and the right branch runs close to the
Graham farmhouse. Both branches converge into one stream
again which adds water to the Blackwater River, Club Run
and Mill Run. It was within the right branch of Freeland Run
that a legend grew.

On December 10, 1898, M. A. Graham and Mrs. Josina
Harr, conveyed their interest in the farm to Joseph E. Graham, Jr., and his wife Lucinda. (The deed is on record in the
clerk's office in Deed Book 19 at page 99.)

Joseph Graham constructed a small shed across the right
branch of Freeland Run and used it to store foodstuffs that
required coolness to preserve. To facilitate this, part of the
floor of the shed was left open so that the cool air from the
mountain water reduced the temperature inside. The run
widened below the shed and at that point he constructed a
small dam and spillway. Into the small pond he placed trout
of various types taken from other parts of the stream.

Graham fed the trout with flies and other items found near
their natural habitat. As time went by the trout began to
swim under the shed. It was there that he trained them. First

he fed them cottage cheese and after that, he used grease. This required the trout to eat the grease from his fingers. The trout became domesticated and Graham placed his hands under their bellies and lifted them into the air. It is said that the trout remained motionless when this occurred.

A most remarkable tale, especially to a trout fisherman—if it is true. There is little doubt that it is. The shed is still there. The offspring of those former fighting giants of the mountain stream are there for anyone to see. Fay Graham, the elder son, still feeds the fish regularly (see Figure 31) but he has not been able to match the feat of his father who died March 21, 1943, at the age of 79 years.

> J. C. Graham—a gentle man—
> Lived hard, worked and prayed.
> He traveled far to reach this land—
> And here he simply stayed.
>
> He built a home of wood and nail,
> Near Freelands Run, close by,
> He captured trout in a pail
> And fed to them a fly.
>
> The trout began to love this man—
> They swam into his lair;
> He fed them grease and cottage cheese—
> He held them in the air!
>
> And so this story must be told,
> It shouldn't be forgotten,
> Of mountain streams and Laurels bold
> A trout's place up in heaven.

A second visit to the valley produced another of the tales that Jack Preble—and others—came to find. The person who related the story attached the condition that his name not be associated with it.

The rim of the valley was reached by the new road and the breathtaking scene once more unfolded. Call it scientific,

geological or what, it is one of the finest scenes on earth. A
soft breeze whispered against the massive rocks at the side of
the road and a large crow moved slowly up and down going
nowhere in the head wind indicating that it wanted a better
view of the majesty below. At Davis that morning, the barber
William Sayger mentioned the name of an elderly man in the
valley who might have information about the flight of the
Brandenburg. His directions were followed and the house was
found without difficulty. Located near the center of the valley on the hardtop road, the ancient frame weathered house
nestled beside a large tract of second-growth timber. An elderly man dressed in heavy denim overalls answered the
knock at the door and the invitation to enter was instantaneous.

It was quickly apparent that the man could add nothing to
the story of the balloon crash. He remembered folks in Davis
talking about it but otherwise it had no meaning to him.

He was questioned about life in the Canaan Valley. He
made it clear that he had no regrets and would live out his
life there. He remembered Jack Preble and knew of the
stories he had written about the valley. Asked if he could
verify any of them he replied, "I reckon most of them are
true, but I haven't seen the book." He was questioned about
the tame trout of Joseph Graham. Verifying this, he stated
that he had been present many times when Graham lifted the
speckled scrappers from the cool mountain water of Freeland
Run.

It became clear that nothing new could be uncovered and
he was thanked for his information. At the door, he said, "If
I told you something that was true, would you believe me?"
After a promise not to attach his name to it, he told the
following story:

"Many years ago, oh, I reckon it was about 1895, I was
about 10 years old at the time (he was nine)—the timbermen

many as 500 on one train, having ridden exposed to the
elements from some way-off point. They were mean men and
my father warned me to keep away from them. At that time
our farm was surrounded by the tallest stands of timber that
any man had ever seen. Some reached 100 feet straight up
before a branch was encountered. Most were so large around
that a grown man could not reach even one-fourth the way
around. I remember the rumbles of the falling trees that
seemed to hang in the valley for days after they fell. I always
felt that those trees did not want to be taken from the valley.
The timbermen had constructed the Lumber Railway out of
Davis, across the northern end of the valley, to the base of
Brown Mountain, taking the timber out as they went. The
railroad was built across the Little Blackwater River to a
point near the bottom of Cabin Mountain. They did not have
steel trestles back in those days. They took those giant trees
and hewed them square and built the best trestles you ever
saw. The railroad was extended to Freeland Run where it
ended. There were many trestles along the side of the mountain at one time. I played on them year after year after the
timbermen had moved elsewhere. The trestle beams were so
large that two boys could hold a foot race on one of them at
the same time. Now I want to tell you this. That railroad is
not there anymore and the tracks have been removed and the
trestles have all rotted away. But will you believe it—those
trains still make the trip from Freeland Run to Davis? I hear
the sounds each night at almost the same time as those little
steam engines struggle to pull the huge logs to the lumber
mill at Davis. The whistle is clear as a bell."

A strange tale but since it concerns the valley, the man
probably hears what he thinks he hears. One cannot kill giants without protests being registered that might last for centuries. What the timbermen took from the valley can only be
replaced by God—and he may never again choose to place at

the mercy of men such majesty. Early visitors to Tucker
County and the valley verified what once was there.

In 1762, one James Parsons traveled through Tucker County after his escape from Indians in neighboring Hardy County.[59] He was greatly impressed by the beauty of the wilderness of Tucker County. All in all, less than 70 men are known
to have visited the rugged real estate prior to the first settle-
ment that came in 1766. The first settler was John Crouch, a
Welshman, who settled near Blackman Flats just across the
Cheat River at Alum Hill.

The first white visitors to the valley were probably the
members of the Fairfax Boundary Line Surveying party in
1746. The party was engaged in running the western boundary of the Thomas 6th Northern Neck Proprietary of Lord
Fairfax and erected the first of five stones called the Fairfax
Stone. Thomas Lewis kept a survey book and made exact
entries of the survey. On Tuesday, October 14, 1746, the
survey party was at the Allegheny Front near what is now the
boundary line of Tucker and Grant Counties. They approached and crossed the Canaan Valley and their survey
book records the event:

"Tuesday 14th one of the Pilots horses being missing a
great part of the morning was Spent in vain hunting for him
Began where we left off the Day Before Thence 100 poles a
Loral Swamp Begins 406 poles X the River of Styx total for
this Day This River was Called Styx from the Dismal ap-
perance of the Place Being Sufficen to Strick terror in any
human Creature ye Lorals Ivey & Spruce pine so Extremly
thick in ye Swamp through which this River Runs that one
Cannot have the Least prospect Except they look upwards
the Water of the River of Dark Brownish Cooler & its motion
So Slow that it can hardly be Said to move its Depth about 4
feet the Bottom muddy & Banks high, which made it Extremly Difficult for us to pass the most of the horses when
they attemp'd to ascend the farthest Bank tumbling with

their loads Back in the River. most of our baggage that would have been Damaged by water were Brought over on mens Shoulder Suchas Powder, Bread and Bedclothes&c. We got all our Bagage over as it Began to grow Dark So we were Obliged to Encamp on the Bank & in Such a place where we Could not find a plain Big enough for one man to Lye on no fire wood Except green or Roten Spruce pine no place for our horses to feed And to prevent their Eating of Loral tyd them all up least they Should be poisoned."[60]

Homer Floyd Fansler commented on the survey entry in his *History of Tucker County:* "In ancient mythology the Styx was a river of the underworld over which the bodies of the dead were ferried by Charon. The entire distance of the line was 76.5 miles and since they have already traversed 68 miles, they only have 8.5 miles to go, and are, therefore, in Canaan Valley in the vicinity of Glade Run."[61]

Henry Fansler is credited with being the first settler in the Canaan Valley. It is believed that—startled upon seeing the valley—he gave it its Biblical name. He was born in 1761 in Berks County, Pennsylvania, the eldest of 10 children. He served in the American Revolution as a soldier in the 6th Battalion of the Pennsylvania Infantry, and later qualified for a $19.05 per month pension. He died in 1843 and was buried near Hendricks, West Virginia, on beautiful Backbone Mountain. His father, Dietrich, is believed to have been a Palatinate immigrant who sailed from Rotterdam, Holland, and arrived in Philadelphia about 1727 or 1728. If this is true the first settler in Canaan Valley was a German.

"To the geologist Canaan Valley is an anticline; to the naturalist it is a nature study; to the scientist it is an enigma; to the tourist it is a scenic wonder; to the artist it is a delightful dream; to a sportsman it is a bonanza; to the farmer it is a gamble; to the layman it is a snow reservoir; and to Henry Fansler it was bitter fruit."[62]

And to balloonists it was a trap!

GOING ACROSS

Blow, winds, and crack your cheeks! rage! blow!
You cataracts and hurricanes, spout
Till you have drench'd our steeples.
Shakespeare, *King Lear*, III, 2

The captain's record tells what happened as the *Brandenburg* encountered Cabin Mountain. "More quickly than it can now be written followed hard collisions with trees, rocks and tree stumps. Upon collision with a boulder our oxygen bottles exploded which we had carefully conserved for the next day for coming greater altitudes. Scarcely had we time to throw out further ballast when suddenly came a lurch over a strong picket fence. The basket turned almost upside down. We threw ballast out and again we raced further on right upon a tree of about 60 meters height. The network was caught in it. The tree was broken down with crashes and with a unified strength we sawed the remaining boughs off. This because of the raging squall-winds and the strong pitching back and forth of the basket required no little effort and exertion. Relieved we looked on as the saw cut through the last hindering boughs. This lightening happiness was however of short duration since in the next moment on the next higher and stronger tree we hung despite throwing out the only possible ballast."[63]

At the opposite rim of the valley the Cooper brothers stood shaken and deeply concerned. Convinced that the flyers had been hopelessly dashed to pieces on the boulders of Cabin Mountain they hurried to give what aid they could. The battle with the dead trees on Cabin Mountain at the far side of the Canaan Valley close to Allegheny Front, drew to a close.

In the meantime other residents of Davis had given chase to the balloons and were either behind the Coopers or in front of them. Driving their father's 1927 Studebaker Commander sedan, Walter M. Raese, R. A. Raese and their close friend, James R. Browning, speeded to the rescue. It is not clear which group first reached the site of the balloon crash. No one was thinking of priorities—only of giving help if they could.

Both cars covered the six-mile run from the rim of Canaan Mountain to the base of Cabin Mountain in record time. After passing Maple Grove School they sped past the homes near Cortland and crossed the bridge over North Branch, down to Cortland School. From there the flat valley pointed them straight across Freeland Run past Cosner School to the Graham farm. Their progress was slowed by the poor condition of the narrow farm road. They crossed the double branches of Freeland Run, and stopped at the Graham farmhouse.

The tall sharp gabled farmhouse sat at the base of Cabin Mountain surrounded by a growth of several tall straight pines. The house was cool in the closing hours of the stormy day. To the right of the house was the small dam across the right branch of Freeland Run in which Joseph C. Graham, Jr., kept his trained trout.

Graham, a slender, sturdy man of 64, was not one to get excited about just anything. Years of hard toil in the lonely fields of the valley had taught him temperance, patience and calmness. He had been concerned about his livestock because of objects thrown about by the high wind. As a result he had not observed the passage of the *Brandenburg* about 2,000 feet to the right of his house as it faced the valley floor.

However he soon learned of it as young Virgie Gaskins, a 5-year-old neighbor, came running up to him. Somewhat out of breath she told him about the big ship that just went over trailing a long rope. She quickly assured Graham that she had tried to catch the rope. (See Figure 32.) Now just a little puzzled—and curious about what the young lady said, Graham stopped his chores, gently picked her up into his arms and calmly asked, "Honey, would you mind repeating what you just said—only say it a little slower this time?"

A CANAAN VALLEY STORY

Rain squalls struck the western edge
   Of the Valley of Canaan.
Harsh winds sang 'cross the ledge
   As early night began.

'Cross the ridge came two brave men
   A ridin' winds of hope.
Raging squalls once more began—
   They sped beneath the slope.

In fields green, just up ahead,
   A small girl ran for home.
The whitefaced calf that she just fed,
   Was suddenly alone.

The little girl then saw the men—
   Thrown about like straw.
She stopped and stood in the wind—
   Her face covered with awe.

The *Brandenburg* was going across
   The Valley of Canaan,
Where timberman and his big boss
   Stripped God's forests from the land.

A landing rope trailed down below—
   The two men dumped their sand.
The five-year-old tried to show
   That she would lend a hand.

She crossed fields over rock and stone—
   Her small arms stretched out far.
She raced and stumbled all alone,
   Like reaching for a star.

Violent winds whipped 'cross the base
Of Cabin Mountain Range.
Despair and fear now found a place
And everything seemed strange.

A picket fence came into view—
Its cross bars split in ten.
The wicker basket—bright and new—
Smashed sideways with the men.

The golden gas bag overhead—
(The trailing rope in tow)—
Crashed in a tree long since dead
And snagged a branch below.

The *Brandenburg* that knew life
In azure skies above,
Now knew danger, fear and strife
In "Land filled tall with love."

The ship carried two young men—
Two knights from castled land—
Along the pitching, dangerous wind
To fabled Land of Canaan.

And so the tale must be told—
A Canaan Valley story—
Of a German airship painted gold,
Just twenty feet from glory.

The wind whistled through the toe
Of a long dead forest stand
And timbermen once more know
The magic of the land.

DOWN

And fast through the midnight dark and drear,
Through the whistling sleet and snow,
Like a sheeted ghost, the vessel swept
Tow'rds the reef of Norman's Woe.
Longfellow, *The Wreck of the Hesperus*

Captain Bertram's log continued: "Now our fate was sealed! Since the ripcord had caught itself, the balloon was torn open so that the gas streamed out. The unavoidability struck us heavily. We had lain continually in front of the other balloons in favorable wind direction and had [with us] upon being stranded, besides the necessities, landing ballast and eight more bags of ballast. Sad and shattered over our fate, we mutually bound up our wounds and made ready mournfully in the middle of those barren and rugged Allegheny Mountains, upon a high, steep mountain to spend the night."[64] (See Figures 33, 34, 35.)

The German flyers witnessed firsthand the ravages of saws, axes and energy of hardened men. The area was barren of tall trees (other than the dead trees that caused their downfall). About the trees stood thick matted underbrush of second growth just taking form.[65]

The captain described the scene as follows: "Around us high trees, parts still alive, part fallen down and rotten. Blocks of granite, broken down trees, tree stumps and shoulder-high briars. It appeared to us almost impossible to salvage the balloon from there." The balloon had cost a lot of money and salvage was uppermost in their minds. It would be difficult to raise the money in an economically disturbed Germany to construct another balloon in the near future and the flyers knew that.

At the foot of the slope where the *Brandenburg* came to rest and about one mile from its position were the rotting trestles of once majestic Lumber Railway. About a half mile to the east was the boundary line that separated Tucker County from Grant County. From that point east the Alleghenies tapered. Three miles further the elevation dropped to 3,982 feet. At the site of Bear Rocks the Allegheny Front began its headlong plunge to the beautiful floor of the Shenandoah Valley of Virginia.

Considering the favorable position of the balloon; the distance that it had covered in a short period of time; the ballast remaining and the sufficiency of the gas supply; one may conclude that Captain Otto Bertram and his aide, Lieutenant Georg Frobel, were only "20 feet from glory." Had the *Brandenburg* gained 20 feet altitude they would have missed the snare that caught them. The Captain continued:

"Suddenly we heard distinctly from below on the slope calls from people. Our looks brightened. We answered and finally shortly before the penetration of complete darkness reached us, five brave men, themselves tired from making their way up the steep mountain slope who by chance had seen our landing and believed us to be shattered on the rocks.

"What followed now could console us somewhat with our fate. A willingness to help which we had not up to this point in our balloon travels known."[66]

J. Stuart Cooper, his brother James and the others had found the flyers. The Raese brothers and Browning arrived at nearly the same time as the Cooper brothers. The five young men were concerned only with giving what aid they could to two fallen flyers. The Germans came to the Land of Canaan; they observed its fortresses and woods and became acquainted with its people.

"A salvage of the balloon was impossible at night so we had to unconcernedly leave our shattered bird with all its feathers hanging since the declaration of our rescuers was that it had been some time since people had entered this barren inhospitable region.

"After a look back and then a many hours long trip down the steep, rugged slope through woods, thick briars, vines, high grass, over racing mountain streams (where we hastily threw ourselves down and quenched our thirst) we continued until day."[67]

The trip from the 4,275-foot crest to the floor of the valley was rugged. The lieutenant had been severely shaken by the crash and the Cooper brothers aided him to the valley floor. The party refreshed themselves by drinking from Idyleman Run—one of many mountain rivulets that feed the slow-moving Blackwater River.

The thick, briar infested underbrush—at places more than head-high—tore the clothes of the rescue party and scratched their once well-polished shoes and boots. The Germans witnessed firsthand two things: the beauty of the Alleghenies and the destruction that had occurred there. "Gaunt skeletons of fire-charred pines with upthrust trunks like masts on spectral ships appear momentarily then are lost in the vapors that swirl around them. Comes the sun and the entire valley is one vast emerald glistening with dew on its million facets. This then, is The Land of Canaan. Behold it! A rugged and beautiful land of broken and tumbled mountains thrusting themselves ever upward into the drifting clouds that pass like phantom ships across the azure skies."[68]

The party continued to the valley at a point about one mile north of the Graham farmhouse. They reached an old log road and followed it the last mile to the site where the cars were parked. Lieutenant Frobel felt better by that time and handed his brass-clasped survival kit to a member of the rescue party with a gesture that indicated that it was intended to be a gift. He could not speak English and they could not speak German.

As mentioned previously, the most valuable piece of equipment carried on the *Brandenburg* was the statoscope. This was an aneroid barometer with a dial marked in meters. It had been used to read the height of their balloon as the flight progressed. (Balloonists who flew without a statoscope relied upon a simple physical trick to tell them if they were rising or descending in the air. A small quantity of sand was clasped in a hand extended over the side of the basket. The flyer released the sand slowly. If sand rose into the palm of the hand the balloon was dropping. If it fell away rapidly the balloon was rising: A primitive substitute for a statoscope.) At the time of the rescue Captain Bertram expressed concern about the safety of the delicate piece of equipment. The fate of the rest of his gear was of no concern. In fact, the two flyers gave most of it away in the next two days in appreciation to those who went to their assistance.

The Raese brothers and Browning drove the Germans to town in their two-seated sedan. And the residents of Davis were awakened early—and in a most unusual manner as reported by the captain:

"Finally we embarked in the car of our driver on a 12-mile trip over terrain which, according to our opinion, a truck could never have traversed. At first our driver had, without us being able to hinder it, made our rescue known by driving through the village and shouting happily: 'We have the Germans; we have the balloonists!' in spite of the advanced time of night."[69]

The need for the services of policemen in Davis had decreased with the passing years. The Saturday night saloon fights of the timbermen ended as the hicks drifted to other parts of the country. Thus only one policeman was on duty when the German flyers arrived in Davis.

The previous night had been uneventful although several persons expressed concern about the whereabouts of the Cooper and Raese brothers and their friend Jim Browning. The policeman saw the two cars speeding out of town and

was not concerned because he knew the young men were
capable of caring for themselves. Also, he knew that two
balloons had passed overhead that evening and simply added
two and two. As a matter of fact he had muttered something
to the effect that "If I weren't on duty I would have gone
with them!" Suddenly sounds of shouting and car engines
reached the officer's ears.

"Everywhere happy calls except for the policeman who
stopped our driver because of the too-great noise. He was
conciliated with us and let us continue, however."[70] As a
matter of fact, the officer did a little news-spreading himself.

"Afterwards in the village, small disputes were settled since
everyone wanted to put us up and be helpful. And we landed
in Davis with an American family by the name of Raese. We
refreshed ourselves with a bath, ate and had a good sleep."[71]

Browning recently provided the following narrative: "I had
no personal knowledge of the James Gordon Bennett International Balloon Race prior to that day (July 1, 1928). I was
seated on the porch of John Raese's home at Seventh Street
in Davis when the balloons were spotted. There were two
balloons about one mile apart. We later learned that one was
the *Brandenburg* and the other the French *Lafayette.* The
Raese family was also present on the porch. The balloons
were nearly side by side as they passed over town. They were
at an altitude of about 800 feet. (The rise in feet from Davis
to the Canaan Mountain ridge was about 700 feet leaving
a 100-foot clearance. This 100 feet would not be enough to
clear the next range.) They approached from the north as
best I can recall. We decided that they were flying too low to
clear the Canaan Mountain. Driving to the top of Canaan
Mountain we could see the balloon dragging the basket up
Cabin Mountain on the opposite side of the valley.

"We then drove to the house of J. C. Graham and proceeded on foot to the top of the mountain. We met Bertram and
Frobel near their balloon. Bertram approached us saying,

'Americans are nice people,' which he repeated several times. We eventually assisted in leading the way to the farmhouse. Lieutenant Frobel was a little 'goofy' from being slammed around in the basket as it was dragged up the mountainside. Frobel did not speak English and Captain Bertram explained his silence as being caused by the rough ride. They brought their German flag with them and later gave it to me as a gift. (See Figure 15.)

"They were very pleased to find that we wanted to help them and not abuse them. We drove to the Raese home and gave them food after they washed. Captain Bertram was anxious to send a telegram to his wife who was waiting for him in a New York hotel (the Pennsylvania Hotel). He was also concerned about the French balloon—wondering if it had cleared the mountain which it had.

"The *Brandenburg* still had ballast in it but the flyers thought that they could clear the mountain without using it. They intended to use it to gain altitude when the sun was lower thus getting high enough to continue the race. They nearly made it but the basket caught, the bag fell and was punctured on a sharp dead tree. If they had been twenty feet higher they would not have snagged the last tree.

"Bertram was a captain in the German Imperial Air Force in World War I and Frobel an artillery lieutenant. I introduced them to German-speaking people as well as to the local priest, Father Murphy of Saint Veronica Church. Father Murphy often joined the Lutheran minister for lunch at the Blackwater Hotel and they spent their lunch hour discussing religion. The priest was Irish and when introduced to the captain said, 'Oh, from the land of Fitzmaurice!' The priest continued, 'That worked out well—the Irish and the Germans—but for some reason, Bertram became provoked."

(Colonel James C. Fitzmaurice of the Irish Free State Air Force, and two Germans, Captain Hermann Koehl and Baron Guenther von Huenefeld, had flown the Junkers monoplane,

Bremen, on the first westward nonstop flight across the Atlantic on April 12 and 13, 1928, and crash-landed on an island off Newfoundland. The crossing from Dublin of 2,124 miles had taken them 36 hours and 30 minutes. (See Figures 6 and 42.) The "Three Musketeers of the Air" began their association at Baldonnel Field, Ireland.)

"At any rate this was the only time that the Germans showed any resentment," Browning continued. "I recall the captain stating, 'That is in the past and we will let it be in the past.' The priest continued the conversation by asking, 'Have you ever been to the British Isles?' Bertram replied, 'I have been to England and I was there when they didn't want me to be.' The priest concluded by saying, 'I am going to Germany soon. If you will give me your address, I will look you up.' The reply was, 'Ask for me in Berlin, they know me there.' "

> *He who has a thousand friends has not a friend*
> *to spare,*
> *And he who has one enemy shall meet him*
> *everywhere.*
>   Emerson, *Conduct of Life*

FLYING FREE ON THE DEVIL'S BREW

Men folks ain't got no feelin
ain't got no time to fill;
Pa spends his time a-huntin
or putterin 'round the still. [72]

As stated previously the prosecuting attorney of Tucker County campaigned on the promise of ridding the county once and for all of any "white lightning" or "illicit hootch" operations within his bailiwick.

The platform either did, or did not, cause him difficulty in getting elected. Who can be sure of such a thing? It was rumored that most of the citizens who would have voted *against* him were in no condition to go to the polls. In any event the new prosecutor squeaked into office by a mere handful of votes. Once elected, he swore on a copy of the New Testament (frayed on all four sides) that he would "uphold the Constitution of the United States, the Constitution of West Virginia, and the laws of West Virginia and the United States," so help him God. The magnitude of the promise chipped a few serious nicks into the edge of his conscience but he did the best he could. After all, no one *really* expects politicians to keep their promises.

Nothing—and nothing it is—throws the fear of the Lord— and the devil at the same time—into a moonshiner more than a federal agent or a crusading prosecutor. Either is bad enough without the other. But stack both up against the moonshiner at the same time and it is enough to cause him to look elsewhere for better territory. Confronted with such a situation some have been known to pack brass coils, copper vats, the "makins" (and a reserve supply of tobacco juice for coloring) and head for inaccessible regions.

Where one is not in a position to move elsewhere such conditions may result in the "product" being hidden between the wall studs of a building. This can be hazardous in cases where a careless carpenter drives an eight penny nail into the bottom of a crock container. (Supposedly it happened in Davis, and the owner and wife, three carpenters, an adjoining store operator and four of his employees were unable to pursue gainful employment for two and one-half days after— rumor, mind you.)

It was further reported that (faced with such uncompromising circumstances) some "unfortunates" buried their supply of jugs in open fields. Hazards there too! A hired hand might accidentally clip the tops from a year's supply on one pass with a plow through the potato field. (The word "accidentally" was chosen carefully to describe this since no one—not even the *lowest* hired hand—would do such a thing on purpose.) Some persons expressed wonder at the early "barnstormers" who found themselves "forced down" in plowed fields. The true reason for this is suggested—and it is a statistic that cannot be controverted—not one flyer was ever lost on such a mission.

The Eighteenth Amendment to the United States Constitution did not apply to the nation of Germany. Lack of jurisdiction over the subject matter. In any event Germans like to drink beer. Lack of proper water purification facilities, coupled with the German habit of dumping human waste into roadside gutters make the drinking of beer a matter of necessity. Faced with a choice of drinks: water that will kill, or carefully brewed beer that is sterilized, the average German— (after deep and serious reflection)—drinks the beer. (In America, scientific and thoroughly efficient water purification systems force inhabitants to find other excuses.)

Returning to the downed German flyers, both asked their

hosts in Davis for beer. They had no reason to know of the 18th Amendment and less cause to fear the prosecuting attorney of Tucker County.

The "product" supplied as the result of the request was received graciously, sampled and rejected as being "too young." A member of the rescue party remarked in a recent interview: "Since the repeal of Prohibition and the return of beer as a legal sales item I know exactly what they meant." ("Brewing your own" was not all that some pretended it to be.)

The repeal of Prohibition was proposed by Congress on February 20, 1933, and ratification followed quickly on December 5, 1933. It had taken many times longer to ratify the United States Constitution than it took to repeal Prohibition! A true testimonial to the unpopularity of a "dry state of affairs."

One other little remembered—yet significant event—occurred in Davis during the visit of the Germans. It involved a certain member of the community who was suspected of living high on some "potent brew." The prosecutor had not been able to obtain evidence to present the case to a grand jury—but he kept trying. The opportunity came one morning as the prosecutor observed the suspect walking sideways out of an establishment in Davis.

The bulge under the right arm of the suspect was about the size of a "bootleg" fifth of whiskey—but how could one be sure? The prosecutor took up the trail.

For some reason the grip on the cargo was relaxed and a full quart of "white lightning" dropped to the concrete sidewalk. Result? The bottle of "moonshine" struck the sidewalk in front of the prosecutor, bounced back into the arms of its unlawful owner who proceeded down the sidewalk, sideways, just as if nothing had happened! If a man had luck like that who would want to press the point? No indictment followed.

RECOVERY

*There was hells of snakes in those days be-
fore the big forest fires and Luke and Buck
collected themselves a nice sackful in one afternoon.* [73]

Tuesday, July 3, 1928, was a beautiful though chilly morning at Davis. The flyers were up early after a night of deep
yet fitful sleep, disturbed by a flaming subconscious desire to
win a race—fanned by the realization that their failure was
due to their own neglect and misjudgment. Time would
ease—but not erase the feeling. And a new thought crossed
the flyers' minds: Would the residents of Davis express resentment or display hostility toward them?

Three residents of Davis had been killed in action in World
War I. Lester F. Hughes died on October 31, 1918; Clyde
Herman Slider, June 18, 1918, (just four days after Quentin
Roosevelt) and Fortunato Valenzio was killed in action on
September 28, 1918, near the war's end. Two other Davis
residents had died in the service from other causes. All of the
victims had been in their early 20's and the townspeople
shared the agonies that came with word of their deaths. [74]

No one can recall any open expression of resentment toward the German military men. (See Figure 36.) The concern
about hostility was unfounded and the German officers
turned their attention to the salvage of their valuable balloon.
Could the airship be rescued?

The ship had crash-landed on scraggy skeleton-shaped remains of yesterday's giants atop a peak on the farm of J. C.
Graham, Jr. That part of Cabin Mountain was almost inaccessible due to heavy undergrowth, crevices, poisonous snakes,

giant boulders and unfriendly rock ridges that blocked the
path of those who penetrated the area. Passage by foot was
difficult even for the most nimble. The German ship had
fallen into a cauldron of uncertainty.

The almost impossible means of passage by foot coupled
with the likelihood that even if freed from the dead trees—
that it could not be brought out—changed the question to
"Could the *Brandenburg* be salvaged at all?" The question of
what to do with the *Brandenburg*, impaled upon dead trees
atop one of the highest—and most rugged mountains in the
Alleghenies (see Figures 33, 34 and 35)—was a simple one to
answer—as it turned out.

Many persons—large, small, medium, old, young and otherwise—responded to the call for assistance. The Germans declared that the salvage of the *Brandenburg* was probably
impossible. But they were soon exposed to simple, forthright
West Virginia ingenuity, manual skill, strength-plus-simple-
determination to do what had to be done. A party of 16
persons had assembled at the Graham farmhouse and took
stock of the tools needed to do the job.

Joseph Graham, Jr., like his father, was not a man to go
into the mountains unprepared. He listened to the captain
carefully, and formed in his mind a view of the approximate
location of the *Brandenburg*. As one faced Cabin Mountain at
the Graham farmhouse, the right knoll crested at 4,375 feet;
the center one where the *Brandenburg* rested, at 4,275 feet;
and the left knoll at well over 4,000 feet. (See Figure 30.)
The topographical map of the range as surveyed in 1919,
showed many places where the 50-foot contour rings touched
which indicated sheer drops. Of what use was land that rose
one-quarter of a mile straight into the air from fields of a
farm? The view from the crests was unexcelled but the land
was worthless to a farmer. It is difficult to imagine land so
inaccessible that the man who owned it had only visited it a
few times—but such was the case. The timbermen had gone

there and stripped part of the timber placing the balance to the torch. While Graham had watched some of the operations after selling the timber to third parties, he had avoided the region.

After determining the approximate size and weight of the airship, Graham made a decision. A means of transportation was required but he rejected the suggestion of using a wagon. He valued the lives of his horses more than that. In addition a wagon would be dangerous to its passengers on the slopes that awaited them. He decided to use his rock and pole sled.

The sled was a huge, handmade flat-bedded affair with wood runners. It was about four feet wide, eight feet long, had side boards and was used to carry away rocks plowed from the fields in the spring. The two runners were surfaced with iron straps. Two good horses could pull it easily on flat ground even though fully loaded with rock.

Other volunteers arrived at the farm even though it was Tuesday—a working day. Earl Graham, Joseph's brother, was there with his brush hook—a curved axe type instrument used in clearing underbrush and slicing small trees up to two inches in diameter. Cromwell Graham insisted that he go too, but at 10 years of age he was a little small to use an axe. The Germans later gave him a nice souvenir for his interest, however.

Joe Ketts, Owen Harr and others volunteered and with them came an assortment of small fry all anxious to assist the Europeans. Fay Graham and Myrtle Graham Edwards, a son and daughter of Joseph, were away at the time and were not present for the recovery.

Joe Graham selected his two strongest horses, "Rocket" and "Faith," and carefully harnessed them to the sled. Rocket, a white horse with dark legs, was the colt of an old favorite of the Grahams: Starlight. Faith was a sturdy solid black animal with a special sheen to her sides and a white mane gave her a distinguished look. Faith was a good, strong horse and always dependable. Rocket was from riding stock and liked to run. About a year before the rescue Audrey Graham had handed a package to Margaret Graham who was riding Rocket sidesaddle. The horse bolted and ran from the church where they were to Frank Harr's barn giving the little passenger quite a scare.

One of the railroad trestles of the timbering days had run close behind the Graham house. Margaret had owned a small riding horse which she often walked across the wide, wooden trestle beams, leading it by its halter. She remarked to Myrtle Edwards years later, "I probably shouldn't have done that because the little horse might have fallen off." She apparently ignored the danger to herself. Myrtle also set the record straight on another valley story. Rumor had it for many years that Frank "Buck" Harr had killed a wild bear in the Canaan Valley with his bare hands. "Buck" Harr had *danced* with a wild bear—he did not kill it. The astonished bear apparently thought only of flight once Frank turned him loose. A man who could dance with a bear just *might* have been able to kill one with his bare hands if he had decided to do so. Meanwhile, the rescue party was prepared to assault the impossible slopes of Cabin Mountain.

Graham chose Faith and Rocket for two good reasons: Rocket anticipated movement thus keeping Faith moving; and Faith, being a solid horse, restrained Rocket. The result was a working team that could keep a heavy load moving steady over extended periods of time.

Gear was carefully lashed to the sled and the rescue team started the assault on the ridges. Years before a log road had been driven part way to the crest and the road was followed as far as possible. However, the going became progressively difficult because of the almost "barbed wire" underbrush. Frequent rest stops were made to allow the horses to cool. During the breaks the small boys scouted the woods on the flanks for whatever they could find. Since this was copperhead and rattlesnake country all members of the party exercised caution and the young lads were constantly warned to be careful.

The captain carried a small pack over his shoulder. That morning he had filled the pack with various sweets and other items purchased in Davis. He frequently passed his pack to his helpers and the young ones soon kept exclusive company with him. Still skeptical about the removal of the ship, the captain was amazed at the cooperation he received. In Germany he had been warned about the high cost of labor in America. He thought it strange that those who had helped him initially and those who labored very hard for him and his aide on the mountain had not mentioned the subject of money. As it turned out, he was the first to bring up the subject. He learned that what he had been told at home was false in the Land of Canaan.

The party reached Idyleman Run and the most rugged part of the ascent began. They paused for a drink from the crystal clear mountain stream, then the older men moved to the front and cut the trees that blocked their path. The underbrush had not been too difficult to get through but the horses could not walk over trees.

The farmers-turned-timbermen felled many trees of moderate to large size. The trees were cut close to the ground in order to allow the rock sled to pass over the stumps. It was necessary to cut many of the trees twice in order to allow them to be pushed from the path of the sled. After several hours of toil, J. C. Graham concluded that it was impossible to take the sled any further. The horses were exhausted; sheer cliffs of jagged rock prevented further progress of the sled; huge boulders were everywhere and solid laurel underbrush blocked every path to their front. And they were a half mile from the balloon.

Two of the medium-age boys were left with the horses and sled and the main party began a new assault upon the obstacles to their front. Two more hours of brush and tree cutting, boulder dodging and just plain hard climbing followed before the *Brandenburg* came into view.

The scene that greeted the rescue party reaffirmed the flyers' belief that rescue of their ship was impossible. The situation was even worse than they had remembered it. Seeing it after the heated excitement of the crash had cooled, the Germans concluded that the situation was hopeless. Even if the balloon was freed from the dead trees that grasped it, it would not be possible to move it down the ridges to the sleds.

The tangle of cotton cloth, netting, ropes and equipment scattered through ghost-like snags that gripped the airship was a scene to remember. The center of the balloon was snagged over a dead tree that stood a full four stories straight into the air on a mountain where clouds drifted lazily just feet above the rescue workers. In addition, the cloth of the balloon had settled over several other tall tree snags and formed what would have been a lovely beach umbrella for some nasty giant. The appendix was draped close to the earth and the netting that rode over the balloon appeared hopelessly snarled as it lay twisted in and out of the snags and underbrush. To make the situation worse some of the netting and gondola ropes were snagged some 30 feet in the air on a tree located 40 feet away from the basket. It was a nightmare that a balloonist could not have envisioned in his wildest dreams.

The captain assembled the work party and expressed thanks for their services. He acknowledged that the work that they had just performed had been both long and difficult and then raised the subject of payment for services rendered.

At first the West Virginians did not understand. Graham remarked to his brother Earl that this was probably some formality that Germans went through in working out a business arrangement. Or maybe it was the language barrier. While the captain spoke fair English, he was nevertheless difficult to understand at times. But suddenly the message came through—the Germans had decided to leave the *Brandenburg* on the mountain.

The initial surprise of the rescue workers turned into just plain hurt feelings. While no member of the party made any reply, the disillusionment was apparent in the expressions on their faces. The Germans had concluded that they were not capable of making the rescue. And if that were true there was nothing to do but leave the mountain, go back to the Graham farm and return home.

The combination of despair upon the part of the Germans, contrasted against the injured feelings of the older men, was completely missed by the young fellows who rolled up ropes, picked up gear scattered from the basket and in general started the rescue that they came to help with.

The flyers looked at the group before them—the group looked at them—both looked at the small fry busy at work and all broke into large grins. The smiles said more than could be expressed in words. The rescue operation proceeded.

One by one the hard, dead, silver crusted, barkless hulks of former living timber were carefully severed. The large niche, or "felling nick," was cut in such a location that the trunk was controlled by manpower and slid from beneath the cotton of the balloon without doing serious damage. Some of the taller trunks were severed several times.

Astonished at the skill of the farmers, the Germans stood by and watched their fallen bird settle gently to the ground as the bars of its cage were carefully cut one by one and rolled aside. The balloon was freed in less time than it had taken to climb the mountain. The rescue party cleared an open space in the underbrush for the purpose of assembling the fabric and netting of the ship. The ties on the basket were carefully unfastened freeing it from the main netting and gasbag.

After removing wood chips, briars and stones from the netting and fabric, all present joined in the job of stretching and folding the gold material. While the rip panel of the balloon had been forced open, the balance of the giant gas-bag showed little damage—a tribute to the skill of those who brought it to the ground. A few punctures here and there could be patched easily with cotton and lacquer. The *Brandenburg* was reduced to a heavy, compact square of material, secured firmly by horsehair ropes that had been taken along by Earl Graham and the Germans knew their ship would fly again.

The resourcefulness of the men prompted the captain to remark to his aide that he better understood the effectiveness of Americans that he had fought against in the "great war." The most difficult tasks often become mere routine when forced upon resourceful men by necessity.

After everything was secured the question was how to move the heavy bundle to the sled below. Joe Graham provided the answer without hesitation. The cloth bundle was inserted in the wicker basket which was tipped to one side. The men rolled the basket down the approach trail as one man guided the end of the bundle that reached beyond the open end of the basket. The sled was reached in record time and the bundle of material was loaded on the front of the sled while the basket was placed at the rear. After the equipment was secured the trip to the valley began.

The weight of the load on the rock sled caused deep ruts to be cut into the dry, hard July soil. There was no concern about a "runaway" and the horses literally pulled the load downhill. Upon reaching the log road the trip continued down the ruts cut that morning until the farm was reached.

Grateful to their many helpers the flyers were liberal with souvenirs. Cromwell Graham was particularly pleased when the German captain gave him the aluminum can in which the flyers had carried coffee. He posed with the balance of the

crew near the line fence that separated the farm of Dr. Dove
from that of Graham. Cromwell made it a point to stand
clear of the sled so his new acquisition would show in the
photo. (See Figure 37.) (The can had a "press-in" aluminum
top and was later used to capture trout in neighboring
streams. For years the can hung on a nail in the shed behind
the Graham house—and eventually vanished—a victim of for-
getfulness that accompanied the passage of time. It was of
little significance after the rescue but would be of interest to
others today.)

A passing truck was commandeered and the *Brandenburg*
was deposited at the Railway Express Office at Davis to begin
a journey back to Germany.

Writing later about the rescue of his ship the captain stated: "On the next morning after hard climbing and unspeak-
able toil, the balloon was salvaged after about 200 trees from
the slope to the valley of the first farm were felled, and the
balloon by means of trucks (sled) from the farm was brought
out."[75]

Jim Browning worked that Tuesday in 1928 and was unable to assist in the rescue. He had just arrived home from
work when the truck brought the balloon into Davis so he
joined the growing crowd. Browning recalls: "The Germans
had heard of high wages in this country and had decided to
abandon their ship on the mountain where it had fallen.
After the rescue, the Graham boys and those who assisted
them refused to take any money for their services and the
Germans asked me what they should do. I told them not to
ask the price but to just give one of them $20. This Bertram
did and nothing further was said about money." One of the
party recalled later that the $20 was split evenly among the
small fry. (The menfolk wanted no pay for helping visitors in
time of trouble.) The flyers told Browning that they expected to pay at least $500 for the salvage and that was one
reason why they had decided to abandon the *Brandenburg.*
The other was that they did not believe it could be rescued.

VISITORS

*From going to and fro in the earth, and from
walking up and down in it.*
Old Testament, *Job* 1:7

On Wednesday, July 4, the German visitors were treated to
a series of car rides to points of local interest. They were
driven to the rim of Canaan Valley which enabled them to
see once more the breathtaking beauty of the valley and the
rugged mountains five miles across that had spelled disaster
to their flight.

They visited one of the most fabulous beauty spots in
America—the falls of the Blackwater River. The rivulets that
the Germans drank from on their descent from Cabin Mountain flowed to the valley floor where streams of various sizes
were formed. The streams dropped into the main channels of
a larger stream which formed the Blackwater River.

The river drained the Canaan Valley and flowed lazily past
Davis—almost parallel with the main street and within a
stone's throw of the center of town. The river moved along at
a pace that barely caused ripples among the brown, tannic
acid-soaked rocks of its bed. After passing Davis, an increasing decline in elevation in the river bed caused a speeding up
of the flow of water. The decline continued until the drop
was greater per 1,000 feet than it was across the entire Canaan Valley. And then a mad plunge began at the falls. (And
so it is today.)

David Hunter Strother, who wrote under the name of
Porte Crayon, brought world-wide attention to the falls. Born
September 16, 1816, at Martinsburg, Virginia (now West Vir-
ginia), he studied art in France and Italy and served in the

American Civil War attaining the rank of Brigadier General. In writing of the falls, he stated: "Gathering the waters among the swampy glades of the broad, level summits of the Allegheny, the Blackwater winds in peaceful obscurity through dense overhanging forests for about twenty miles. Swelled with numerous tributary brooks and rivulets, it at length attains a width of 50 yards and a considerable volume of water. Then its placid face begins to break into dimples and wrinkles, and its sluggish current freshens into a frolicsome race with the red deer that haunts [sic] its banks. Suddenly emerging from woodland shades, like a bold youth taking leave of his paternal shelter, the stream makes a wild leap into the abyss of life, and never thereafter knows peace or rest until engulfed in the Lethean pools of the Black Fork of the Cheat."[76]

The flyers visited the falls with John Raese, father of Richard A., Robert and Walter Raese. The visitors posed for photos and then descended to the base of the falls. Wood steps had been constructed down part of the sheer walls that lined both sides of the gorge where the Blackwater made "its leap into space." (The ruggedness of the abyss cannot be appreciated by one who has not seen it firsthand.) As the bottom of the stairs were reached, the flyers found that they were still five stories from the pool below the falls and continued downward over hazardous boulders and dangerous crevices until the base of the falls was reached. The breathtaking beauty left them wide-eyed. Nature bestowed more than a normal share of uncut beauty there for man to behold.

The flyers scampered to a large rock just to the right of the center of the falls and photos were taken. (See Figure 38.) (This very clear detailed photo led to the discovery of the airline that the captain had been associated with. The emblem on his hat was clear enough that an enlargement showed the wording on the insignia.)

Almost an hour was spent at the base of the falls and one

resident of Davis remembers that the Germans were impressed more than before with the ruggedness and wild beauty of Tucker County. Their experience on the mountain coupled with what they witnessed in the Blackwater gorge,
convinced them that few scenes on earth equaled it.

Two years before the visit of the Germans, the West Virginia Photo Company of Parsons sent a team of photogra-
phers into the gorge to take a panoramic photo during one of
the times of peak water flow. The result was one of the more
remarkable early views of the falls. (See Figure 39.) (The
entire photo is too large to reproduce on a normal book
page.)

The 1926 party experienced difficulty in reaching the base
of the falls. The pine stairs (which were about 3.5 feet wide)
dropped precariously down the sheer sides of the fabulous
canyon at a 45-degree angle. While there were 2x4 railings on
the sides of the stairs, no one was foolish enough to rely
upon them. Some 50 feet above the lower pool the stairs
ended. The descent was completed without the aid of anything but care and caution. The resulting photo discloses a
sign painted on the left wall of the gorge as one faced the
falls. The sign was six feet long, two feet high and stated
"1910—Starr." The significance of it is unknown.

In later years (after proper drilling) boulders in the gorge
were blasted apart to make it easier for one to descend to the
bottom of the falls. But even today the descent from the end
of heavy wooden stairs is difficult. Man has had perpetual
difficulty in negotiating the ruggedness of the Land of Canaan.

After the group returned to Davis many townspeople
stopped by to wish the flyers well. The overall reception
offered them was one of kindness, warmth and well-wishing
all typical of the residents of Tucker County. One resident of
Davis during the visit recalls that the Germans had not tasted

ketchup and were impressed with it as a supplement to the
food served them. But falls, friends, food—all faded.

As all events of men, the visits came to an end. Arrangements were made to allow the flyers to journey from Davis to
New York then to destinations unknown to newfound
friends in West Virginia.

Browning accompanied Bertram and Frobel on the motor
trip to Oakland, Maryland, where they departed by passenger
train. The subject of payment for the rescue was mentioned
once again. "I apologize for asking," said the captain, "but
may I have a receipt for the $20? I was instructed to keep
records of all expenses." Browning complied, writing a receipt on the back of an envelope. The group took their leave
at Oakland as the flyers departed on the Baltimore and Ohio
Railroad train. In his shirt pocket (completely unnoticed at
the time) the German captain carried a receipt which read:
"Received of Otto Bertram, for services of 12 men for one
day's work in removing racing balloon from Cabin Mountain—$400.00. (Signed) James R. Browning." (Browning re-
marked recently that he hoped the captain had been paid the
larger sum—a little "friendly fraud.")

The balloon and equipment had been shipped to New
York by Railway Express the previous day. Attached to the
basket and cloth bundles were shipping labels that contained
two brass eyelets. The front of each label read as follows:
"Gordon Bennett Race, 1928, von Chemnitz-Sud. Please send
it to the German-General Consulate—Vera—Fork." The reverse of the identification tag stated: "Owner, Mr. Otto Bertram, balloonist of the German balloon, 'Ernst Brandenburg.' " (The captain later sent the shipping labels to
Browning as a souvenir.)

And so two foreign nationals started homeward—and returned to lives altered by the friendship they found in the
Land of Canaan. The last paragraph of the captain's narrative
contains a ring of sadness: "We had the good fortune to

spend two further nights under the hospitable roofs of their houses. A grateful parting from the dear people, another drive around Davis, and then northward we traveled the way back to New York in the conviction that we had done all that we could have done."[77]

And so the story of the "German airship painted gold" has been related. The balloon had been within 19 feet of clearing the dead snags on rugged Cabin Mountain. If that had happened the ship probably would have flown to Florida—and a new world record. The Germans had been just twenty feet from glory. Perhaps a member (or two) of another generation will recall that the *Brandenburg* flew in the beauty that was, and is, Canaan Valley. If so, they might remember the final report issued by the captain:

And they told him, "We came to the land to which you sent us; it flows with milk and honey, and this is its fruit."[78]

AFTERMATH

All are architects of Fate
Working in these walls of Time;
Some with massive deeds and great,
Some with ornaments of rhyme.
Longfellow, *The Builders*

About sixteen months after the International Balloon Race, "The Roaring Twenties" skidded to a tragic close. Once-prosperous businessmen hurled themselves out of windows; others ended their lives by gunfire. The stronger members of society simply faced up to the reality of the loss that they had sustained. Future generations were, and will in the future, be shocked when learning of the crash of '29—but in the meantime, things happened in those days.

The ninth Olympic Games began at Amsterdam, running from July 28 to August 12. The first such games had taken place in 776 B.C. The new Model "A" Fords that zipped along freshly paved highways rolled on four 50 x 30 tires (measured differently than those of today). Other events tied 1928 to the age of "computerized corporations," "mass merchandising"—and space exploration.

In August, 1928, Bert R. J. (Fish) Hassel and Parker Cramer tried to prove that a circle route for long distance air travel was best. They planned to fly *The Greater Rockford* from Rockford, Illinois, to Sweden by way of the Arctic. (Their prediction proved true as bombers flew the suggested course in World War II.) *The Greater Rockford* did not finish the 1928 trip. After exhausting its fuel the plane crash-landed on ice 60 miles from Sondstrom, Greenland. The *Rockford* was left where it fell but the flyers escaped uninjured.

For forty years the *Rockford* lay upside down on the ice.

The U. S. Air Force spotted the plane and photographed it in 1946—the first time humans had seen it since 1928. Because of the interest of Robert Carlin of National Airlines at Houston, a Greenlander Sikorsky helicopter (after proper preparation) lifted the *Rockford* from the ice on September 11, 1968. The old machine was in an amazing state of repair, probably because of the cold and ice. Carlin laid plans to restore the craft—possibly to place it into the air—providing a significant link between modern times and the forgotten year of 1928. In the months prior to the flight of the *Rockford*, a little-noticed event occurred in Germany.

The Amnesty Act of July 14, 1928, permitted a strange man to be freed from captivity in Germany. After six months' imprisonment Rudolph Hoess stood on the steps of Potsdamer Station in Berlin, staring incredulously at "plain people" passing by—persons in pursuit of everyday goals. (He was credited with arranging the gassing of 2,000,000 "plain persons" from 1941 to the end of 1943.)

Norman Thomas, six-time Socialist Party candidate for President of the United States, made his first bid for the White House in 1928. He received 267,420 votes that year. By 1932 his popularity had increased so that he received 884,781 votes. Slipping to 187,342 votes in 1936, he registered 116,796 votes in 1940. On December 19, 1968, at the age of 84, he died in his sleep—the White House reserved for others. He never came close to winning one electoral vote.

On the 1928 automobile scene, Chevrolet made big inroads because of Ford's transition from the "T" to the "A". It had resulted in a period of time during which Ford did not have cars to supply the dealers. The Chevrolet "Cabriolet" with fold-down top and popular "rumble seat" came out in May. Offered in combinations of red, black and gold, the Chevrolet was a success. Its four cylinders had overhead valves and a stroke of four inches. The motor generated 35 horsepower at 2,200 R.P.M. The brakes were mechanical and the gear ratio was 3.81. With 4.50 x 21 inch tires and body by Fisher, 931,000 "Chevys" were sold by the close of 1928. The Cabriolet sold at $695 F.O.B. factory. The new competition posed serious problems to those in command at the Ford complex.

Tucker County voters split almost evenly in the presidential election of 1928, with 1,447 persons voting Democratic and 1,421 voting Republican—a margin of only 26 votes!

At Uniontown, Pa., Simon Johns and Bros. advertised the sale of fireworks for the 1928 Fourth of July—wholesale only. Howard Mason Gore, a Republican, served as governor of West Virginia. The state's U. S. Senatorial representatives were Matthew Mansfield Neely, a Democrat, and Guy D. Goff, a Republican.

As records later disclosed, 344 persons were born in Tucker County in 1928 while 115 deaths occurred. Marriages totaled 80 and divorces ran below the national average at 14. (The decline in population is well-illustrated by statistics some 30 years later. Births showed 164, deaths 90, and marriages 35 stacked up against 8 divorces.) National averages had no application to those who lived in Tucker County—a tribute to the "land" as well as its "people." On the industrial scene an amazing invention had been introduced. Color television (in a very crude form) had been demonstrated in 1928. Practical use for the machine waited for future generations, however.

So the affairs of 1928 wound to a conclusion. In the meantime, Bertram found time to correspond with his newfound friends in America.

On December 3, 1928, the captain wrote to Jim Browning expressing gratitude for the "hospitable reception which I found in your in-laws' home . . . I take the liberty to send as a remembrance . . . a small Christmas gift. It is Nurnberger gingerbread which is probably world famous."

On March 11, 1929, the captain wrote of the next race in

America (scheduled for October 1 at St. Louis). He waited for an answer from the German government since he needed approval before he could enter the race.

Freight charges from New York to St. Louis concerned Bertram. He inquired, "I ask you if it is not possible to take a freight auto from New York to St. Louis—how much would be the price of such auto? The last time I was at Detroit there were many old autos to buy for $100." In the letter he stated that he planned to take an American reporter on the flight as an aide. "It will lower the cost," he commented.

October 3, 1929: Bertram expressed regrets for his inability to travel to America in 1929. The race date had been set back to September thereby causing Bertram to cancel. "This month is the best of my business." He ended the letter by expressing hope that the next races would be in Germany, and voiced a desire to show Germany to his American friend.

Correspondence with Bertram ceased as the Nazi power play engulfed Europe in a flame of death and destruction. Little is known of the activities of the captain during the Second War other than from two sketchy sources. Richard Collier, in his memorable book, *Eagle Day*, lists in the appendix the name of Hamptman Otto Bertram as a flyer operating out of La Haure Oye Plage with the III/J.G.2, called the Jafu 3, commanded by Oberst Werner Junck. The book contains no other mention of the flyer. Bertram was born in 1883 and was 57 years of age in 1940: a little old for a fighter pilot— but yet he flew.

The other source was his wife Martha who wrote several letters beginning in 1948. The strong hand of the wife of an aging military man related the suffering she endured following the war.

On March 22, 1948, she confessed: "I am so sorry, I must tell you that he is not ever at home since nearly 2½ years. He is in Russia as a war prisoner. We are now married 38 years and I am so unhappy that this pass to him in his old days. Otto gets on this year 65 years and I am over 59 years old."

She continued, "Today we have lost all, the Russians took our freehold property. In the war (Second World War) he was called as flyer as commander for the rescue service in Denmark as field officer. Therefore, the Russians took him away on February 21, 1946. In war, he saved others by flying friends or enemies, they were all equal to him, no matter what country they belonged." (Could the captain have remembered other days in the mountains of West Virginia?)

A tender note closed the letter when she stated, "I wish I could help him to become free, because I love him so much. But I am sorry that I can do nothing in this case."

June 19, 1948: The lot of Martha Bertram worsened under Russian rule: "I am quite alone now, I get only our —— (word not distinguishable) and this is so few to live and even too much to die."

Writing of Otto on August 6, 1948, she stated: "I am sure he will work again hardly . . . but as an old good sailor and captain and flyer, he will not be easily suppressed."

With no heat in her meager quarters in Chemnitz, she reported on November 5, 1949, that "it would be really a great world for us to have good shoes again." Looking forward to the possible return of Otto after almost five years, she reflected: "You must know he was always diligent in his business, always the first in the mornings and the last in the evenings and always with good humor and smiling. In the morning still singing or fifing, oh, he is a really fine boy." She closed by asking a prayer for his return.

Good news came on December 14, 1949. Otto had been released and was at Celle, Blumlage. His wife was in the East Zone at Karl-Marx-Stadt—the new name for Chemnitz. He visited her, however, for just a few moments as the Russian transport carrying him to the West Zone, stopped in Karl-Marx-Stadt.

Martha escaped to the West, leaving what little they owned behind. On October 27, 1950, she wrote that they had been reunited for almost a year. Her flight was discussed briefly when she wrote: "We came with walking out of the East Zone; it was very difficult and when we begin in November with one room, first we must buy a bed-couch for two, or two bedspreads, and we will be happy. We begin again like quite young married people, with nothing, and we were married now 40 years." Philosophically, she sadly commented: "It is a long time if you see time in front, but a short time when you see it backwards." Perhaps some day, she closed, they could return home and regain what they had lost. Hope that exists in a human being is difficult to shatter.

On July 4, 1951, she wrote, "here the life is difficult and we hope for the reopening of our old firm in West Germany." Showing a remarkable economic eye (even in those times), she theorized, "When the war with Korea is ended, perhaps we could get industrial iron, steel and so on."

Two poignant letters written by Bertram tell a large story in few words. They follow in their entirety (however the name of the person who received the letters has been concealed):

> Celle, December 16, 1951
> Blumlage 27

Dear ——:

The year 1951 shall not be finished, before you get an answer to your letter. Next to I thank you verry much for it, also for the nice pictures from your house. I would be so glad, to come to you to a visit, and to see you and speak you in your home. I am sorry, that is not yet possible now. Perhaps, there will be one day a Gordon-Bennett-Race for Balloons, which will bring me again near to you. Now it was 23 years ago. In the East Zone I have all the pictures of the trip to America. Have you still any pictures of this time. The young man, who accompanied me, has died long time ago, and only the remembrance of America is remained and the good

friendship between you and me . . . My really great possession is all lost in the East Zone, only with the naked
life my wife came secret over the green frontier. To you
I had send the report of my suffering through prisons
and Russia. It was very difficult in my age to begin
without nothing once more. No dressing, no linnen, no
furnitures, and ill to through this martyrdom in Russia.
With much troubles and work I began to erect, and we
still take pains to form a new life. The Americans have
helped a great deal of Germans in this bad time; but you
cannot imagine what a wretched life the most of the
fugitives must bear. 8,000,000 people came over from
the East Zone to the West Zone till now, and more are
coming still. The towns are still bombed through the
war, the dwellings are so rare and all overfilled. But the
diligence of the Germans hope to bring our Nation again
high, when it will be possible to prevent a new war. In a
short time there is Christmas. We both wish you a good
festival and a happy New Year. If you will have time, we
will be fond of a letter from you.

With our best regards, we are
yours
(Signature)

(20a) CELLE, den   3rd March 55
Blumlage 27
Telefon 4387

Dear Mr. ——:

You will certainly give me the permission to call you
like this, as you are the only one who was really main-
taining the old America connexion. First of all I am
desirous to give you many thanks for your kind and
long letter and the photographs enclosed with it, photographs which I unfortunately lost during the escape. A
very nice souvenir on the landing in the U.S.A. On the
photographs I am still looking very young, but in the
meantime, 27 years, more than a quarter of a century
having been passed and what has one to go through
during that time? A second world war, prison, house of
correction, prisoner of war for four years with the Russians, loss of the total of my fortune and then refugee to
Western Germany. If I would send you a photograph of
me as I am looking like now, you would think it would
show "Old Moses" or "Ramses" and not the young

aviator of the year 1928. So are times changing and only
the remembering of good old times is remaining and the
bad things one must forget. But we would be much
appreciated to hear from you and your wife, that you
are satisfied in every respect, which is really the main
point in life, and chiefly one is in good health. We, as far
as we are concerned, as refugees, at an age of 72 years
have to work to earn our daily food. Very often it is not
easy, but we are happy anyway not to live amongst the
Russians and their communistic management anymore.
Only people, who have really suffered this are in the
position to talk about this and know what "Liberty"
actually means. My voyage to the U.S.A., which I intended to do, could unfortunately not be effected, but
perhaps you could come to Germany for a visit. We
would be very pleased to show you our own nice still
remained and rebuilt Germany.

Will you please be kind enough and remember us to
—— and giving them our very best compliments and you
yourselves be greet from
                Yours, thinking of you in anticipation
                          (Signature)

A telegram was sent to the last address of Bertram on
February 19, 1969, and a letter was received as a result.
Dated April 22, 1969, and written in the strong hand of Martha Bertram, it said in part: "I received your wire from February 69. I did not answer before, because I had to think
about your request first . . . I am 80 years old now, on account of the war and the Russians my husband and I lost
everything. We both had to leave our home and our Fa. M.
Schmieder & Co. Iron and Steel, etc. en gros—and begin here
at Celle quite a new life without anything. My husband
worked hard, he died in 1960. I was alone but he bequeathed
me some money so that I could live . . . The life of my husband was very interesting even at the age of 17." Unfortunately, further contact with Mrs. Bertram became impossible
and a source of material about the life of a German flyer was
ended. And so, the flight of the *Brandenburg*, written upon a

small page in the giant book of humanity, has taken its place upon the endless bookshelves of time. It will soon fade into the obscurity that so carefully hides the forgotten events of yesterday.

TODAY

I've shut the door on yesterday
And thrown the key away—
Tomorrow holds no fears for me,
Since I have found today.
—Vivian Y. Laramore

The research required to write the story took more than one year and required 6,000 miles of travel. Out of it one minor dispute arose concerning the 7.65-caliber pistol owned by J. S. Cooper. Cooper (who operated a general merchandise store in Davis in 1928) recalls that someone showed him a photo a few days after the Germans departed. The photo disclosed several German military men at the graveside of Quentin Roosevelt. The handle of a pistol was visible in the photo and the broken top edge of the handle was identifiable matching the pistol that Cooper owns. (See Figure 8.) Cooper signed an affidavit to attest to the accuracy of what he remembers. (See Figure 41.)

The dispute concerns which of the two officers carried the pistol at the burial. Sketchy accounts in books and newspapers state that Roosevelt was buried by "German aviators." The books are in dispute as to which German caused his death. Since the pistol came from the survival kit carried by Frobel it is possible that it was his property. Since Roosevelt had been downed 10 miles behind the German lines in World War I, it is possible that he had fallen near an artillery unit. On the other hand, since the records state that he was buried by "German aviators," it is possible that Bertram had been associated in some way with the "Flying Circus"—the unit credited with the kill. The answer may never be found and yet the incident related in this story may ultimately lead to the answer. An advertisement was placed in the *Parsons Advocate* in 1969, asking if any resident of Tucker County might know the whereabouts of the photograph J. S. Cooper mentioned. No response was made to the ad. Yet, the photo may be resting between the pages of a forgotten album, or stuffed into the ancient papers of some family in Davis. Hopefully it has not been destroyed. The discovery of the photo would help to complete the picture of an incident that leaves a blank space upon at least one page of American history.

The captain's log was carefully kept and preserved and he used it to write a detailed account of his flight for an unknown German newspaper. A copy of the newspaper story was forwarded to Browning who made it available for translation. This article allowed a factual account of the events of the flight to be related and provided a way of determining the path flown by the Germans.

The flight line of the *Brandenburg* from Pittsburgh to Cabin Mountain was arrived at with reasonable certainty. (See Figure 40.) The approximate point of the crash on Cabin Mountain was located by eyewitness testimony of the Cooper brothers as they stood on Route 32 south of Davis on the side of Canaan Mountain. It was there that the Cooper brothers saw the *Brandenburg* dragged up the side of the mountain. Crossing the Canaan Valley to the old Graham farm they concluded that it was the middle mountain of three in a row where the balloon came down. After locating this peak on a geological survey map a line was drawn to the center of Pittsburgh, Pa. It was determined that the line ran North 21 degrees West. This meant that the craft had followed a path of South, 21 degrees East as it crossed the western part of Pennsylvania and the eastern part of West Virginia.

The line crosses the eastern ridge of Davis near the church where the balloon was first sighted by the Cooper brothers.

This accounts for the lack of information by residents of Thomas, West Virginia; the balloons never crossed Thomas, but rather passed east of it.

A side view of the crossing of Tucker County—based upon one-fourth-inch elevation intervals taken from the geological topographical map—is significant. This view was drawn from a single line across Tucker County based upon the course of South, 21 degrees East. The side view gives an approximation of the terrain of the county as the flyers crossed it. (See Figure 24.) The difficulties that faced them as they passed Davis are graphically shown as Canaan Mountain rises in front of them like a wall—with Cabin Mountain waiting in the distance.

The encounter with the picket fence is explained by the fact that the *Brandenburg* was dragged up the slope of Cabin Mountain. The fence simply impeded their progress. After the encounter with the first tree, the ship was dragged nearer the top where the rip panel of the balloon was forced open as the rip cord became snagged on a dead limb. This panel was designed for deflating the balloon after landing and thus the sudden, unplanned discharge of gas, sounded an end to the flight. A mere puncture by a snag would not have caused the collapse; but fate was against them.

The balloonists could not control their approach to Tucker County. The turbulence literally shaped their destiny as they rode those "winds of hope." If the *Brandenburg* had traveled only five miles on either side of the path it followed, down drafts of the valley could have been avoided.

Today at Dearborn, where the flight of 1928 began, amazing things await a visitor. First at Edison Institute and Ford Museum, there is faithful evidence of the history and growth of Ford Motor Company. In particular, the affairs of Ford in 1927 and 1928 can be revisited firsthand. And evidence of the death of a "king" can also be seen.

America was on wheels and in the air in 1927 because of

Edsel's father. The Model "T" filled the need for efficient, inexpensive travel in America but the "T" lived too long. At first Henry Ford refused to believe this. Hadn't this car enabled him to pay his workers the sum of $5.00 per day—the first business to do so? Hadn't this vehicle allowed him to keep his plant closed on Sundays enabling his workers to enjoy a day off? And hadn't he been able to market a product for a sum millions of Americans could afford to pay? And hadn't this car provided him and his son with a fortune far beyond anything they might have hoped for?[33] But Edsel had insisted. The "T" was through in spite of its brilliant record. Kings die hard.

Equipped with new transmissions, and powered by six cylinders, Chevrolets and others were passing the "T's" as though they were standing still. The drivers of Fords did not fail to notice this. Edsel had insisted and Henry had been stubborn—but Edsel finally won out. In the end Henry still insisted that the "T" was good for three or more years.

As president of Ford Motor Company Edsel designed the Model "A" and saw it into production. His genius was proved by this feat although in the long run, he remained under the shadow of his famous father. Edsel knew that the three-speed sliding transmission, which had arrived in the past few years, sounded the death knell for the Model "T." As stated the changeover in production caused a period of time in which Ford lacked cars to sell. Chevrolet, backed by General Motors, came to the front. Buick, Dodge and others made serious inroads into the market. Because of this, Ford Motor Company was in financial trouble. Had Edsel made a mistake? The answer came when Ford introduced the famous Ford Phaeton late in 1928 and it created a sensation. Some dealers had managed to obtain early Model "A's" and showed them before Ford did so officially. This caused concern to the Ford people but mushrooming sales dimmed memories. A new age of "Fordism" had arrived.

And Ford history is preserved for all to see. The Edison Institute, Henry Ford Museum and Greenfield Village are modern tourist attractions at Dearborn. "A living history of America" is a fitting title for this panorama of Americana. Situated on 260 acres of Dearborn, the magnificent collection is located just minutes from the center of Detroit. Over 1.5 million persons visit annually—a tribute to the far-sightedness of Henry Ford. There is much to see and do and remember and to believe in.

"The careful choice of penny candy in the General Store, hushed appreciation of a building where scientists or housewives lived in centuries past, studious understanding of a steam engine or power loom which advanced the Industrial Revolution, reading of historic documents, pure personal enjoyment of beautiful silver, pewter, china and glass—all these are among the reasons adults and children come to Henry Ford Museum and Greenfield Village again and again.

"As the seasons change, schedules change. A visitor who one day in July enjoyed the crowds, the steamboat, Model 'T' rides and blooming Village gardens, may come again for a November walking tour, a January sleigh ride, or an evening lecture, a Sunday film or week-day forum in the Museum."[79]

Those visiting this complex of Americana during May 22-24, 1969, were treated to the added spectacle of the *County Fair*. This "annual fair at Greenfield Village embodies many of the features that made these occasions festive: displays of livestock, athletic contests, demonstrations, side shows, and the award of prizes for entries of home arts, crafts, and collections. The County Fair of Yesteryear is history at its liveliest, made available to all youngsters as an extension of the educational services of the Henry Ford Museum." John H. Brickner, Assistant Superintendent of Maintenance, although busy supervising a display on the lawn of the Wright Brothers' home, was kind enough to help answer an important question: What happened to Ford Airport? First he suggested that a walk be made down Christie Avenue across the Ackley Covered Bridge and then down South Dearborn Avenue to the location of the Cape Cod Windmill. This giant "knight killer" had been brought to Greenfield Village from West Yarmouth, Mass. The walk that Brickner suggested takes one past the Cotswold group: reconstructed English stone houses, sheds and blacksmith shops that Ford brought from England stone by stone.

Standing on a rise near the huge windmill what appeared to be the surface of a runway could be seen partially in the level field lying almost due south. Yet, it certainly did not look like an airport.

Skipping lunch Brickner invited us to accompany him. He drove down Bagley Avenue, across Main Street where he met Robert C. Koolakian, the youthful curator of Ford Museum. At the time, Koolakian was driving a green Ford Model "A" pickup truck. After a cordial welcome by him the drive continued down Bagley Avenue. Turning at the Lapeer Machine Shop, we proceeded around the Harahan Sugar Mill past the Tripp Sawmill to the rear of the Education building that houses both the Ford Museum and the Edison Institute. (Ford's admiration for his friend Edison prompted the name.)

After entering the massive building from the rear, Brickner walked quickly through the power plant section with its polished brass valves and heating turbines. The huge electrical heating complex serves the main buildings.

Entering the back of the museum a panorama of the interior unfolded. Power plants, airplanes, a full-size ship, steam engines—a collection that staggers the imagination.

In the airplane collection sits a low wing plane with the word "Junkers" painted on the side in black. This is the *Bremen* that prompted a German, and an Irish priest, to become embroiled with each other in far-off Davis, West Virginia, in 1928. To reiterate, the first east-west crossing of the

Atlantic had been made in the plane on April 12-13, 1928, just 77 days before the start of the balloon race at Ford Airport. (See Figure 6.)

The *Bremen* has six small pipe manifolds running out of each side of the hood which then curve to the rear. At the point where the wing joins the fuselage the thickness is a full 20 inches. This low wing monoplane has curved-up tips at the end of each wing. Compared with the polished sheen of modern planes, the corrugated washboard hide of the craft is surprising. (See Figure 42.) The small windows of the cockpit are smashed in as though some huge object had dropped upon it at one time. It had been caused at the time of the landing of the *Bremen* at the end of its historic flight. On the right side of the plane is found "D1167-Bremen." Painted on the right rudder is "W33B/2504." The elevator of the ship is made of sandwiched, riveted aluminum. There is no airfoil to the elevator and control wires are missing.

A small 1½ inch x 2 inch brass plate riveted to the lower left forward edge of the fuselage—but behind the engine— carries the following:

"Fabrik No. 2504
28.7.27
Bremen."

It is the birth certificate of a famous airplane.

The propeller is two-bladed with surprisingly little pitch. The Junkers' triangle symbol is located on the front of each blade. The relatively small prop pulled the *Bremen* and its three brave passengers on a trip that exceeded 2,000 miles. It was one of the first all-metal low-wing monoplanes and three flyers were very lucky.

Across the aisle from the *Bremen* sits the *Stinson-Detroiter.* The first diesel-powered flight was made in the plane on September 19, 1928. The engine had been designed by Captain L. M. Woolson and the plane was flown by Walter Lees, a Packard pilot.

Near this plane sits a white and red striped airplane inscribed "U. S. Air Mail, Varney Speed Line, In Southwest Division." The first mention of Ford Airport since entering the building was made. Brickner remarked, "This plane landed at Ford Airport in 1968. After being disassembled it was brought here and reassembled." But where was Ford Airport?

Brickner led the way straight across the vast building, past the souvenir stands to the main entrance. He passed the cornerstone under the giant chandelier, said "hello" to several guards and turned up the carpet-covered stairs that led to the second floor. After passing the first car made by Ford (preserved under glass), he passed several giant blown-up photos of Ford, Edsel, Henry II and other famous persons. (On the second floor of this amazing building the Henry Ford personal history exhibit is found.) Unlocking a heavy door, Brickner proceeded inside. A long series of carpeted offices with glass-top walnut desks occupy the rooms behind the door. While not plush by some standards, the offices were well-furnished and obviously efficient working areas. To the right of the first office was a table-desk affair that contained literature to be distributed to visitors of this "open book of American history." (A visit there exceeds the adventures of "Alice in Wonderland" by a wide margin. When one steps into the front entrance of the vast complex, he is walking upon the printed lines of paragraphs taken from the best American history books.)

The mystery of the whereabouts of Ford Airport was beginning to mount. Since it had been a major airdrome in the mid-east in 1928 it was highly unlikely that it had been swept away by urban housing, or replaced by the monstrous building in which we now stood. It was even more unlikely that the airport would be found on the second floor of the Edison Institute and Henry Ford Museum!

A fleeting recollection brought before the mind's eye a map of the Dearborn section of Detroit. Sprawling across one side of the map was a huge block of real estate, blocked in by thousands of streets, and listing such names as Dearborn, Dearborn Heights, Inkster, Allen Park, Melvindale, Lincoln Park and others. Two main roads—Southfield Freeway and Detroit Industrial Freeway—pour thousands of cars into the area each hour. In the center of the vast conglomerate of humanity and industrial activity is a vast parcel of land called "Dearborn." Looking at this parcel from the south it could be broken up into three rough areas. To the left Ford Field, Edsel Ford High School, Levagood Park, the Dearborn Country Club and the Sacred Heart Shrine. To the right Ford Motor Company—River Rouge Plant (with guided tours)—the Civic Center; the beautiful 13-story Ford Central Office Building (the point from which the guided tours begin); Loverix Park; Fordson High School and St. Alphonsus High School. In the center Henry Ford Community College, University of Michigan, Dearborn Center, Henry Ford Museum and Greenfield Village State Historical Site. Adjoining this, Ford Proving Grounds identified on the north by Village Road. A high, thick red brick wall acts as a barrier and the road separates the visitors' area from the flat, inner, highly-secret fields of Ford Proving Grounds.

The oval track of the proving grounds is shaped like a giant kidney with the dished-in side of the "kidney" cuddling Village Road which in turn provides an "Iron Curtain" for the footloose who visit Greenfield Village.

But where was Ford Airport?

In the center of Ford Proving Grounds are found many concrete pads and speedways. "Some have been repaved as many as twelve times," Brickner noted. Competitors in the automobile industry have taken photos from the air in hopes of predicting the shape—and style—of the newest Ford cars. Since Ford was—and is—a leader, competitors are inclined to spy.

Brickner wheeled to the right and entered a very narrow

opening. Carefully plastered (as was the remainder of the room) the shallow niche in the wall appeared suitable only for storage of wet umbrellas, overshoes and other miscellaneous gear of those who visited the office. Brickner instantly disappeared. He had moved into the wall through a narrow opening that had been constructed there. The opening was not visible from the office.

A very narrow, spiral steel staircase was encountered. Twenty-three narrow spiraling green metal steps wound their way to the next level where a large square room was found. With clear cautions from Brickner to "avoid that large round metal circle," the climb continued to the left. (One who might step upon the large circle would find himself falling through the majestic chandelier below and onto the cornerstone that bears the signature of "Thomas Alva Edison.")

The adventure continued. A series of 45-degree-plus ladders were encountered. Troop transports and other sailing ships are known for similar inconvenient ladders that separate the main decks from the living compartments below. Designed to move a man quickly to a hold, or to the deck, these stairs are always steep whether approached from below or above.

The ladders became uniform in number of iron steps as the platforms grew smaller. The platforms, or rooms, showed signs of invasion by many winged creatures.

One ladder led to a room surrounded by four circle-shaped glass clock faces, marked off in reverse Roman numerals from midnight to noon. The translucent surfaces of the four faces permitted light to flood the surfaces of the brass clock works located in the center of the room which systematically ticked away the seconds and minutes. Four round brass arms extended from the central works to the gears found at the base of the hour and minute hands of each of the four clock faces. The central works, being of Seth-Thomas manufacture, will record accurate time for years to come. The brass works of the timepiece carry the date of manufacture—1928.

Negotiating two more ladders, Brickner reached the level he was seeking. The size of the rooms had steadily decreased as the climb had progressed. Any room above the one where we stood would be too small for any practical use. Above was the columned portion of the steeple that supported the cupola roof. The curved small part of Ford's Independence Hall was capped by the long, tapering point that reached skyward.

One small porthole-type window admitted light to the front of the small room. At the backside of the room was a smaller than ordinary door which provided an exit. Brickner found—as he expected—that the door was swollen shut. It was soaked by the water that swirled about the tower during periods of rainfall. The roadblock was removed by a firm kick near the knob. Noon-hour sun flooded the room making it difficult to see for a few moments. Upon stepping carefully through this door a balcony was encountered. Railed by wood beams painted white, the balcony circled the tower on all four sides. Below, the giant ribs and skylights of the massive roof of Edison Institute covered thousands of feet of land. Constructed in long flat-topped humps, the roof contained the skylights that helped illuminate the fabulous collection below. Proceeding to the left, Brickner was walking upon the tin roof of the middle steeple, which was painted a dull red. The metal of the roof gave way slightly under foot making a "popping sound" as the foot was lifted again.

Upon reaching the front of the tower, an impressive view unfolded. Now close to 200 feet above the ground, the view was the highest possible in the entire Ford complex—except for the Ford Office Building far to the left and behind Greenfield Village. In the left front distance, the skyscrapers of downtown Detroit peered through the haze that enveloped them as though making subtle inquiry into the state of affairs at Dearborn.

The low and large buildings of the Ford research and development facilities spread across open fields to the right. Surrounded by walls and massive iron fences, the castle-type gates carried signs with the pointed warning: "No cameras allowed." Below, across the main entry road, hundreds of automobiles were parked in the free parking lot for visitors. A constant stream of persons, large and small, and most camera-laden, moved in lines both to and from the entrance building.

Greenfield Village spread to the immediate left in all of its historical glory. One of the great accomplishments of man, the village of history is a must for every American. The strength of America lies in its heritage—and its heritage is here to see, to touch and walk within.

Directly in front was Ford Proving Grounds. The view of the restricted testing area was perfect. (See Figure 43.) Test cars were parked to the right. In the far right center, a man-made mountain rose from the floor for testing purposes. Ringing the proving grounds was the test track where the latest designs are placed to grueling rituals of destruction. Crossing the great expanse were two long lines of wide concrete. They crossed at an odd angle and it suddenly became apparent what John Brickner wanted to show. Ford Airport is now Ford Proving Grounds! (See Figure 43.)

The airfield is capable of being used by even large craft but few planes land there today. The old dirigible mast is gone— one minor victim of the changing times. The runways are there in form only and have been paved over many times. Ford executives keep their planes at the main Detroit Airport. A symbol of the good old days, a small windsock hangs unceremoniously at the far end of the field. Perhaps the Ford test drivers occasionally glance at it to determine if the wind is playing a part in the performance of the autos they are testing. But Ford Airport is no more.

Dearborn contains many items that tie it with Germany.

However, the balloon race story told here has not been one of them. The event was barely mentioned in the *Ford News* in 1928, apparently overshadowed by other events of the times. However, one of the autos in the car collection of some 300 pieces ties Dearborn solidly to Germany and World War I. It is possible that what is reported here was not intended for publication and for this reason, the informant is not disclosed. Before discussing the car itself, a thumbnail introduction is in order.

Edison Institute is divided into four basic blocks of exhibits with each block containing an unbelievable quantity of displays. As one enters the museum, the right-hand block contains the wheeled vehicles. To the far right are found bicycles, motorcycles, tire machines and engines. Next come sleighs, carriages, automobiles, locomotives, buggies, boats, trains (full size), trucks, wagons and, at the end of the aisle near the right back wall, aircraft. It is here that the *Bremen* and the other displays sit and hang from the ceiling. The automobiles are formed in several rows and include a Tucker, all types of Fords and many, many others. Between two of these rows, hidden by the cars in front of it, is a strange auto, sitting on blocks. There are no signs to identify it and one must climb over the aisle ropes to reach it.

The auto has an open driver's seat up front with a spare tire mounted on the right side. A large press-handle chromed brake occupies a place on the right fender. Oil drips from the auto at two places and pans catch the oil on the floor. The passenger section of the long machine is enclosed with a flat (bullet proof?) window separating passengers from the driver. There is an extra seat in the rear upon which a person could sit, back to the driver. An ancient Parisian-type phone connects the rear compartment with the front. On each side at the rear are oval windows much like those on the 1929 Ford Business Coupe.

The inside of the auto is lined with red velvet folded

drapes that at one time closed all view from the outside when drawn. The large tires are smooth as glass and never carried any tread. The door handles on the inside are of intricately carved ivory. The interior is all inlaid with teak, French walnut and other scarce wood. White inlays dot the paneling.

The door handles on the outside are shaped like dragons and appear to be solid silver. The wheels are spoke type and chrome plated. Three exhaust vents run from each side of the long tapering hood. The front of the auto is pointed, much like early racers. It is a unique machine—fit for a king. Sitting only 75 feet from the *Bremen*—it was the personal car of the Kaiser Wilhelm. Undoubtedly museum authorities plan an appropriate display for the historical item. In the meantime, it sits almost hidden—resting in the glory of better military days.

The *Brandenburg's* flight line that had so precisely tied the "Land of Ford" to the "Land of Canaan" has taken its place among the almost forgotten events of days gone by. The teeming throngs that saw the race begin; the youthful Germans who flew the ship; Henry Ford, Edsel and many of the others have passed down the footpath of time. But the story remains—the flight line is still there and the link survives.

Part of the link is the Davis Power Plant on display at Ford Museum. Personal contact with Robert C. Koolakian at Dearborn brought a negative answer on the question of the power plant. Stating, "We do not classify our accessions according to place of origin," he apologized for not being of further help. A subsequent letter from Henry E. Edmunds, Director, Ford Archives, dated June 25, 1969, states: "In answer to your second inquiry about a power plant from Davis, W. Va., our Registrar's office reports that it has no record of it under that name. I am sorry that I cannot be more helpful."

A copy of Cooper's letter has been forwarded to Ford Museum and will no doubt allow the power plant to be prop-

erly identified for those who may be interested in seeing it in
the future.

Today Detroit and Windsor—the international sister
cities—are teeming with industrial—and night life—activity.
Canada's southernmost city, with about 200,000 population,
has more night life per capita than any U. S. city. Entertainment is a major industry there. Four major nightclubs offer
floor shows with perpetual big-name entertainment. Windsor-
ites also take great pride in education and culture and the
University of Windsor continues a remarkable growth pattern. The Hiram Walker International Museum on Pitt Street
West and the Willistead Art Gallery in the Walkersville section
are major attractions. At the Windsor Raceway on Highway
18 West, harness racing is conducted all winter long. Mario's
of Windsor on Quellette Avenue, is a favorite dining spot.

In downtown Detroit, the Cedars offers three shows night-
ly in exotic Middle Eastern surroundings. Racing is popular at
such tracks as the Wolverine Raceway and Hazel Park. The
Dee-Cee will carry you on a sight-seeing boat tour while the
Leland House at 400 Bagley advertises that it has nine law-
yers, five reporters, four starlets, 41 airline hostesses, five
football players and many more (416 others) living there.
The sister city area is ablaze with lights day and night, flooded with people and autos constantly—bustling with industrial
activity—and yet mindful of the past and the things that
happened there in an age gone by.

At Newton Falls, *The Herald*, advertises "Ninety-Four
Years of Service to the Area," and reports on the matters of
modern times. Citizens chastise city council and the city
manager over traffic problems; new sewer construction is
costing more than expected; some 400 fail to file city income
tax returns; the sewage disposal plant is seeking more workers; the zoning commission refuses to grant a variance; dogs
are inoculated at a scheduled time and life goes on as new
generations prepare to take the place of the old.

At another Ohio town, 200 miles west of Newton Falls, rests another of the parts of the story that are scattered to the winds. At the Wright-Patterson Air Force Base, Dayton, in the main U. S. Air Force Museum building, sits a little noticed trophy. This trophy was made of silver and shows five nude females with handsome figures—but hideous faces—climbing the spire as though reaching for stars shining through spiraling clouds above.

The trophy was cast in Belgium many years ago by Minkelers and donated by the Aero Club of Belgium. It is the James Gordon Bennett International Trophy that came to America permanently upon the strength of Kepner's win in 1928. The plate on the front lists his winning flight as having covered 460.9 miles.

Today as one drives from Richfield, Ohio, up Route 21 to Cleveland, Mike Zappone's Cortina is observed on the left. It is designed similar to an Italian villa at Cortina d'Ampezzo which is located just across the Austrian border from Italy and only a stone's throw from the border of Germany and Austria. At the main entrance of Zappone's restaurant is an arched door constructed with mortar and brick. Enclosing the front of this arch is a locked iron gate. Inside are large bottles with candles surrounded by the melted drippings of thousands of former tapers. On the wall is an "X" shaped rack of wine and champagne. The Alpine atmosphere is complete with stag horns, two-seated booths and overhead carved beams. In the corner of the large room is a medieval-type table with huge black chairs. Candles in amber goblets cast a red glow across a wine rack causing stained glass windows behind to shimmer in the night. Oval glass windows set in brick provide light from the outdoors while cast-iron bars grasp carved containers holding arrangements of beautiful flowers. It is almost Brandenburg country.

At Pittsburgh today, a great physical change is taking place. The almost Herculean efforts of those farsighted members of the Allegheny County, Pittsburgh, DAR of 1900 have blossomed into fruits that they hoped for—but might never have thought possible. Sparked by the "Renaissance of Pittsburgh"—a knock-down drag-out operation that forced the cleanup of the city—a flame was ignited that has engulfed the debris that once so horribly covered the "Golden Triangle" in the heart of the magnificent city.

The "mopping up" started in 1895. Limited to a very small area around the blockhouse initially, it has swept from the redoubt to the forks of the rivers. While two rusting relics of bridges still span each river near the point (see Figure 45), new gleaming bridges further back arch to the North Side, to a new stadium and to the new Fort Pitt tunnels. Now that the new bridges are in place the old will come down, leaving a magnificent open parcel of land for final development of Point Park.

At Gateway Center—home of KDKA radio and television, the Pittsburgh Hilton and others—the concrete span across the point carries a steady flow of traffic in all directions. Approaching Point Park from between the skyscrapers of the city, one encounters gently curving walkways which lead toward dull-yellow bronze plaques that describe what is in front of the visitor. The ancient moats are exposed once again in their original locations and those so inclined can walk along the weathered brick walls as they slant and turn across the clipped grass lawns that surround them.

The curving walls converge under a gentle curved concrete arch over which the heavy traffic flows almost unnoticed. Under this arch a wide, gently arched footbridge spans shallow water that runs under it. In the water are thousands of round stones side by side, resembling a cobblestone street of other years submerged by a heavy rainfall. Leaving the underpass one encounters branching walkways that spread across the lovely fields of Point Park. Immediately to the left is the old blockhouse serving as a souvenir shop. Beyond it and

close to the highway is the Fort Pitt Museum. Here, the early
years of Pittsburgh can almost be relived.

> The Forks of the Ohio River, modern Pittsburgh's
> "Golden Triangle," was an eighteenth-century magnet
> attracting Indians, trappers, land-hungry men, and the
> imperial armies of Britain and France. So intense was
> the competition that, within ten years, four successive
> forts were built on the site. The last one, Fort Pitt,
> symbolized England's victory and the removal of the
> French and Indian barrier to westward expansion. In the
> next 50 years, Pittsburgh boomed with the business of
> merchants and traders who provisioned the flatboats
> and wagons of the settlers who headed west.
> The Fort Pitt Museum, built on the site of one of the
> bastions of the original Fort Pitt, recounts this tale of
> men and events and emphasizes the most colorful chap-
> ter in the history of the Forks, the French and Indian
> War, whose outcome helped determine the destiny of
> colonial America.[80]

At the top of the museum, reached by an angled walkway,
is a reconstructed bastion of hewed timber and earth housing
brass-barreled ship-type cannons that guard the fields of the
park below.

Immediately inside the museum is an artist's rendition of
the completed park. Capped by a circular fountain reaching
high into the air, the park is circled by broad concrete walkways where young and old can walk and enjoy the river
scenery, the passing boats and the concert bands that occupy
river barges there. (See Figure 44; compare with Figure 45.)

Set against a backdrop of some of the finest skyscrapers in
America, the park symbolizes the strength of America (as
well as the determination of Americans) and points the way
to a magnificent future. But the days of the Pittsburgh of
1928 will never be again.

At Salem, Lisbon, Pittsburgh, and Davis, West Virginia, the
complex affairs of men in a modern society continue to some
form of conclusion. Crimes are committed, divorces are

granted, and the young are trying to learn all of the things that the old had difficulty learning. And the flight of the *Brandenburg* serves as an invisible line that ties all of these cities, towns and persons together. The bond is slight and some might refuse to acknowledge that the bond exists. And yet (as in all affairs of man) that which has happened is history and history remains to be viewed occasionally—if at all—by those who would look at it. But so it is with all events—large and small. Some of man's tales are told and most are not. But in the end, everything that could be said becomes part of the same story.

April 9, 1969, was a muddy, sunny day. Outside Davis drifts of banked snow dotted the shady sides of the hills and crevices. To the left, the old road and iron bridge over which the Coopers, Raeses and Browning raced on their rescue mission, sits abandoned and in advanced stages of deterioration. The new road has been finished for many years and takes one on a more direct route to the top of Canaan Mountain.

Further on and closer to the valley rim, a few homes have been constructed among large piles of broken stones that line the road on both sides. At various points signs indicate that hiking trails are available to those who would travel the rugged country on foot. At the edge of Canaan Mountain, the vast valley unfolds below like a giant billiard table surrounded by a crowd of humped-over players. (See Figure 46.) A sign gives the elevation as 3,846 feet. A soft wind blows in a northeasterly direction and a mild rustle runs through the barren trees on the side of the nearest ridge. Mixed with the mild wind comes a strange silence. The sounds of a busy day elsewhere are not heard here. A strange feeling crosses one's mind once this is realized. The hushed silence continues until broken by the harsh roar of a heavily loaded tractor trailer or car beginning its climb up the side of Canaan Mountain from either direction.

At the Graham farm, Myrtle Edwards lives in a new home

near the old Graham residence. Her sister has constructed a split-level home on the family property to the right of her house and on a little knoll. The view of the valley is splendid from there. From the picture window of Myrtle's home, Cabin Mountain looms up to 4,000 feet and fills the small colonial panes of the glass. She points to the range and remembers the trestles long since gone. The logging train that came down the length of Cabin Mountain past the house where she now lives is part of faded history. (See Figure 47.)

A ski resort complex is planned for one ridge on Cabin Mountain and the acquisition of property is under way. The screaming of logging trains; the crash of timber and smoke and ashes of loggers' fires will be replaced in the wintertime by the laughter of new generations on the ski slopes of Cabin Mountain.

In the summer, horseback riding has become a favorite pastime. In coming years the former wilderness of the grand valley will be nothing but a memory.

The second growth of timber is under way and the dead trees that captured a German airship so many years ago provide nourishment for new life. Clouds drift lazily through thin tops of young pines. The rivers, rivulets and streams join forces to continue the spectacle of Blackwater Falls. A fifty-six room, Bavarian style, state-operated lodge permits a spectacular view over the 500-foot deep Blackwater Canyon. With ice skating and tobogganing in the winter, horseback riding and trail hiking in the summer, it is a year-round vacation spot. (See Figure 48.)

At Weiss Knob and Cabin Mountain skiing draws the young from across the nation. Coolness in the summertime provides relief for those who suffer from sinus and hay fever problems and many come for that purpose alone.

A 1,500-foot sled run, with rope tow, is operated at Blackwater Falls State Park. The park also offers ice skating and the sled run often doubles as a ski slope. The

natural beauty of Blackwater during the winter makes it
the perfect setting for the annual Tucker County Alpine
Festival . . . Lodging is available at Blackwater Lodge,
the park cabins and at hotels and motels in the area.

West Virginia skiers will have a new facility by the
1970-71 season, Canaan Valley State Park, near Blackwater Falls. Construction has been started on the complex which includes a main slope lift of over 3,000 feet
with an intermediate 925-foot lift for beginners.

The main base facility will consist of a ski fitting and
rental area, pro shop, lounge and sales area, snack bar
and dining room, first aid and nursery facilities. Also
included in plans are a campground with 34 sites.[81]

A bright future awaits Davis and Canaan Valley. Someday
soon the population will begin a rise that will pass the all-
time high realized during the timbering days and the "Gem of
the Alleghenies" will be polished (once more) to a brilliant
luster.

And so (as Vivian Y. Laramore beautifully stated), we
must close the door on the flight of the *Brandenburg* and
throw the key away, *cause tomorrow holds so much for us—*
we *should* be happy with today.

Figure 1. Unidentified Tucker County youths following a "wreck."—Origin of photo unknown

Figure 3. The Wright Brothers' Cycle Shop as it now stands at Greenfield illage, Dearborn, Michigan. It was brought here from Dayton, Ohio, and recon-ructed.—Photo by author

Figure 4. The famous Wr? Spirit of St. Louis, in which Lindbergh flew the Atlantic. From

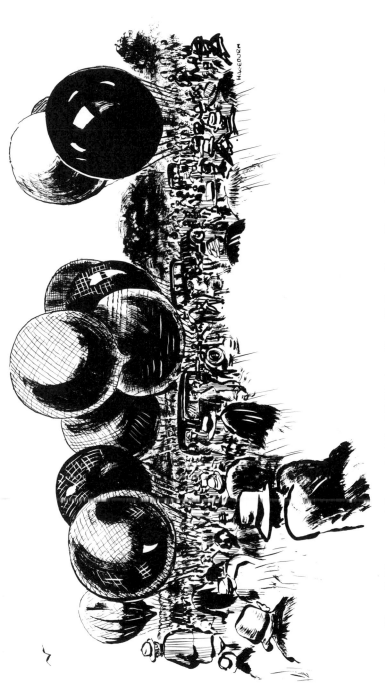

Figure 5. The scene at the start of the 1928 International Balloon Race.—Drawing by O. Dale Hagedorn

Figure 6. The *Bremen*, manufactured by "Junkers" as it now sits at the Edison Institute.

23127

Figure 7. Lt. Frank Luke of Arizona, "The Balloon Buster."—Photo by
U. S. Signal Corps, No. 111-SC-23127

Figure 8. Bayard 7.65 automatic, serial number 137820. Notice broken handle on top of right grip. Forward of ejector is the number "24."—Photo by Superior Photos, Morgantown, West Virginia

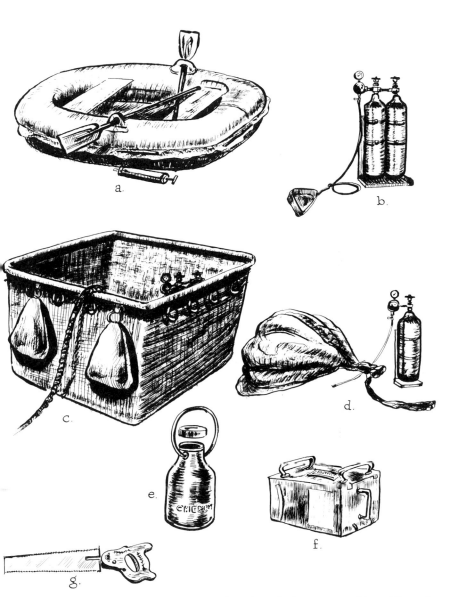

Figure 9. Equipment carried on the *Brandenburg:* a. rubber life raft;
b. oxygen bottles and face mask; c. the wicker basket with ballast; d. hydrogen
bottle with small balloon; e. aluminum liquid can with sealed top; f. statoscope
with glass bubble and g. the saw used in an attempt to save the flight.—Drawing
by O. Dale Hagedorn

Figure 10. Lieutenant Quentin Roosevelt, second from left, returning from his Nieuport 28 after combat flight. Issoudun, December 12, 1917.—Photo by U. S. Signal Corps, No. 111-SC-80210 in the National Archives

Figure 11. Chaplain Francis P. Duffy, Colonel Frank A. McCoy and Lieutenant William P. T. Preston, holding services at the grave of Roosevelt, August 9, 1918, some 26 days following his death. The names of the enlisted men are unknown.—Photo by U. S. Signal Corps, No. 111-SC-18910 in the National Archives

Figure 12B. This photo was taken just seconds after Figure 12A. Both observers landed safely.—Photo by U. S. Signal Corps, No. 111-SC-19118 in the National Archives

Figure 12A. Rare World War I combat photo of American observation balloon under air attack with the observers leaving the stricken balloon by way of parachute. See Figure 12B.—Photo by U. S. Signal Corps, No. 111-SC-19116 in the National Archives

Figure 12C. Enemy observation balloon falling from the sky in flames. Photo taken from French artillery

Figure 13A. Lieutenant F. J. Grant, maneuver officer, discussing enemy position with Lieutenant R. K. Patterson, observer. Second Balloon Company, Montreuil, July 8, 1918. Notice the striking "WW II appearance" of Patterson, and the map holder on side of gondola.—Photo by U. S. Signal Corps, No. 111-SC-16950 in the National Archives

Figure 13B. Observation balloon, crew and filling apparatus, France, 1918.—Photo by U. S. Signal Corps, No. 111-SC-10276 in the National Archives.

Figure 14. "The Land of Castles." American Second Division Officers on the Rhine, 1918.—
Photo by U. S. Signal Corps. No. 111-SC-44308 in the National Archives

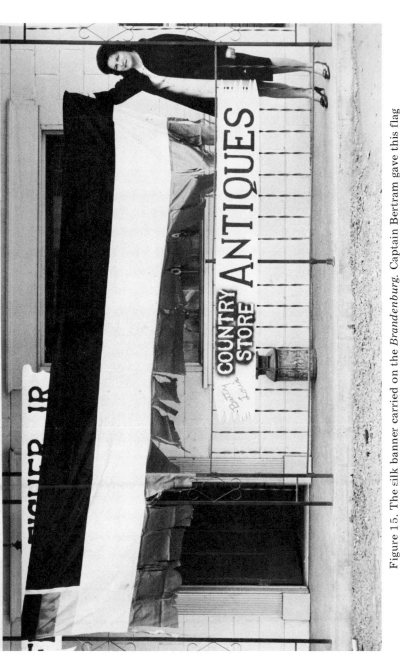

Figure 15. The silk banner carried on the *Brandenburg*. Captain Bertram gave this flag to James Browning as a souvenir.—Photo courtesy of James Browning

Figure 16. Equipment carried on the *Brandenburg:* a. the Bayard automati b. the drag rope; c. fish hooks carried in the emergency kit; d. flashlight; e. wo blankets; f. the sheath knife of the lieutenant and g. the captain's pack.—Dra ing by O. Dale Hagedorn

Figure 17. Lake Erie as seen from a point approximately where the *Brandenburg* made Cleveland land-fall.—Photo by author

Figure 18. The Trumbull County covered bridge, located at Newton Falls, Ohio.—Photo by author

Figure 19. The main street at Newton Falls.—Photo by author

Figure 20. Salem, Ohio. The flight pattern of the *Brandenburg* was
at right angles to this main street.—Photo by author

Figure 21. Lisbon, Ohio. Notice the white steeple of the courthouse.—
Photo by author

Figure 22. The mighty Ohio River as seen from East Liverpool, Ohio. Across
the water is Chester, West Virginia. Notice the mountain ranges.—Photo by
author

Figure 23. Blackwater Coal Company tipple, Davis, West Virginia, 1925.—Source not known

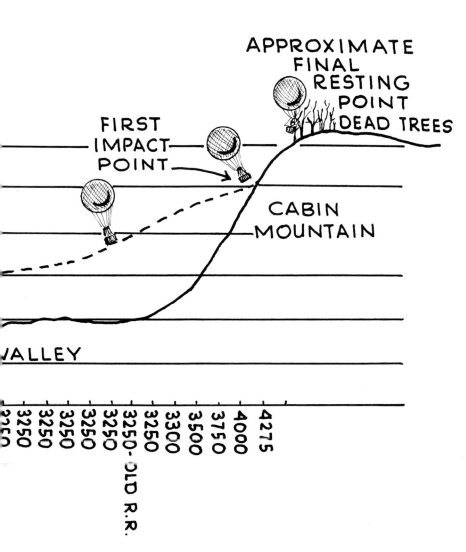

APPROXIMATE
FINAL
RESTING
POINT
DEAD TREES

FIRST
IMPACT
POINT

CABIN
MOUNTAIN

VALLEY

3250
3250
3250
3250
3250
3250
3250-OLD R.R.
3250
3300
3500
3750
4000
4275

Figure 24. Side angle drawing of the path of the *Brandenburg* as it crossed Tucker County. At the left of the drawing are the altitudes in feet. Along the bottom edge are the elevation readings taken from a geological survey map. Cabin Mountain looms ahead like a giant wall.— Drawing by O. Dale Hagedorn

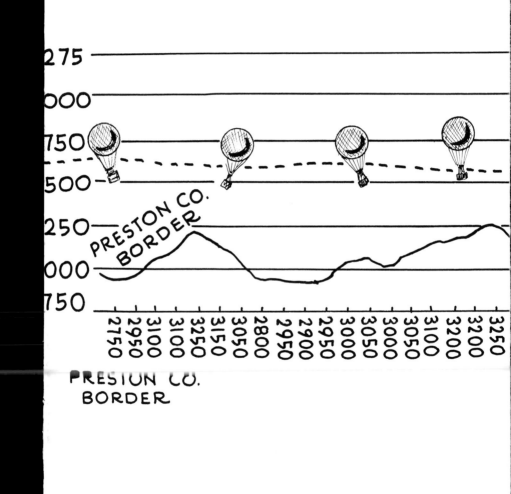

275

000

750

500

250

000

750

PRESTON CO.
BORDER

2750
2950
3100
3100
3250
3150
3050
2800
2950
2900
2950
3000
3050
3000
3050
3100
3200
3200
3250

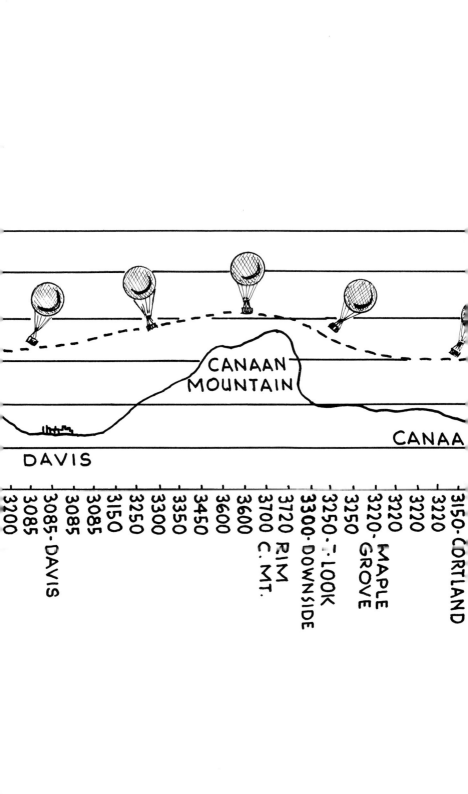

CANAAN
MOUNTAIN

CANAA

DAVIS

3150-CORTLAND
3220
3220
3220-MAPLE
3250-GROVE
3250
3250-LOOK
3300-DOWNSIDE
3720-RIM
3700-C. MT.
3600
3600
3450
3350
3300
3250
3150
3085
3085
3085-DAVIS
3085
3200

Figure 25. The Verzi Saloon, Davis, West Virginia, 1910. Notice the empty beer kegs waiting shipment to the brewery. The Pennsylvania House in the first building to the left in the photo. — Origin of photo unknown

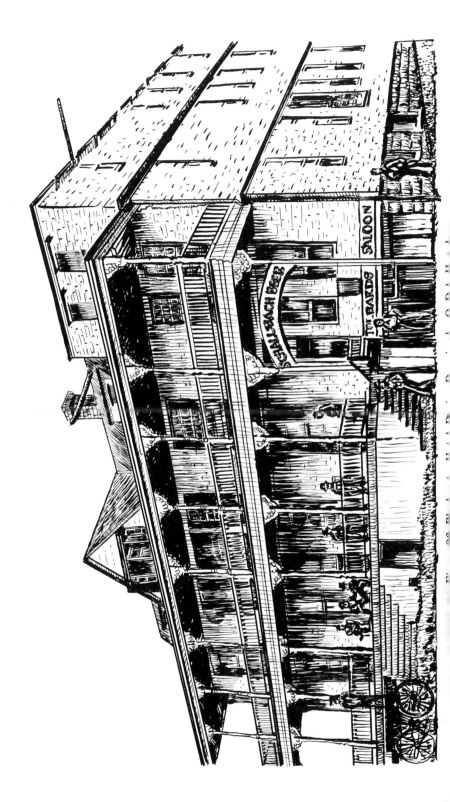

Figure 23 Ballard's Hall. Drawing by Robin Loznak

Figure 27. Davis, West Virginia, as the town is approached from the Thomas de. Notice the lack of trees and the mountain range in the distance.—Photo by uthor

igure 28. The Saint John Lutheran Church is on the right on Third Street. This street is parallel with the line of flight of the airship.—Photo by author

Figure 29. Photo taken July 1, 1928, on Seventh Street, Davis, West Virginia, of one of two racing balloons passing overhead. It is not known whether this the *Brandenburg* or the French *Blanchard.*—Photo courtesy of Robert Raese, Davis, West Virginia

Figure 30. The Canaan Valley as seen from the floor. Notice Cabin Mountain about five miles to the front, and the three giant knobs rolling into the sky from the valley.—Photo by author

Figure 31. The pond where J. C. Graham trained his trout. On the left, James Cooper, who is obviously interested in what he sees in the pond; in the center, Fay Graham who is feeding these trout and Mrs. Betty Goodwin on the right. Notice the sled in the back of the photo and the action within the water. —Photo by author

Figure 32.

"The *Brandenburg* was going across
The Valley of Canaan,
Where timberman and his big boss
Stripped God's forests from the land "

Figure 33. The *Brandenburg* is down. Notice the netting in the tree to the right.—Photo courtesy of James Browning

Figure 34. Notice the top valve cover. Captain Bertram with hand on hips at center of fallen balloon.—Photo courtesy of James Browning

Figure 35. Another view of the stricken airship. The top valve cover is clear visible here. The captain is leaning on his ship.—Photo courtesy of James Brov ing

Figure 36. Captain Bertram (holding the statoscope from his ship) and Lieutenant Frobel. The auto is a 1926 Studebaker Commander owned by John Raese. The license number is 33-959. July 2, 1928.—Photo courtesy of Walter Raese

Figure 37. "Faith," "Rocket," the rock sled carrying the balloon, the rescue party and Cromwell Graham standing to the left holding his "souvenir," July 8, 1896. The rock sled carrying the balloon and Cromwell Graham standing to the left

Figure 28. The lieutenant and the captain at Blackwater Falls, July 3, 1928. They both enjoyed American cigarettes. —Photo courtesy of Robert Raese

Figure 39. The beautiful Falls of the Blackwater. — Photo by West Virginia Photo Co. — Thomas, W. Va.

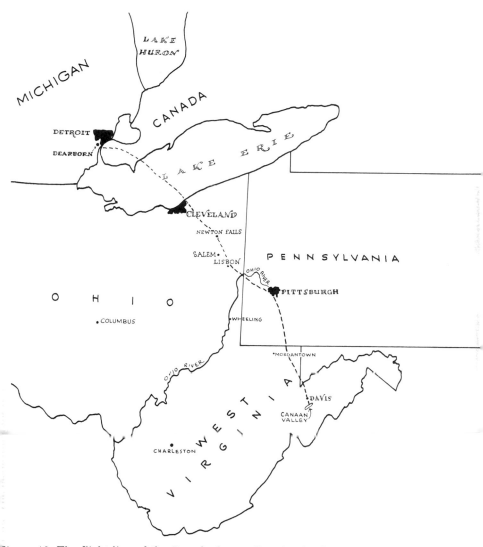

Figure 40. The flight line of the *Brandenburg*.—Drawing by O. Dale Hagedorn

A F F I D A V I T

STATE OF MARYLAND,
COUNTY OF _Garrett_ :

    This day before the undersigned Notary Public appeared J.S. Cooper, who after being duly sworn according to law, stated as follows:

    1. That on Sunday, July __1__ , 1928, in the latter part of the day at about _6:30_ P.M., he observed two racing balloons in the vicinity of Davis, West Virginia, in Tucker County. One balloon carried two men who were dumping sand over the side of the balloon basket.

    2. That he followed these balloons believing that both would not clear the mountain range near Davis, this being the highest municipality in the State of West Virginia.

    3. That he traveled to a mountain range about _12_ miles from Davis, and proceeded up the mountain through briars and heavy underbrush, causing damage to his clothes and shoes.

    4. That he came upon the balloon that had been dumping sand, finding it being snagged on tall, barren trees that had been long dead.

    5. That there he found two German aviators in the process of bedding down for the night and their names were Captain Otto Bertram and Lieutenant George Frodnel.

    6. That this balloon found there was the official entry of Germany in the James Gordon Balloon Races that had started from Detroit on June 30, 1928, and this balloon carried the name "Bradenburg."

    7. That a 7.65 caliber "Bayard" pistol, made in Belgium, bearing serial number 137820, was in the survival kit given him by one of the aviators as they came off the mountain.

    8. That this pistol further carried the carved number "24" on the right front.

    9. That Captain Otto Bertram told him that he had carried this pistol at the burial of a fallen American aviator by the name of Roosevelt and that his burial was made in France during World War I.

    10. That Captain Otto Bertram told him that he had flown for Germany in World War I and had been machine gunned in the leg.

J. S. Cooper
J.S. Cooper

    Taken, subscribed and sworn to, before me in my said County, this _6_ day of March, 1969.

Notary

My Commission expires:

Figure 41. Affidavit of J. S. Cooper.

Figure 42. The *Bremen*, another view. —Photo by author

Figure 43. Ford Airport, now Ford Proving Grounds. Taken from the tower

Figure 44. An artist's conception of "Point" at Pittsburgh after it is completed. This is a snapshot of the painting that hangs inside the museum at Point Park.—Photo by author

Figure 45. Compare with the artist's conception, Figure 44. This photo was taken at Grandview Avenue on Mount Washington at the intersection of Plymouth Avenue, Pittsburgh, Pennsylvania.—Photo by author

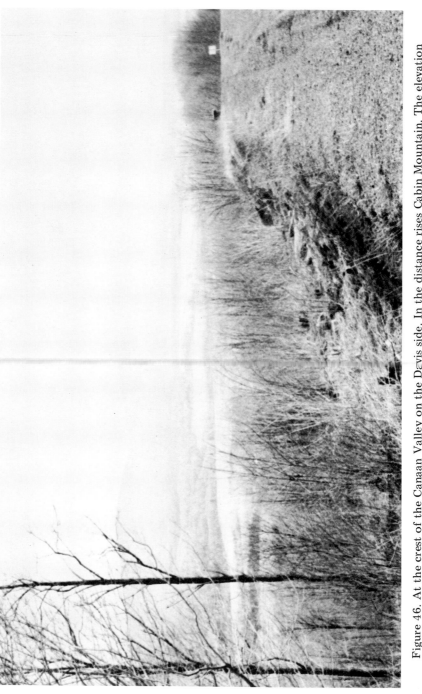

Figure 46. At the crest of the Canaan Valley on the Davis side. In the distance rises Cabin Mountain. The elevation

Figure 47. Winter in the Canaan Valley, 1969. Left to right: J. S. Cooper, Fay Graham and James Cooper. In the background Cabin Mountain begins its rise from the Graham farm.—Photo by author

Figure 48. Mark, John, Matthew and Luke Goodwin (left to right) from the wooden walkway overlooking a summertime Blackwater Falls. July 3, 1969, 41 years after the visit of the

NOTES

1. Aeronaut—the pilot or navigator of a balloon or dirigible. From "aero" and Greek "nautes"—a sailor.

2. I am indebted to Frederick Lewis Allen and his books, *Only Yesterday* and *The Big Change 1900-1950*, as sources of material for this chapter.

3. Frederick Lewis Allen, *The Big Change 1900-1950*, page 128.

4. Frederick Lewis Allen, *Only Yesterday*, page 21.

5. *Ibid.*, page 99.

6. On July 2, 1918, Ernest Udet, Commander of the Bavarian Bluetails, downed Lt. Walter B. Wanamaker of the U. S. Army. The air battle was fought over the Chateau-Thierry battlefield of France. On September 6, 1931, Wanamaker, a judge in Akron, Ohio, went to Cleveland to see Udet perform as a stunt flyer in the air races. Udet presented to Wanamaker a portion of the tail of his World War I plane bearing the number *N6347*.

7. The story of her death at the hands of the Japanese was not uncovered until the 1960's.

8. In later years an airplane owned by Amelia Earhart crash-landed off the center of the main street of Davis, Tucker County, West Virginia—but that is another story.

9. *The Newton Falls Herald*, Newton Falls, Ohio, Vol. 47, No. 23, June, 1928.

10. Letter from Mr. J. S. Cooper, Oakland, Maryland, dated June 2, 1969.

11. II Kings, 2:11.

12. *Amusing Things of Physics and Geometry*, Father Galien of Avigon.

13. Copy of letter at the United States Air Force Museum, Dayton, Ohio.

14. *Ibid.*

15. "The Fuhrer ordered Göring to bring the gallant island nation to its knees. The air assault was given the code name Adlerangriff—the Attack of the Eagles; and its opening day was to be Adler Tag: *Eagle Day.*" Richard Collier, *Eagle Day.* Avon Books, 1969.

16. Euripides, fragment.

17. The account is in the files at the Air Force Museum, Dayton, Ohio, and is published here for the first time. However, *The Detroit News*, Sunday, August 19, 1928, in the Metropolitan Section, carried a report of the flight, as told by Kepner's aide, Lieutenant William O. Eareckson to Dexter Haynes.

18. The "cap" rested in the rafters of a barn in West Virginia for almost forty years—to finally become a victim of the garbage pile.

19. As mentioned earlier, Captain William E. Kepner, as a major, piloted Explorer I as it lifted for outer space. After rupture of this giant bag, the pressurized capsule plunged earthward with two men within. Kepner heroically saved his trapped aide as he booted him from the capsule's hatch. Both parachuted to earth, "to fly again."

20. James R. Browning, Letter, dated May 7, 1969.

21. Bob Blake, Salem, Ohio, Letter, dated May 15, 1969.

22. D. R. Bates, "Composition and Structure of the Atmosphere," reprinted in *The Earth and Its Atmosphere*, Science Editions, Inc., New York, 1961, on page 97.

23. Adapted from Standard Pressure Tables.

24. Estimated from the temperature-altitude graph for atmosphere, Bates, Note 22 above, page 104.

25. Bates, above, page 97.

26. Eddie Rickenbacker, *Fighting the Flying Circus*, page 184.

27. *Ibid.*

28. The letter was sent to Mr. Heytz on October 3, 1969.

29. "Here rests on the field of honor, First Lieutenant Quentin Roosevelt, Air Services, USA, Killed in Action, July 14, 1918."

30. S. J. Duncan-Clark, *et al.*, *History's Greatest War*, E. T. Townsend, 1919, page 17.

31. Section VI, of Peace Terms and League of Nations. Duncan, *ibid.*, page 362.

32. H. H. Windsor, "International Balloon Race of 1907," *Popular Mechanics* (January, 1952), page 170.

33. At the death of Ford in 1947, his estate was appraised at $600,000,000.

34. All quotes about the *Brandenburg* and its adventures were taken from the Flight Log, carefully recorded during and after the flight by Captain Bertram. The record was fortunately located in Germany—it was not available in America.

35. Contemporary news report.

36. Numbers, 13:1-20.

37. Captain's Log.

38. Contemporary news report.

39. Contemporary news report.

40. The *Brandenburg*, at 1,600 meters, was reflecting the first rays of the July 1 sun.

41. *Neue Berliner Zeitung*, Berlin.

42. Corley McDarment, "Why Men Go Up in Balloons," *The Saturday Evening Post* (July 17, 1926).

43. *Ibid.*, page 20

44. Captain's Log.

45. James H. Lord, *An Economic Profile of Tucker County, West Virginia*, W.V.U., 1967, and the source of material for this chapter.

46. Stuart E. Brown, Jr., *Annals of Blackwater and the Land of Canaan (1746-1880)*, page 35.

47. Roy B. Clarkson, *Tumult on the Mountains*, McClain Printing Company, Parsons, West Virginia, 1964, page 15.

48. C. L. Perkins, *West Virginia Wildlife*, 7:5-7; 18-19;23, 1929.

49. Clarkson, page 8.

50. Brown, page 4.

51. *Tucker County Republican*, August 9, 1895.

52. Jack Preble, *Land of Canaan*, McClain Printing Company, Parsons, West Virginia, 1965, page 2.

53. Pamphlet: Mountain State Historical and Natural Museum, Davis, West Virginia, owner Joe McCleary.

54. *Ibid.*

55. J. S. Cooper missed his date—and so did the future Mrs. James Cooper and Mrs. Walter Raese. Today they realize that their menfolk played a part in West Virginia history that evening.

56. From the Captain's Log.

57. Preble, page 5.

58. Phillip Pendleton Kennedy, *Blackwater Chronicle*, 1853.

59. Homer Floyd Fansler, *History of Tucker County*, McClain Printing Company, Parsons, West Virginia, 1962, page 47.

60. *Ibid.*, page 77.

61. *Ibid.*, page 78.

62. *Ibid.*, page 596.

63. Captain's Log.

64. *Ibid.*

65. "For fortune hunters came and went, wasting priceless forests and the very ground beneath the trees. Since the establishment of the United States Forest Service, a great effort has been made to reclaim and reforest the exploited land. So successful have been these earnest efforts that once again the desert blossoms like a rose, the cool breezes rustle through forests of second growth spruce, hemlock, oak and beech, and the clear sprawling streams teem with fighting trout. It is once more the Land of Canaan." Preble, page 4.

66. Captain's Log.

67. *Ibid.*

68. Preble, page 5.

69. Captain's Log.

70. *Ibid.*

71. *Ibid.*

72. Preble, page 94.

73. Preble, page 96.

74. Seventeen more residents of Davis gave their lives in the Second War on battlefields that reached from the Philippines to Pearl Harbor; from France to Sicily; and from Italy to Germany itself. One of these young men, Cleon Wilson Raese, Jr., age 24, died in England of wounds on July 1, 1944, just 16 years to the day after the balloon crash near Davis. Two residents of Davis, Dominick Vozzo and Argil Harper Warner, and one resident of Canaan Valley, Ernest Wolford, died on German soil.

75. Captain's Log.

76. David Hunter Strother, "The Mountains," *Harper's New Monthly Magazine,* 1873, Porte Crayon.

77. Captain's Log.

78. Numbers, 13:1-20.

79. Brochure, Greenfield Village.

80. Brochure, Point Park, Pittsburgh.

81. *This Week* (Charleston, West Virginia: December 7, 1969), page 25.

BIBLIOGRAPHY

Books

Allen, Frederick Lewis. *Only Yesterday.* New York: Perennial Library, Harper and Row, 1931.

Barrett, William E. *The First War Planes.* Greenwich, Conn.: Fawcett Publications.

Bates, D. R., ed. *The Earth and Its Atmosphere.* New York: Scientific Editions, Inc., 1961.

Biddle, Major Charles J. *Fighting Airman: The Way of the Eagle.* New York: Ace Books, Inc., 1968.

Brown, Stuart E., Jr. *Annals of Blackwater and the Land of Canaan (1746-1880).* Berryville, Virginia: Chesapeake Book Company, 1959.

Cameron, Lou. *Iron Men With Wooden Wings.* New York: Belmont Productions, Inc., 1967. 174 pages.

Clarkson, Roy B. *Tumult on the Mountains.* Parsons, W. Va.: McClain Printing Company, 1964.

Collier, Richard. *Eagle Day.* New York: Avon Books, 1969.

Duncan-Clark, S. J. *History's Greatest War.* E. T. Townsend, 1919. E. J. Townsend and Underwood, 1919.

Eby, Cecil D., Jr. *Porte Crayon. The Life of David Hunter Strother.* Durham, N. C.: Seeman Printery, 1960.

Editors of American Heritage. *Men of Science and Invention.* New York. Perennial Library, Harper and Row, 1960.

Fansler, Homer Floyd. *History of Tucker County, West Virginia.* Parsons, W. Va.: McClain Printing Company, 1962.

Freidel, Frank. *Over There.* New York: Bramball House. MCMLXIV.

Hall, N. S. *The Balloon Buster: Frank Luke of Arizona.*

McWhirter, Norris and Ross, Dunlap. *Illustrated Encyclopedia of Facts.* New York: Bantam Books, 1969.

Millard, Joseph, ed. *True Civil War Stories.* Greenwich, Conn.: Fawcett Publications, Inc., 1961.

Morrow, William. *Morrow's Almanack, for the Year of Our Lord 1927-1928.* Rahway, N. J.: Quinn & Boden, 1927.

Platt, Frank C. *Great Battles of World War I: In the Air.* New York: Signet Books, 1966.

Rickenbacker, Eddie V. *Fighting the Flying Circus.* New York: Avon Books, 1967.

Roosevelt, Kermit, ed. *Quentin Roosevelt, A Sketch with Letters.*

Sweetser, Arthur. *The American Air Service.* 1919.

Thomson, David. *World History from 1914 to 1961.* New York: Oxford University Press, 1964.

Time Incorporated. *Time Capsule/1925.* New York.

Time Incorporated. *Time Capsule/1928.* New York.

Von Mises, Richard. *Theory of Flight.* New York: Dover Publications, Inc., 1959.

Magazine Articles

Airways, "Do's and Don'ts on Mountain Flying," March, 1969.

Flying, "Free Balloons Make Comeback," September, 1953.

Flying, "The Fine Old Art of Free Ballooning," June, 1955.

Holiday Inn Magazine, "Indy's Lighter Than Air Balloons," May, 1969.

Sports Flying, "The Greater Rockford Returns," May, 1969.

PERSONAL INTERVIEWS

James R. Browning
Morgantown, West Virginia

Reba I. Browning
Morgantown, West Virginia

R. A. Raese
Morgantown, West Virginia

Walter M. Raese
Morgantown, West Virginia

Pauline Raese
Morgantown, West Virginia

J. S. Cooper
Oakland, Maryland

Katherine Cooper
Oakland, Maryland

James C. Cooper, Jr.

Louise Cooper

Martin Luther Cooper

Fay Graham

Myrtle Edwards

William Sayger

Charles G. Worman

Mr. and Mrs. John J. Deutsch
Severna Park, Maryland 21146

(And many others who
chose to remain unnamed.)

CORRESPONDENCE MAILED OUT

February 13, 1969	Telegram, Martha Bertram, Celle West Germany
February 15, 1969	United States Air Force Museum
February 15, 1969	The German Consulate Washington, D. C.
March 3, 1969	J. S. Cooper Oakland, Maryland
March 8, 1969	Gemeinschaft "Alte Adler" Mühlig-Hofmann, West Germany
March 12, 1969	German Embassy Air Attache Washington, D. C.
March 17, 1969	Mrs. Ben Graham Fort Lauderdale, Florida
March 21, 1969	Hamburger Kreditbank Celle, West Germany
March 22, 1969	S. & D. Book Store, Inc. Indiana, Pennsylvania
March 23, 1969	J. S. Cooper
March 23, 1969	Mayor Davis, West Virginia
March 23, 1969	Mr. and Mrs. James C. Cooper, Jr.
March 29, 1969	National Archives Still Picture Branch Washington, D. C.
May 2, 1969	Joe McCleary Mountain State Museum Davis, West Virginia

May 7, 1969	Henry Ford Museum Dearborn, Michigan
May 8, 1969	O. Dale Hagedorn Anmoore, West Virginia
May 10, 1969	Bob Blake *The Salem News* Salem, Ohio
May 15, 1969	The Pennsylvania Hotel New York City
May 15, 1969	General Services Administration National Archives and Records Service ATTENTION: Collections Officer Washington, D. C. 20408
May 15, 1969	Fay Graham Canaan Valley Davis, West Virginia
May 15, 1969	S. & D. Bookstore, Inc. 16 S. 11th Street Indiana, Pennsylvania 15701
May 15, 1969	*The New York Times* New York City
May 15, 1969	Don Kersten Fort Dodge, Iowa
May 15, 1969	Robert C. Raese Davis, West Virginia
May 26, 1969	Bob Blake
May 26, 1969	Detroit Chamber of Commerce Detroit, Michigan
May 26, 1969	Wide World 50 Rockefeller Plaza New York City
May 29, 1969	Henry Ford Museum William Clay Ford, President Dearborn, Michigan
May 29, 1969	J. S. Cooper

May 31, 1969	Shultzie Book Store 80 4th Avenue New York City
July 11, 1969	Henry E. Edmunds Ford Archives Ford Museum Dearborn, Michigan
July 11, 1969	J. S. Cooper
July 22, 1969	Bob Blake
July 28, 1969	Stan Kloc Bureau of Business Research College of Commerce West Virginia University Morgantown, West Virginia 26506
July 31, 1969	Bob Blake
August 6, 1969	United States Air Force Museum Wright-Patterson Air Force Base Dayton, Ohio 45433
August 18, 1969	National Aeronautic Association Washington, D. C.
August 18, 1969	Director, Air Force Museum ATTENTION: Royal D. Frey
August 30, 1969	Air Force Museum
September 11, 1969	Air Force Museum Charles G. Worman, Historian
October 1, 1969	Lieutenant General William E. Kepner 1220 Madison Street Clarksville, Tennessee
October 2, 1969	Mr. and Mrs. James R. Browning
October 3, 1969	Burdick Heytz 4493 E. White Street Fresno, California
November 11, 1969	Lieutenant General William E. Kepner
January 25, 1970	*The New York Times*

CORRESPONDENCE RECEIVED

March 5, 1969	Werner H. Nuehrenberg, Major German Air Force
March 6, 1969	J. S. Cooper Oakland, Maryland
April 22, 1969	Martha Bertram Celle, West Germany
April 23, 1969	Ernst Matthiensen Dresdner Bank Celle, West Germany
May 15, 1969	Bob Blake *The Salem News* Salem, Ohio
May 15, 1969	Joe V. McCleary Mountain State Historical Museum Davis, West Virginia
May 20, 1969	Robert C. Koolakian Curatorial Assistant Communications and Power Department of Collections The Edison Institute Dearborn, Michigan
May 21, 1969	Shirley Baig *The New York Times* New York City
May 23, 1969	John C. Chambers Resident Manager The Statler Hilton (Formerly Pennsylvania Hotel) New York City
May 28, 1969	Meyer Goldbert Wide World Photos, Inc. 50 Rockefeller Plaza New York City 10020

June 2, 1969   J. S. Cooper
                               Oakland, Maryland

June 3, 1969   James W. Moore, Chief
                               General Services Administration
                               National Archives and Records Division
                               Washington, D. C.

June 3, 1969   Douglas H. Duer
                               S. & D. Bookstore, Inc.

June 4, 1969   Bob Blake

June 25, 1969   Henry E. Edmunds, Director
                               Ford Archives
                               Dearborn, Michigan

June 25, 1969   Robert C. Raese
                               Davis, West Virginia

June 25, 1969   James R. Browning
                               Morgantown, West Virginia

June 25, 1969   Mrs. James R. Browning
                               Morgantown, West Virginia

July 24, 1969   Bob Blake

August 1, 1969   John W. Bingham
                               Education Division
                               National Air and Space Museum
                               Smithsonian Institution
                               Washington, D. C. 20560

August 11, 1969   Department of the Air Force
                               Air Force Museum
                               Wright-Patterson Air Force Base
                               Ohio 45433

August 27, 1969   Department of the Air Force
                               Air Force Museum

September 4, 1969   Air Force Museum
                               Charles G. Worman, Historian

September 19, 1969   Air Force Museum
                               Charles G. Worman, Historian

October 10, 1969   Lieutenant General William E. Kepner
                            1220 Madison Street
                            Clarksville, Tennessee

November 3, 1969   O. D. Hagedorn

PERSONAL VISITS

United States Air Museum, Washington, D. C.

Cleveland, Ohio

Salem, Ohio

Newton Falls, Ohio

East Liverpool, Ohio

Chester, West Virginia

Oakland, Maryland

Davis, West Virginia

Canaan Valley, West Virginia

Blackwater Falls, Davis, West Virginia

Detroit, Michigan

Dearborn, Michigan

Windsor, Ontario, Canada

Point State Park, Pittsburgh, Pennsylvania

Air Force Museum, Wright-Patterson Air Force Base, Ohio

Dayton, Ohio

Smithsonian Institution, Washington, D. C.

Parsons, West Virginia

German Embassy

Germany
    Ulm
    Munich
    Nurnberg
    (and other towns)

INDEX